A RIGHT APPROACH
ECON

MARGARET THATCHER'S UNITED KINGDOM

PETER HARDY

Hodder & Stoughton

LONDON SYDNEY AUCKLAND TORONTO

In memory of Gretl

British Library Cataloguing in Publication Data
Hardy, Peter
  A right approach to economics?
  1. Great Britain. Economic policies
  I. Title
  330.941

  ISBN 0–340–53585–7

First published 1991

Typeset by Wearside Tradespools, Fulwell, Sunderland
Printed in Great Britain for the educational publishing division of Hodder and
Stoughton Ltd, Mill Road, Dunton Green, Sevenoaks, Kent by Clays Ltd, St
Ives plc

CONTENTS

ACKNOWLEDGEMENTS

The author would like to offer grateful thanks to Joan Buckeridge for her expert secretarial assistance and great patience. Thanks are also due to the following for help, advice, support, provision of information and proof reading: Jack Hardy, Susan Hardy, Nicholas Baker MP, Bryan Cassidy MEP, Tom Wheare, John Baker, Neil Boulton, David Bourne, Maggie Barlow, Paul Crocker, David Crush, Nicki Crush, Brian Deakin, Andrew Duncan, Richard d'Silva, Ed Finley, Tim Gascoine, Ronald Hird, Mark Kingston, Mark Laurence, Paul Mitchell, Robert Ogilvie, Mike Pyrgos, Peter Snow and Mike Suffield.

The illustration on the front cover was designed by Sophia Jundi, a pupil at Bryanston School studying A-Level Art.

The Publishers would like to thank the following for permission to reproduce material in this volume:

Argyll Foods plc for the extract from the Argyll offer document for distillers (1985–86); Barclays Bank plc for the information from Barclays Bank Economics Department; Central Statistical Office for the material from *Social Trends 20*; Centre for Business Strategies for the table from *Does Privatisation Work?* by M Bishop and J Kay; Child Poverty Action Group for the extract from their booklet; the Conservative Party for extracts from various Conservative Party Election manifestoes, Mrs Thatcher's speech after her 1987 General Election Victory and Nigel Lawson's resignation speech; The Economist for two tables from *The Economist*, 16 July 1988 and 'The Mother of Privatisation' from *The Economist*, 16 September 1989; Employment Institute for the material from *Regional Policy and the North-South Divide* by H Armstrong and J Taylor (1988); The Financial Times for their copyright material; General Synod of the Church of England for the material from *Living Faith in the City* (1990) and *Faith in the City*; Professor John Goddard for the material from his book *North South*; Guardian News Service Ltd for material from *the Guardian*, 12 January 1988, 6 September 1989, 28 February 1990, 15 July 1988, 1 November 1989, 14 February 1990, 24 October 1985 and 9 March 1988; HMSO for the figure from *Economic Progress Report*, January–February 1987, 'Leading world maufacturers of telecommunications equipment' from *Monopolies and Mergers Commission's Report*, the table from the 'Public Expenditure White Paper', January 1990, the material from *Regional Trends 24* (1989), the National Audit Office Report on Urban Development Corporations, 1988, 'Urban Regeneration and Economic Development: the local Government Dimension' from the Audit Commission Report, 24 January, 1990, Crown Copyright; the Liberal Democrats for the extracts from 'Britain United'; the Labour Party for the extracts from their 1987 election manifesto; Lloyd's Bank plc for the extract from 'De-industrialization in the UK' by A Thirlwall from the *Lloyd's Bank Review*, April 1982; London Weekend Television Ltd for the extract from *The Walden Interview*, 5 November 1989 – LWT; Marxism Today for the extract from *Marxism Today*, January 1987; Newspaper Publishing plc for 'Average gain in income 1979–1989' from *the Independent*, 13 May 1989 and 'Rover Group: making more from less' from *the Independent on Sunday*, 1 April 1990; David Owen for the extract from his book *A United Kingdom*; the Royal Bank of Scotland plc for the information from the *Royal Bank of Scotland Review*, March 1989; the Sunday Telegraph for the material from *the Sunday Telegraph*, 15 April 1990; Times Newspapers Ltd for the chart from *The Sunday Times*, 18 March 1990, the map from *The Sunday Times*, 29 October 1990, © Times Newspapers Ltd 1990, the extracts from the article by Sir Hector Laing from *The Times*, 2 June 1990, 'Industry still lagging, says NEDC chief' by Colin Narborough from *The Times*, 5 April 1990, the material from *The Sunday Times*, 14 June 1987 and *The Times*, 19 June 1987 and 2 September 1987.

Every effort has been made to trace and acknowledge ownership of copyright. The publishers will be glad to make suitable arrangements with any copyright holders whom it has not been possible to contact.

The Publishers would also like to thank the following for permission to use copyright illustrations:

Barnaby's Picture Library (page 136); FT/Syndication International (pages 28 and 38); Massimo Giachetti/Camera Press London (page 104); Popperfoto (pages 2, 51, 141, 148, 146, 154 and 158).

Introduction

The Conservative party under Margaret Thatcher was elected to office in 1979 and remained in power throughout the 1980s, winning re-election in both 1983 and 1987. It is true the Conservatives faced a divided opposition throughout the period and that, as a result of Britain's **first past the post** electoral system, a share of the vote just in excess of 40 per cent became a landslide victory in terms of seats in both 1983 and 1987. For much of the time the Labour opposition was divided and appeared to be dominated by the trade unions and the left-wing of the party. The public perceived a Labour party which had not learnt the lessons from the mistakes made in its previous term of office. Nationalisation, interventionism and high taxation were economic policies with which the Labour party was associated for much of the 1980s.

Right-wing thinking dominated economic and political debate throughout the decade. In particular, Margaret Thatcher proved to be so dominant within the Conservative party that her name became associated with the more radical right wing parts of the Conservative programme. *Thatcherism* was associated with an attempt to get Britain 'back on its feet again' by practising free market economics and by reducing the power of the trade unions. As state aid was withdrawn and market forces were allowed to operate, the 1980s witnessed a significant rise in unemployment to levels which would have been unimaginable in the previous decade.

The 1980s started with a two-year period of recession, which was followed by sustained growth throughout the decade. This allowed the government to claim that it had achieved a turnaround in the fortunes of the economy and even to claim that an 'economic miracle' was taking place. However, towards the end of the decade, problems with both the balance of payments and inflation reappeared – reminiscent of difficulties experienced in the 1960s and 1970s. This questioned whether the high growth of the mid 1980s could be sustained.

This book considers various aspects of policy which have been important under the Conservative government. It is divided into four sections. The first section, 'A Right Approach', looks at how industry has fared during the 1980s in the light of various aspects of government policy. It starts with a focus on manufacturing industry, which suffered badly during the recession of 1979–81. Critics claim that this represented mismanagement of government policy. Conservatives, however, claim that this period of time laid the foundations for the subsequent industrial revival and associated productivity gains. Conservative ideology is underpinned by a belief in market forces and the benefits of the free market and competition.

Competition policy is then discussed, with particular reference to merger policy. A case-study approach is adopted as a means of discussing some of the

Margaret Thatcher, Prime Minister 1979–90

major issues. Privatisation has been heralded as one of the most important ways of increasing competition in the economy by exposing industry to market forces. The Conservatives' privatisation programme is assessed and, in particular, the issue of whether privatisation has increased competition rather than simply raising money for the government is considered. The motor industry can be seen as a test case for Thatcherism in the 1980s. The industry has been chosen for an in-depth case study to consider various aspects of policy, including the government's attitude towards foreign investment and privatisation.

Opponents of the Conservative government argue that the benefits of economic growth during the latter part of the 1980s have not been evenly spread. The government has been accused of not giving enough care to those least able to help themselves and also of presiding over a situation in which prosperity has not been spread fairly across the country. These aspects are considered in Parts Two and Three respectively.

The Welfare State was established after the Second World War in order to provide 'care from cradle to grave' for all the population. However, the cost of providing the various benefits and services has risen enormously and the increasing scope of the Welfare State has led to criticisms that a **dependency culture** has been created.

The changing nature of poverty is considered together with the Conservative government's proposals to alleviate it. Criticisms that Conservative policy has (both directly and indirectly) contributed to an increase in poverty are investigated. Both health and housing have been the subject of major reforms during the 1980s. The National Health Service has often appeared to be 'underfunded'. How to decide on the resources to be allocated to the NHS is assessed, as are the attempts to introduce greater choice and efficiency into the Service at the risk, according to critics, of undermining its whole ethos. As part of the government's drive towards a 'capital-owning democracy' and 'popular capitalism', the government has encouraged moves to sell off council houses and to increase owner-occupation, but its opponents argue that it has failed to attend to the real housing needs of the nation.

In Part Three, the phenomenon of the 'North-South divide' is studied. Does it exist and has it widened during the 1980s? The political implications of the North-South divide are then discussed. This is followed by an assessment of the government's regional policy reforms and also of the problems of the inner cities – named by Mrs Thatcher as one of the key areas for attention during the third term.

The book concludes with 'An Overview of Thatcherism in the 1980s', which is a consideration of the main strands of macroeconomic policy during that period.

Note: The words which appear in **bold type** in the text are defined in the Glossary on pages 194–202.

PART 1

A RIGHT APPROACH

1 *De-industrialisation or Industrial Revival?*

- Aspects of de-industrialisation
- Causes of de-industrialisation
- Does de-industrialisation matter?
- An industrial revival?
- Comment

ASPECTS OF DE-INDUSTRIALISATION

Serious concern has been expressed about the health of manufacturing industry in the UK and this has been raised particularly in the debate about whether 'de-industrialisation matters'. Although there has been concern about UK manufacturing for many years – some people tracing the causes of problems back to the Industrial Revolution – discussion came to the fore during the recession of 1979–81 (refer to Figure 1.1).

The economy has recovered since 1981, showing increasing strength during the 1980s, and manufacturing growth has contributed to that. The Conservative government claims that the industrial recovery is a tribute to the success of its policies, which have placed great reliance on market forces, the profit motive and the role of the private sector. Critics blame the government for the 1979–81 recession and claim that the lack of a clear **industrial strategy** throughout the Conservative period of office has weakened the country's **industrial base**, thereby questioning whether the industrial revival is likely to be sustained in the long term.

Before these arguments are considered, it is necessary to attempt to clarify the meaning of the word *de-industrialisation*, as there are many different interpretations, which can lead to different conclusions.

Between 1960 and 1986, UK manufacturing as a share of gross domestic product (GDP) declined from 32.1 per cent to 21.8 per cent. Such a measure compares the size of the manufacturing sector with that of the whole economy. However, these figures must be treated carefully, as a declining percentage may

Figure 1.1: Shares of the world trade in manufactured goods

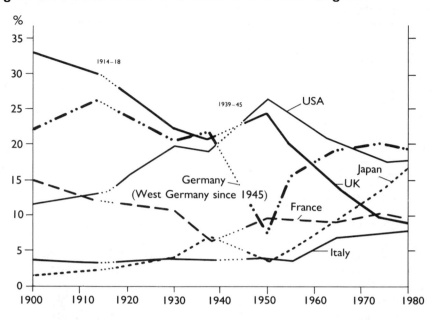

Source: UN data and 'Maizels'
From: Barclays Review, November 1987

simply represent the buoyancy of other sectors compared to manufacturing, rather than a decline in manufacturing itself. (Similarly a rising percentage during a recession could reflect the possibility that manufacturing had declined by less than other sectors.)

All advanced industrialised countries (even Japan) have experienced a relative decline in their manufacturing sectors, ie a reduction in the share of GDP accounted for by manufacturing. This is associated with increased spending on services, which occurs as individuals and society as a whole become more prosperous. The figures referred to above compare with a decline from 40.3 per cent to 33.1 per cent for West Germany, from 29.1 per cent to 22.2 per cent for France and from 33.9 per cent to 29.3 per cent for Japan during the period from 1960 to 1986. However, a consideration of Table 1.1. demonstrates that the UK and the US finished with the lowest shares of manufacturing as a share of GDP and that the decline over the period of time considered was greater than for the other countries involved.

However, a more serious situation occurs if a country experiences an *absolute decline* in the level of manufacturing output, rather than a *relative decline* as described above. During the deep recession of 1979–81, manufacturing output declined by 14 per cent. Since then manufacturing output has recovered, but only reached the level of June 1979 in July 1987. The all-time

Table 1.1: Percentage share of manufacturing in GDP (value added in manufacturing as a percentage of current price GDP)

	1960	1970	1975	1980	1985	1986
			%			
Canada	23.3	20.4	19.2	18.8	—	—
USA	28.6	25.7	23.4	22.5	20.3	19.9
Japan	33.9	35.9	29.9	30.4	29.8	29.3
France	29.1	28.7	27.4	26.3	22.1	22.2
W Germany	40.3	38.4	34.5	33.0	31.9	33.1
Italy	28.5	28.9	29.7	30.5	23.8	23.4
UK	32.1	28.1	26.3	23.1	21.3	21.8

Source: *Economic Progress Report* (June–July 1985) and *National Accounts of OECD Countries*, Vol II, Detailed Tables (1988 edition)
From: *Royal Bank of Scotland Review*, March 1989

peak of manufacturing production (June 1974) was not exceeded before June 1988.

Instead of considering *manufacturing output*, we shall now consider *manufacturing employment* as a criterion for assessing the health of manufacturing industry. The share of manufacturing employment as a proportion of total employment in the UK declined between 1960 and 1986 from 36 per cent to 22.5 per cent (refer to Table 1.2). The actual number of job losses in manufacturing between 1979 and 1986 was just less than two million (refer to Figure 1.2) and, of course, for the people made redundant, especially those in areas of high unemployment who may be **occupationally** and **geographically immobile**, this represents the real meaning of de-industrialisation, far better than other more sophisticated explanations.

Although movements in output and employment are related, differences occur which are based on productivity growth. Thus, in a time of rapid technological progress and productivity growth, a 'reasonable' rate of growth of manufacturing output may be associated with a decline in the level of manufacturing employment. This highlights the problems of definition – on a *level of employment* basis, the situation described represents a case of de-

Table 1.2: Employment in manufacturing as a percentage of total civilian population

	1960	1970	1975	1980	1985	1986
			%			
Canada	23.7	22.3	20.2	19.7	17.5	17.3
USA	27.1	26.4	22.7	22.1	19.5	19.1
Japan	21.5	27.0	25.8	24.7	25.0	24.7
France	27.5	27.8	27.9	25.8	23.2	22.6
W Germany	37.0	39.4	35.6	34.3	32.0	32.2
Italy	23.0	27.8	28.2	26.7	23.2	22.9
UK	36.0	34.7	31.0	28.4	23.1	22.5

Source: *OECD Labour Force Statistics* and *ILO Bulletin of Labour Statistics*
From: *Royal Bank of Scotland Review*, March 1989

Figure 1.2: Employment in different sectors as a percentage of the employed labour force

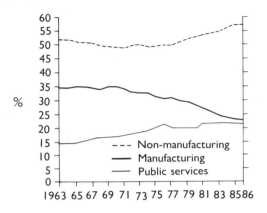

Note: Non-manufacturing includes agriculture, forestry and fishing, energy and water supply, construction, hotel and catering, transport and communiction, retail distribution, banking, shipping and insurance, and other services (e.g. recreational services).

From: Economic Progress Report (January–February 1987)

industrialisation, but on a *level of output* basis, this is not so.

Reference must also be made to the UK foreign trade position. There has been a long-term decline in the UK share of world trade in manufactured goods. In addition, **import penetration** of the UK market for manufactured goods has increased, especially in high-technology, durable consumer goods (eg cars, video recorders). One would expect, however, both a declining share of world trade and rising import penetration in a world economy which has become increasingly liberal in its attitude to trade throughout most of the post-war period. The rapid development of many of the Newly Industrialised Countries, such as Singapore and South Korea, has contributed to this, but the deterioration in the UK trading position, compared with most of the Organisation of Economic Cooperation and Development (OECD) countries, has been marked. The UK share of world trade in manufactured goods (refer to Figure 1.3) has deteriorated from 9 per cent in 1970 to 6 per cent in 1986 (compared with over 30 per cent in 1900). At the same time, import penetration of manufactured goods has risen from 24 per cent in 1976 to 34 per cent in 1986 and the increase is considerably greater in some sectors (for example, in the motor industry).

For Britain rising import penetration of manufactured goods has not been matched to the same extent by rising export sales (refer to Figure 1.4). As a consequence, Britain's balance of trade in manufactured goods deteriorated sharply, resulting in a deficit in 1983 for the first time since the Industrial

Figure 1.3:   UK export performance in manufactured goods

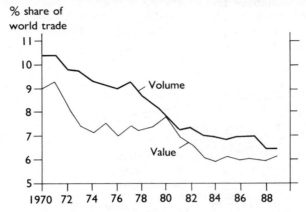

Source: Financial Statement and Budget Report 1989–90
From: Barclays Economic Review, November 1989

**Figure 1.4: Exports and imports of manufactured goods at constant
(1985) prices**

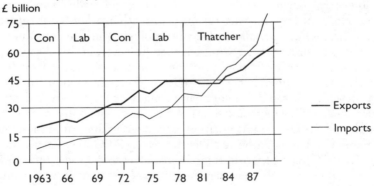

Source: Godley from Pink Book and NI Review
From: Guardian, 6 September 1989

Revolution. A surplus of manufactured goods of £5.4 billion in 1980 turned
into a deficit of £6.1 billion by 1986 and deteriorated to £16.1 billion by 1989

(refer to Figure 1.5). For a country which has traditionally covered a deficit on trade in food and raw materials with a surplus on manufacturing, the long term balance of payments position has given cause for concern. This is especially so now that North Sea oil production has peaked, causing the surplus gained from oil exports to decline.

Figure 1.5: UK balance of payments in manufactured goods

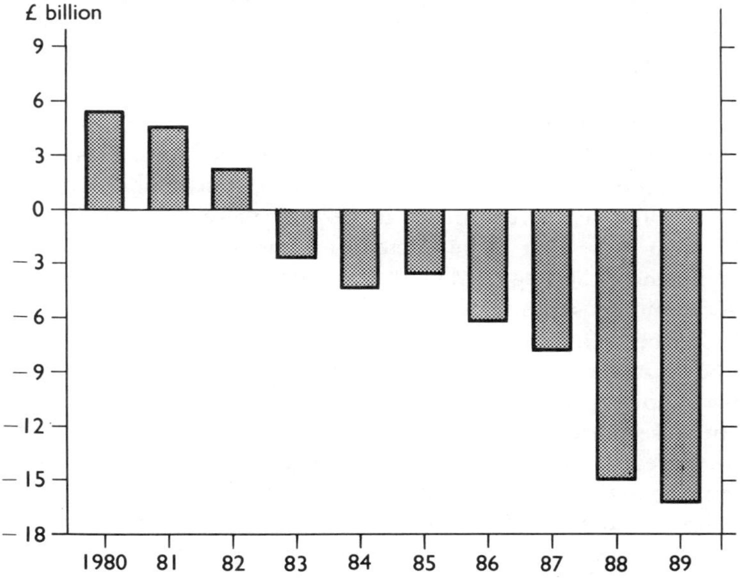

Source: Central Statistical Office

CAUSES OF DE-INDUSTRIALISATION

Loss of competitiveness in the period 1979–81

Critics of the Conservative government argue that, although the British economy had been showing certain symptoms of de-industrialisation over a long period of time, the government's mishandling of exchange rate policy in the period 1979–81 resulted in a grossly overvalued currency. This led to uncompetitive exports and a loss of export markets, and rising **import penetration**. The recession that followed caused a massive 'shakeout' of manufacturing industry, during which the least competitive firms went bankrupt. The background to this is considered.

Although the 1974–79 Labour government had retreated from its policies for intervention in industry and had in 1975 adopted an **incomes policy** as a counter-inflation weapon, international confidence in sterling continued to decline, precipitating the sterling crisis of Autumn 1976. The Labour government negotiated a rescue package with the IMF, involving a loan. However, in order to obtain the IMF loan, the government had to agree to public expenditure cuts and targets for the rate of growth of the money supply, both of which were contrary to the existing policies of the Labour party. International confidence in sterling returned, partly due to the belief that the IMF-imposed policies would control the left-wing of the Labour party, and at the same time impose fiscal and monetary discipline on the economy. Sterling recovered from its low point of $1.56 in Autumn 1976 and, aided by capital inflows during 1977 (which were initially attracted by high interest rates) appreciated during the year. Although the upward trend was not maintained throughout the whole of 1978, further appreciation in the exchange rate occurred during 1979 and this trend was maintained until 1981.

The commitment to money supply targets, first established after the IMF rescue of 1976, was strengthened in 1979 by the election of the Conservative government – the first to be elected on a monetarist platform. The Medium Term Financial Strategy (MTFS) was introduced in the 1980 budget; this produced money supply targets for the next four years and was the main plank of the government's counter-inflation strategy. The central premise of those who advocated monetarist policies was that there was a correlation between money supply growth and the rate of inflation, and that changes in the money supply caused changes in the rate of inflation. Thus in order to control inflation it was necessary to control the rate of growth of the money supply. By announcing medium term targets (ie four years ahead) for the money supply, it was hoped that **inflationary expectations** could be gradually reduced thus helping to reduce wage claims and thereafter the rate of inflation itself. This process is termed the **transmission mechanism.**

However, wage settlements during 1980 accelerated instead of moderating as the government had hoped. Thus industry's borrowing requirement rose at the same time as the government was trying to control the money supply. Rates of interest therefore rose, raising the cost of borrowing, thereby imposing an extra burden on industry. As a consequence of these high rates of interest, and also inspired by confidence in the Conservative government in general and by Mrs Thatcher's tough policies on industrial relations and inflation in particular, foreign capital flooded into Britain, thereby further pushing up the exchange rate. Throughout 1980 industry was faced with high wage settlements, high interest rates and an appreciating currency, all of which contributed to a worsening of the competitive position of British industry.

Another explanation given for the rapid rise of sterling was the existence of North Sea oil. The UK changed from being a net importer of oil into a country self-sufficient in oil in 1980 and, thereafter, into a net exporter. As a direct consequence the current account of the balance of payments improved. North Sea oil also conferred **petrocurrency** status on to sterling – a petrocurrency is a currency whose value is significantly affected by the fortunes of the oil industry in that country. Foreign funds, attracted by the benefits offered to a country producing oil when its competitors were not, flowed into the UK, thus increasing the demand for sterling.

At this point it becomes evident why it is so difficult to give a clear explanation for the rise in sterling – foreign capital did flow into the country, but whether it was attracted principally by high interest rates or as a result of North Sea oil, is impossible to tell.

As a consequence of the rise in the exchange rate during the period 1978–81, British firms found in harder to compete in foreign markets, whilst at the same time foreign firms were able to compete more effectively in the British market, thereby increasing import penetration. This led the House of Lords' Select Committee on Overseas Trade to conclude in their 1985 Report that

> a combination of tight monetary policy under the Medium Term Financial Strategy, as part of the government's anti-inflation policy, accompanied by a high exchange rate, resulted in the loss of a significant part of Britain's manufacturing base.

In 1979 the government abolished **exchange controls** on British capital invested overseas in a successful attempt to encourage a capital outflow which generated some downward pressure on the exchange rate. (The interest, profits and dividends (IPD) earned on the money invested overseas would, moreover, contribute to the balance of payments when the benefits of North Sea oil diminished.) However, the government refused to contemplate any further measures which would have reduced the appreciation of the exchange rate during the period 1979–81. Much was made of the benefits of the 'strong' pound and this was seen as the key to entry into the *virtuous circle* of high growth and low inflation. A *virtuous circle* is characterised by the imposition of an **external discipline** on wage-bargainers, who are no longer able to rely on a declining exchange rate to regain the competitiveness lost by the granting of inflationary wage claims. Thus firms would be forced to improve productivity if they wished to remain competitive with foreign firms. It was hoped that the removal of an inflationary climate would create stability and economic growth as seen, for example, in the West German 'economic miracle' for much of the post-war period.

Some economists have argued that the decline in manufacturing was an inevitable consequence of the production of North Sea oil, through the exchange rate mechanism described above. Others have argued that it would have been possible for the British economy to have enjoyed the benefits of North Sea oil without suffering de-industrialisation at the same time if the government had done more in order to try and prevent the exchange rate from rising.

If one accepts the argument that North Sea oil contributed to some extent via the rise in the exchange rate to the decline in manufacturing and to the deterioration in the trade balance in manufactured goods, then one is forced to ask what will happen when North Sea oil starts to run out? If manufacturing does not recover, then North Sea oil will have caused long-term harm to the British economy, as well as having contributed to the short-term manufacturing decline. The House of Lords' Report on Overseas Trade (1985) examines very carefully and rejects the Treasury view that, 'as oil declines manufacturing automatically will recover'. The Report argues that:

> it is unrealistic and dangerously short-sighted to expect the decline in the surplus on the balance of trade in oil to result in an automatic recovery of exports of manufactued goods or of a diminution in imports for a number of reasons:
>
> (a) The decline in manufacturing and in the trade balance in manufactures was not the inevitable consequence of the advent of North Sea oil and because the effect of North Sea oil on the exchange rate movements is uncertain.
>
> (b) New industries and new products usually grow out of long established activities and require a long time scale for development.
>
> (c) Lost markets will be difficult to regain.
>
> (d) Lost manufacturing capacity will take a long time to restore.

The government, furthermore, has been criticised for its misuse of North Sea oil tax revenues. The creation of a special fund to channel the revenues into specific projects for expanding the economy or strengthening the **industrial base** was rejected. Those in favour of the fund argued that it would have been sensible to use the revenues from North Sea oil – a short-term windfall – to improve the strength of the economy for the time when North Sea oil runs out. However, this view assumes more government intervention in industry, contrary to the views and ideology of the Conservative government. The government treated North Sea oil revenues in exactly the same way as other taxes collected.

The objectives of the government's fiscal policy were to reduce the public sector borrowing requirement (PSBR) as a proportion of national income and to reduce the nation's tax burden in order to increase incentives. The government has been accused of squandering the North Sea revenues by reducing the PSBR, cutting taxes and paying the dole to those made unemployed due to its exchange rate policy. There is therefore a very clear divergence of opinion between those who advocate direct investment in industry to regenerate the economy and those who believe that the government should use the revenue to help to create the *correct environment* (ie low PSBR and low taxation) in which industry is then able to prosper, thereby regaining lost overseas markets.

Absence of an industrial strategy

The debate over the use of North Sea oil revenues reappears in the wider debate on the use of government expenditure. In particular, it arises in the question of whether or not the government should have adopted an **industrial strategy** during the 1980s in order to encourage industrial development.

The phrase *industrial strategy* has different meanings, but generally involves an interventionist government industrial policy providing support for certain industries. The support is likely to focus on key sectors of industry in an attempt to spot winners. Government funds may be provided for research and development and for other approved expenditure. This type of approach was used to a greater or lesser extent by governments in the 1960s and 1970s in the days when **demand management** was considered appropriate. In contrast to this, the Conservative government has adopted a *laissez-faire* non-interventionist approach to industry, improving the **supply side** of the economy and relying on market forces to improve efficiency. Critics have argued that a more interventionist approach would have been beneficial.

Other causes of de-industrialisation

There are other explanations for de-industrialisation, many of which overlap, which view it as a longer term phenomenon. Although the problems of manufacturing industry have been particularly highlighted during the early 1980s, problems have not only been present under the Conservative government. Indeed Conservatives counter the arguments earlier in this chapter about the causes of the recession of 1979–81, with claims that it was caused to some extent by the problems created and stored up during previous (Labour-dominated) years. The contribution of post-war governments' economic policies to the problems of industry is now briefly considered, together with the role of both trade unions and management during this period.

Interventionist governments

During the period from 1945 until the mid 1970s, governments adopted the Keynesian policies of **demand management**. The principle aim was to ensure that full employment existed. However, the economy tended to *overheat* during periods of expansion, creating excess demand and leading to inflation, a surge of imports and balance of payments difficulties. In order to solve these macroeconomic difficulties, governments were forced to adopt a deflationary fiscal policy in order to reduce demand in the economy. A period of growth followed by contraction was known as a **stop-go cycle** and, in view of the uncertainties created, the long-term investment plans of industry were reduced. As described earlier in the chapter, the Conservative government has rejected demand management as a tool of economic policy and has reduced the role of the state in the running of the economy.

Further criticisms of the role of the government come from those who support the **crowding out** argument. This argument suggests that the growth of the public sector, far from supplementing the private sector (as in the Keynesian analysis), was at the expense of the private sector. In order to finance the larger public sector, it is necessary either to raise taxes, possibly adversely affecting incentives, or to increase government borrowing, which is likely to lead to a rise in interest rates and a consequent decline in private sector investment. An alternative explanation of this argument is that the crowding out that occurs is more direct and that the expanding public sector attracts labour away from the private sector.

Governments of the last forty years have also been criticised for a lack of consistency in their approach to industry. According to David Owen in his book *A United Kingdom* (Penguin, 1986), 'the overall effectiveness of policies for industrial recovery after 1945 has been reduced by institutional instability and the lack of a broad political consensus on the general shape of industrial policies'.

Militant unions

Trade unions have been accused of being responsible for many of the industrial problems in the UK and the Conservative government has legislated to reform unions, resulting in a completely changed climate of industrial relations, including a dramatic decline in the number of strikes and improved working practices. There were, however, two major industrial disputes during the Conservatives' second term which sum up the conflict between the new approach of the Conservative government and the attitudes of many traditional unions. The Miners' Strike of 1984–5 was a clash between (*i*) the management's belief in its **right to manage** and its desire to close down what it termed 'uneconomic pits', and (*ii*) the NUM's defence of employment and local communities. The News International dispute at Wapping in 1986–7 was a conflict between the management's desire to introduce new technology and to reduce restrictive practices and overmanning, and the print unions' desire to preserve employment and to protect traditional patterns of work.

The failure of the unions in both of these major 'set piece' industrial confrontations fuelled the hope among Conservative supporters that unions would adopt a much more reasoned approach to industrial problems. They also hoped that unions would be more willing than previously to accept new technology and improved working practices (leading to improved competitiveness) and that strikes and other disruption would no longer be major problems in a new era of industrial peace.

Poor management

British firms have been accused of failing to invest sufficiently in industry. This means that it is difficult for firms to improve efficiency when producing existing products, which results in a decline in Britain's ability to compete, or to respond quickly to demand for new products. This is particularly true in view of the relatively limited amount devoted to research and development (R and D) (especially civilian R and D) compared with other countries.

The quality of British management has been questioned in terms of its perceived unwillingness to take risks, and of its tendency to ignore the importance of *non-price factors* when attempting to sell British goods (eg quality, delivery dates, after-sales service). Relatively little emphasis has been placed on the need for market-orientated design for consumer goods. In addition British management has been accused of **short-termism** (ie a failure to take decisions in which long term considerations are taken into account).

The above categorisation of the causes of de-industrialisation under the three headings is designed to aid clarity, although the causes may well be interdependent. Thus, for example, a failure to invest, by causing a lack of competitiveness and declining sales, may result in a union, keen to protect its members' jobs, resisting any moves towards the introduction of new technology, which might create unemployment in the short term. Similarly, although low investment might be seen to be a major cause of de-industrialisation, it may itself be affected by government's **crowding out** of the private sector or by the behaviour of trade unions.

Attitudes to industry

The House of Lords' Report on Overseas Trade complained of

> a general lack of awareness of the importance of manufacturing and of a healthy performance in international trade and it is reflected in the inadequate social esteem accorded to industry and trade in modern British Culture.

This attitude was seen to be in marked contrast to the attitude towards industry in many of Britain's competitors, especially in Japan. Partly as a response to this concern *Industry Year* was launched in 1986 as a contribution towards overcoming some of these problems.

British banks have been accused of failing to lend sufficient amounts to industry and of adopting a short-term approach, ie **short-termism**. This militates against long-term investment projects and, in particular, research and development (where the returns may only materialise after a number of years) and contrasts with the long-term approach adopted by banks in many other industrialised countries.

A poor industrial base

Others have argued that the UK, the first power to industrialise, relied for too long on the protected markets offered by the Empire whilst other countries were faced with the open competition of world markets. Thus efficiency lagged behind and innovations were not made. As a result British industry lost opportunities, particularly in the area of high technology, thereby weakening the **industrial base** and reducing the long-term ability to compete. EC entry in 1973 abruptly exposed Britain to the full force of European competition, but British firms have tended not to establish a sufficiently powerful distribution and marketing support system within the EC.

DOES DE-INDUSTRIALISATION MATTER?

The decline of any sector in an economy will contribute to a decline in national income and employment unless other sectors grow to take up the slack created. Therefore, the decline of a sector – especially one as large as manufacturing – can never be seen as a good thing in itself unless scarce labour is being freed to work in a more productive sector, as has happened to agricultural employment in most western countries during the twentieth century.

The debate over 'whether de-industrialisation matters' is polarised between those who believe that specific policies should be adopted to revitalise the industrial sector, in view of the central importance of industry to an economy, and those who claim that there is nothing special about industry and that the market will deal with questions about expansion or contraction for any particular sector, including the industrial sector.

The latter point of view might be termed the government's viewpoint. The then Chancellor of the Exchequer, Nigel Lawson, told the House of Lords' Committee on Overseas Trade: 'The government's general philosophy is that it is industry's job to make itself competitive, it is the government's job to provide an overall climate'. A similar point of view was put forward by David Henderson in the 1985 Reith Lectures. He complained about 'structure snobbery', which occurs when economists, politicians or civil servants attempt to identify certain sectors in the economy which are deemed worthy of special support (ie to 'spot winners'), thereby distorting the market process. This is especially true if chosen 'winners' prove to be 'losers'.

The opposing view is held by Sir Hector Laing (then Chairman of United Biscuits) who, in his submission to the House of Lords' Committee claimed:

> 'The present Government has, in effect, made a virtue of not having a vision of the future of British industry, and a positive policy of distancing the state from the industrial sector. I think the Government should acknowledge that the nation does have an industrial problem in which it has a serious policy interest.'

It is necessary to consider why it is that manufacturing is considered by some to be so important and also whether the service sector (and other sectors) could adequately replace manufacturing, in terms of output, employment and exports.

First, manufacturing is considered by some to be the *driving force* or *engine of growth* of the economy, possessing 'certain growth inducing-characteristics that other sectors of the economy do not have' (A. Thirlwall, 'De-industrialisation in the UK', *Lloyds Bank Review*, April 1982) with a greater scope for productivity growth than in service industries.

Secondly, the success of the service sector should not be seen as being independent of the manufacturing sector; rather, the success of the two is linked. For example, the banking and insurance sectors require advanced computers in order to remain competitive. If the British computer industry is unable to supply them, imports will increase, causing a deterioration in the current account of the balance of payments.

Thirdly, whereas most manufacturing products are tradeable in the world, there are many services which are not. Therefore, a further shift from manufacturing to services could cause a deteriorating balance of payments position.

The Chairman of the British Invisible Exports Council told the House of Lords' Committee that he did 'not see the growth (of services) as being to a major extent a substitute for decline in general industrial activity'. Concern about the service sector's ability to compensate for any decline in manufacturing was raised when a deficit of £713 million for invisible trade was reported for the last quarter of 1989. This represented the first deficit on record, although it is, at the time of writing, too early to say whether it establishes a new trend.

AN INDUSTRIAL REVIVAL?

During the 1960s and 1970s, the UK had a very poor record of productivity growth, measured in terms of *output per person employed*. This applied to both the manufacturing sector and the economy as a whole. Reference to Table 1.3

Table 1.3: Average annual percentage change in output per person employed (a) across the whole economy, (b) in the manufacturing industry, in each of the G7 countries

	Whole economy[(a)]			Manufacturing industry[(b)]		
	1960–70	1970–80	1980–88	1960–70	1970–80	1980–88
UK	2.4	1.3	2.5	3.0	1.6	5.2
US	2.0	0.4	1.2	3.5	3.0	4.0
Japan	8.9	3.8	2.9	8.8	5.3	3.1
W Germany	4.4	2.8	1.8	4.1	2.9	2.2
France	4.6	2.8	2.0	5.4	3.2	3.1
Italy	6.3	2.6	2.0	5.4	3.0	3.5
Canada	2.4	1.5	1.4	3.4	3.0	3.6
G7 average	3.5	1.7	1.8	4.5	3.3	3.6

Source: (a) UK data from Central Statistical Office. Other countries' data from OECD except 1988 which are calculated from national GNP or GDP figures and OECD employment estimates.

(b) UK data from Central Statistical Office. Other countries' data from OECD except France and Italy which use IMF employment data. 1988 data for France and Italy cover first three quarters only.

From: *Economic Progress Report*, April 1989

indicates that, when compared with the other G7 countries (the seven leading industrialised countries), Britain's productivity growth in manufacturing was the lowest of the seven countries considered in both the 1960s and 1970s, and productivity growth for the whole economy was second lowest in each decade (only the US delivered lower figures). However, when considering the period 1980–8, Britain's productivity growth in manufacturing (averaging 5.2 per cent per annum) was the highest of the G7 countries and, for the economy as a whole, was second only to Japan. The results of this 'productivity miracle' were hailed as a great success, allowing the Conservatives to claim that a sustained turnaround had been achieved in Britain's economic performance in general and in manufacturing industry in particular during the 1980s, as a result of the economic policies applied.

The growth of productivity started during the recession of 1979–81, which resulted in a sharp rise in unemployment, as overmanning was reduced during the shakeout of labour. As the least productive jobs were lost, there was a consequent improvement in the productivity of the economy. However, more significantly, productivity growth which started during the shakeout, has been maintained during the subsequent period of output growth in the economy, during which time massive **restructuring** and **rationalisation** of the British economy have occurred. This was associated with an improvement in working practices and industrial relations generally. The twin spurs for these changes were the threat of higher unemployment and the Conservative government's industrial relations legislation.

The rate of growth of the economy during 1987–8 was approximately 5 per cent per annum and this followed a period of sustained growth, commencing in 1981 (at the end of the 1979–81 recession). During this period output rose by an average figure in excess of 3 per cent. Manufacturing output, in the three months to May 1988, was 6.5 per cent higher than a year earlier (CSO figures).

This was matched by a rise in manufacturing productivity of 6.6 per cent over the same period of time, which helped to keep the rise in *unit wage costs* to 2.4 per cent, despite a growth of earnings of 8.5 per cent. Manufacturing productivity growth compared favourably with an estimated 3 per cent increase for the economy as a whole, supporting the view that a manufacturing revival was taking place (refer to Figure 1.6).

However, doubts were voiced about the durability of the manufacturing revival. Britain's workforce is less skilled than that of our competitors, reflecting an inadequate level of resources devoted to training over many years compared to other countries. In addition British firms have invested relatively little in high technology and in research and development (R and D) and this has been associated with a long-term deterioration in the **industrial base**. Supporters of the Conservative government claim that this view ignores the dramatic changes in productivity and industrial relations that have taken place during the 1980s. The ability of British industry to maintain the improvements made will be an indication whether the **supply side** revolution has been effective and whether the short-term revival may become a long-term renaiss-

Figure 1.6: Industrial output showing seasonally adjusted monthly figures

—— INDUSTRIAL PRODUCTION

—— MANUFACTURING

From: Guardian, 15 July 1988

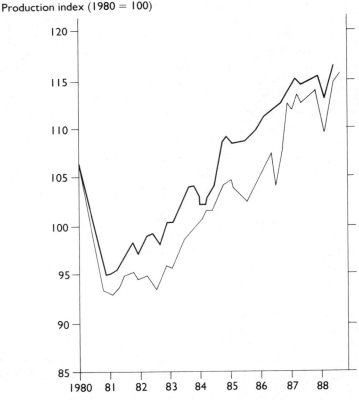

Production index (1980 = 100)

Note: Industrial production includes manufacturing, mining, construction, energy (including North Sea oil and gas extraction) and water supply.

ance. However, short-term problems rather than any longer term difficulties, brought about a halt to the levels of manufacturing growth seen during the 1980s. Despite the relatively high UK growth rate of the late 1980s, the growth of demand was greater and this resulted in a surge of imports to meet the excess demand (demand from both consumers and businesses). The current account deficit that developed during 1987 and 1988 was initially seen as a sign of success, as it was attributed to the high UK growth rate. However, demand was further stimulated by government fiscal and monetary actions during the same period. The government reduced income tax rates significantly both in 1987 and 1988 and also relaxed monetary policy in the aftermath of the 1987 stock market crash, at a time when access to credit was that much easier anyway, due to deregulation and liberalisation of the capital markets.

The 'overheating' of the economy that resulted from the pressures of excess demand (ie supply was unable to meet the extra demand, despite the supply side improvements and the increases in output which had occurred) resulted in a current account deficit of £14.7 billion in 1988 and £20.3 billion in 1989. In addition, inflationary pressures were generated in the economy and inflation rose from a low point of 2.4 per cent in September 10.9 per cent, an eight-year high.

The government attempted to reduce both inflation and the current account deficit by raising interest rates, in order to reduce spending in the economy. Interest rates were raised in steps from 7.5 per cent in May 1988 to 15 per cent in October 1989. Although the economy proved to be remarkably resilient during 1989, resisting government attempts to slow it down, forecasts in the 1990 budget anticipated GDP growth of one per cent and manufacturing output growth of zero per cent in 1990, compared with 1989 outcomes to 2.25 per cent and 4.75 per cent respectively. Falling sales and profits, together with an increasing number of bankruptcies during 1990, led to fears that the recession experienced during the early 1980s would recur in the early 1990s.

COMMENT

The government has rejected the idea of a specific *industrial policy* or **industrial strategy**, as attempted during the 1960s, and has instead adopted a stance of non-interventionism. In an attempt to do this, it has reduced the role of the state and has concentrated on improving the commercial environment in which firms operate, by improving the **supply side** of the economy and increasing the role of the market and encouraging the *profit motive*. Its policies have been based on a rejection of Keynesian **demand management** policies and the adoption of *monetarism* with the central objective of controlling inflation, although concentration on money supply targets has been less in the period after 1985 as the government relied more on interest rates in order to achieve monetary control.

As part of its privatisation programme, the government has sold many nationalised industries to the private sector, with the aim of increasing competition (refer to Chapter 3). Foreign investment in the UK has been encouraged, (see Chapters 2 and 4), both in recognition of the jobs directly created and also because of the competitive spur provided for many British firms (for example, in terms of improved working practices). The takeover process has been accepted as a further stimulus to efficiency in the economy (unless market power is increased) – it is hoped that inefficient firms will be liable to takeover by other firms, whose managements see scope for improvements in profitability (refer to Chapter 2). Other supply side measures adopted to stimulate industrial recovery have included the provision of incentives to personal enterprise in the form of a reduction in the rates of tax on income (see Chapter 6), encouragement of business invesment by reductions in the rate of Corporation Tax (with special schemes for small businesses in particular), measures to reform trade unions in an attempt to improve industrial relations, and the abolition of unnecessary controls by various measures of liberalisation (eg the supply of telephone equipment) and deregulation (eg bus and coach services) (refer to Chapter 3). Direct government aid to industry has, however, been reduced and this has included a reduced level of aid to the regions (see Chapter 10).

A study of manufacturing industry in the 1990s will be necessary in order to say whether progress made, in terms of improved productivity and profitability, as a result of supply side measures adopted, can be sustained.

2 Competition Policy

THE THEORY OF COMPETITION POLICY

Competitive markets are essential if the market system is to operate effectively. In a monopoly situation, the producer may be able to use his market power at the expense of the consumer, although the likelihood of this happening will be moderated if close substitutes for the product exist or if the monopolist fears entry of new, but similar, products into the market, attracted by high prices and the profits being made. It is relatively rare for a firm to have an absolute monopoly of the market, but there are many instances where a small number of large firms dominate a market – this is called an **oligopoly**. Such firms may act overtly (and illegally) or covertly (still illegally, but hard to detect) as if they were in a monopoly situation. Agreements or understandings could cover price-fixing and/or sharing out the available work without resorting to competition (which would have resulted in lower prices). In order for the agreement to stick, no single firm must break ranks, encouraged by the prospect of greater market share by lowering its price, or else a free-for-all may develop producing a *competitive* price, as if the market had been operating smoothly.

The operation of such a price-fixing agreement can be seen in the way that the price of oil has been fixed by the Organisation of Petroleum Exporting Countries (OPEC) cartel. High prices were maintained from 1974 onwards in the face of inelastic demand for oil from oil-importing countries, but an oil glut in the 1980s put pressure on individual countries to reduce their prices in order to gain market share. Despite attempts to prevent this by OPEC, the price of oil plummeted in 1986. Even if there are no formal agreements to interfere with the market, implicit understandings may be reached, in which case the behaviour of the firms involved might, in practice, be the same as if a formal agreement had existed.

The smaller the number of large firms in an industry, ie the more **concentrated** it is, the more likely it is that the competitive process will be interfered with. However, it must be pointed out that not all monopoly suppliers act against the public interest (eg it is not suggested even by the most ardent advocate of privatisation – refer to Chapter 3 – that the water supply or sewage disposal industries should provide competitive services to each household; the duplication of resources in these cases would be extremely wasteful to society), nor do all oligopolies abuse their position. The actual *concentration* of an industry is hard to assess precisely and there are many different measures of it (eg if we say that the *five firm concentration ratio* is 85 per cent, this means that the largest five firms in the industry control 85 per cent of the market; a *two firm concentration ratio* of 100 per cent indicates that two firms completely dominate the market).

In view of the existence of highly concentrated industries, and if governments are concerned that large firms might abuse their powerful positions, two approaches may be adopted when formulating competition policy: the *behaviour* of the firm in the market may be considered and/or the *structure* of the market itself may be considered.

When viewing *behaviour* the firm is, in effect, given the benefit of the doubt and assumed to be operating in a competitive manner unless and until some cause for concern is expressed. Any complaint concerning price-fixing or the adoption of other uncompetitive practices, such as the existence of measures designed to prevent other firms from entering the market, may be investigated. In practice it is often hard to detect such anti-competitive behaviour. The government's proposals on restrictive practices, published in a green paper during March 1988, prohibited all agreements between companies that distorted competition. This was designed to replace the existing arrangements whereby restrictive agreements had to be registered centrally, and it thereby brought the UK into line with the EC. The existing blanket exemptions, as applied, for example, to professional bodies, was to be ended.

The alternative approach to competition policy involves the government trying to influence the *structure* of the market in which the firm is operating – in other words, creating an environment in which a competitive structure, rather than a monopolistic or oligopolistic one, is more likely to exist. Those who believe that it is important to consider the structure of the market rather than the behaviour of firms argue that it is far better to deal with problems before they arise.

If there is concern that the structure of an industry might lead to uncompetitive practices, then the following options are available:

(*a*)   break up large firms into smaller ones

(*b*)   ensure easy access to the market for new firms

(*c*)   prevent firms from amalgamating (ie merging).

Breaking up large firms plays no significant part in UK competition policy although in the US the telecommunications company AT & T was split up into regional competitors. In order to ensure easy access for new firms wishing to enter the market, the Restrictive Practices Court and the Office of Fair Trading try to ensure the absence of barriers to entry. However, although it is possible to overcome many types of barrier, there will always be some that cannot be eliminated. Entry into an industry with high **fixed costs** and **economies of scale** will always be difficult (eg aircraft construction). Governments may adopt various industrial, regional and fiscal policies designed to increase the incentive to entrepreneurs to set up new businesses and possibly also to reduce the 'red tape' involved.

In view of the problems involved with breaking up large firms and the difficulties likely to be encountered in trying to control their behaviour, competition policy in the UK has tended to concentrate more on the preservation of a competitive market structure. This has been done by ensuring easy access to the market for new firms, by a consideration of anti-competitive practices and by investigating some mergers, thereby preventing the emergence of monopolies.

These policies are carried out principally by two institutions – the Office of Fair Trading (OFT) and the Monopolies and Mergers Commission (MMC). The OFT was established by the Fair Trading Act (1973). It acts as a watchdog in the market and observes and collects information on trading practices. In particular, the Director General of Fair Trading (DGFT) has a brief to monitor monopolies, mergers and takeovers and restrictive trade practices. The MMC (formally known as The Monopolies Commission) was established in 1948. Its brief is to protect the 'public interest' by considering suspected anti-competitive behaviour of firms and to investigate proposed mergers. The MMC is not able to initiate investigations itself; either the DGFT or the Secretary of State for Trade and Industry has to refer a case to it. The MMC has no power to enforce its recommendations; action depends on the Secretary of State, if he wishes to follow up the recommendations.

Various criteria have been used to define the 'public interest', including the effect on competition, potential efficiency gains, employment implications, the effect on the regions etc. What is 'in the public interest' and what is 'against the public interest' (there may, of course, be actions which fall into neither category) has been interpreted differently at various times.

The remainder of this chapter is devoted to a discussion of mergers.

Economic theory tells us that there are three types of merger, although in practice it is sometimes hard to categorize a merger as a particular type. A *horizontal merger* occurs when firms producing the same product (ie at the same stage of production) join together. Such a merger may confer the benefits of size (**economies of scale**) on the combined firm. This means that production may be achieved at lower 'unit cost' (ie lower average cost). This may be achieved either by spreading **fixed costs** or **overheads** (eg by sharing research and development expenditure) or by **rationalisation** (ie cutting out inefficient production capacity). On the other hand, a merger between two large firms will increase the concentration in the market and may, as a consequence, increase monopoly power. Moreover, a merger may occur as a defensive measure, in which, for example, a firm, threatened by a dynamic fast-growing competitor, will attempt to merge with a third firm in order to eliminate the threat. On the other hand a horizontal merger may be the best way to **restructure** an industry (see GEC/Plessey merger below), in order to enable British firms to face foreign competition more effectively.

A *vertical merger* occurs when two firms at different stages of the production process join together. This occurs between a firm and either a supplier or an outlet. Thus a car manufacturer might merge with its headlamp supplier and a brewer might acquire public houses. (The 1989 Monopolies and Mergers Commission Report on the Brewing Industry concluded that the operation of 'tied houses' by the large brewers was contrary to the public interest and proposed a limit on the number of public houses that each brewer could own, although the Commission's proposals were significantly modified by the government.) Such mergers do not necessarily confer great increases in market power to the firms involved and are often intended to guarantee supply of component parts or a secure outlet for sales.

The third type of merger is a *conglomerate* or *diversified merger*. This occurs when firms operating in different industries amalgamate. Although this is unlikely to affect market power, neither is it likely to confer the benefits of economies of scale, although the management of the predator company, may claim efficiency gains due to superior management techniques (refer to the section on conglomerates later in this chapter). Such a merger may be viewed as an attempt to spread risks into different markets. (Sometimes such a merger may be partially financed by selling off parts of the company – see later in the chapter.)

There are several different approaches which a government may adopt when deciding on its merger policy. On the one hand there is the completely *free market* approach, which views mergers in a favourable light. A merger may occur when a firm is operating inefficiently and new management will be installed with the aim of increasing efficiency and profitability. Furthermore the threat of losing independence by means of a hostile merger (ie a takeover) is claimed to provide a spur for management to strive for greater efficiency. (Although theoretically it is easy to distinguish between a merger and a take-over, in practice it is less so and the words are generally used interchangeably.)

On the other hand, there is the approach which views mergers as highly undesirable and which doubts the claims made about efficiency improvements made as a result of mergers. The rising concentration of industry and the possible adverse effects on monopoly power are viewed as the factors of paramount importance. Such views are held by economists who consider the beneficial effects of the threat of a takeover to be minimal when compared with the damaging effects of **short termism**. This occurs when a firm continually has to 'look over its shoulder' and concentrate on short-term performance targets in order to try and maintain its share price, rather than planning for the future. In such a situation, investment generally, and research and development spending in particular, might suffer.

The third approach to merger policy is the *cost-benefit* approach. This approach accepts that in any merger there will be certain benefits and certain disadvantages (ie costs) and that some sort of assessment has to be made in order to consider the overall impact.

Although the emphasis of policy changes with different governments, British merger policy has been based on the cost-benefit approach, although there are free market approach overtones. Mergers are generally viewed favourably, except for a limited number deemed to be 'against the public interest'. In 1984 Norman Tebbit, the then Secretary of State for Trade and Industry, said: 'I regard merger policy as an important part of the government's general policy of promoting competition within the economy in the interest of the consumer and efficiency and hence of growth and jobs.' Tebbit clarified the position and laid down guidelines that the effect on competition should be the only criterion for deciding whether to block a proposed merger, although in practice this guideline was not always fully adhered to.

There are those who argue that the 'burden of proof' should be reversed and that companies wishing to merge should have to prove that the merger is 'in the public interest'. Thus all those mergers where the effect was neutral would not be allowed. The alternative view is that merger policy, far from being too lax, is too tight and that companies should be encouraged to merge in order to be able to face foreign competition. These issues are now considered by adopting a case-study approach.

THE NEED TO FACE FOREIGN COMPETITION

A study of the bids by GEC for Plessey

A study of the GEC bid to takeover Plessey outlines clearly the conflict that can exist between maintaining competition in the domestic market and **restructuring** an industry to enable it to compete with foreign competition, by allowing **rationalisation** to occur and encouraging the combined group to exploit **economies of scale**. The Monopolies and Mergers Commission did not allow the 1986 bid to proceed and rejected GEC's claims arguing that: 'We do not consider that it is possible in the field of electronics to establish a direct link between company size and competitive performance'. It was accepted, however, that the rationalisation of the two companies' development of the System X telephone exchanges would be an advantage.

Encouraged by the Labour government of 1964–70 and the attempt of the Industrial Reorganisation Corporation to restructure parts of British industry, GEC took over AEI and English Electric and successfully reorganised the ailing electronics industry during the 1960s by rationalisation, elimination of duplication and elimination of excess capacity. GEC, under the guidance of Lord Weinstock, built itself up into the largest manufacturing employer in the UK, producing a wide range of products from telecommunications to defence electronics. After various failures to takeover other companies, both in the UK and abroad, and following criticisms for sitting on a 'cash mountain', GEC launched its £1.3 billion bid for Plessey in December 1985, partly as an attempt to counter criticism that the company had 'lost its way'.

The Ministry of Defence argued strongly against the merger on the grounds that GEC and Plessey were the two largest suppliers of defence electronics in the UK. Competition had recently played an increasing part in the MOD's procurement policy by the use of **competitive tendering**. An increase in GEC's dominance in the market would cause damage to the UK defence industry. 'There was a risk that merger would produce a company that would try to exploit the domestic defence market, buying up further competition in a bid for total domination' (MMC report).

British Telecom produced evidence which differed from that of the Ministry of Defence and which clearly highlighted the fundamental conflict of views which can occur in such a merger. Like the MOD, BT cited GEC and Plessey as its two largest suppliers. The UK telecommunications industry was fragmented and suffered because it was unable to reap economies of scale. In addition research and development teams were widely dispersed. Hence rationalisation made sense, but, in addition, it might be necessary to develop international partnerships as well. BT conceded that, if a merger did not take place, the System X collaboration could also exist if either company purchased the other company's interests or if a joint company were set up. (In fact, following the abortive takeover, GEC and Plessey announced in 1987 the formation of a joint company: GEC Plessey Telecommunications (GPT) to develop System X.) The fear was that if the two companies, both minnows in the international market (refer to Table 2.1) failed to pool their resources they would sink further down the list of world telecommunications manufacturers.

The MMC rejected GEC's claim that the merger would have created a

Table 2.1: Leading world manufacturers of telecommunications equipment

Company	Telecommunications sales* 1984 £m
AT & T (US)	7,590
ITT (US)	3,500
Siemens (West Germany)	2,530
Northern Telecom (Canada)	2,460
L M Ericsson (Sweden)	2,380
NEC (Japan)	2,010
Alcatel-Thomson (France)	1,935
GTE (US)	1,710
Philips (Netherlands)	893
GEC (UK)	746
Fujitsu (Japan)	744
Plessey (UK)	677
Italtel (Italy)	470

* Figures for GEC and Plessey include overseas sales and same equipment, eg business systems, classified to other industries in Government statistics. Figures for other companies may also include business equipment.
Source: Monopolies and Mergers Commission's report on proposed merger of GEC and Plessey (HMSO)

company which would have sustained the UK's position in world markets into the next century, and implied that GEC should rely more on **organic growth** (ie internal growth) than on growth by acquisitions. Questions were also raised about the importance of the size of firm as a determinant of industrial performance. On the other hand it can be argued that, by rejecting the bid, the MMC were more concerned to maintain the existence of *competition* (as measured by the number of firms in the market) rather than enhance the *ability to compete* (as claimed by those arguing that a merger would lower unit costs). This latter attitude was summed up by Sir Michael Edwardes in a letter to the *Financial Times* (19 December 1986):

> The decision to refer to the Monopolies Commission mergers like those suggested by United Biscuits and Imperial, Guinness and Distillers, and GEC and Plessey raises important strategic issues for Britain. In all three cases the effect would have been to create merged units of a size able to compete with the many powerful US, European and Japanese companies now increasingly dominating the world scene; for example, the Leyland/Bedford trucks merger provides a scale that neither could achieve on its own. It is a nonsense to inhibit that sort of **synergy** on the basis that together the merged units have a logically dominant position in the relatively small British market. That type of 'Little Englander' policy displays an ignornace of commercial reality which will cost us all a very high price in the longer term. By being doctrinaire and parochial, it is easy to have a whole host of companies competing in the same home market; but how many will be effective (or even in business) in ten years' time? Equally important, how many of them will be strong enough to avoid being taken over by foreign companies in the long run? To trade in a heavyweight world market Britain must think big. It needs an industrial strategy founded on commercial logic rather than shortsighted bureaucratic principles. A review of Britain's policy on mergers is overdue.

(The proposed mergers between United Biscuits and Imperial and between Guinness and Distillers are referred to later in this chapter; the proposed Leyland/Bedford trucks merger is considered in Chapter 4.)

As a counter to this strongly argued view, it is worth mentioning that it assumes that 'biggest is best' and that the potential benefits of **synergy** will actually accrue. The history of the British car industry (refer to Chapter 4), which has seen a whole series of mergers, is one example which shows that the potential benefits of mergers are not automatically secured.

However, GEC returned to the fray in November 1988, launching a joint bid for Plessey with Siemens of West Germany, which valued Plessey at £1.7 billion. Although the bid was cleared by both the Monopolies and Mergers Commission and by the European Commission, GEC and Siemens were delayed by the need for detailed negotiating with the Ministry of Defence on various aspects. The battle proved to be one of the most long-drawn-out takeovers ever, involving many twists and changes of fortune. Plessey unsuccessfully attempted to put together a consortium takeover bid for the much larger GEC and there were abortive negotiations between the two companies for the sale to GEC of Plessey's stake in GPT. GEC/Siemens raised their bid to £2 billion in August 1989 and this proved sufficient to end the long running battle. However, whereas GEC/Siemens had originally proposed that their joint bid would result in a series of joint ventures between them, it became increasingly clear subsequently that the bid was, according to Sir John Clark, Plessey's Chairman, 'no more or less than a simple old-fashioned attempt to carve up one of the leading British electronics companies' between GEC and Siemens'.

At the same time GEC was involved in forging links with other firms by means of establishing joint ventures. The Plessey takeover coupled with these collaborative ventures has radically restructured Britain's electronics industry in the run up to the completion of the Single European Market in 1992.

A study of the bid by British Airways for British Caledonian

When the recently privatised British Airways (BA) launched a takeover bid for Britain's second largest airline, British Caledonian, in July 1987 (shortly after the General Election) it used arguments similar to those put forward above by Sir Michael Edwardes to justify its action. BA argued that it needed to acquire its smaller rival in order to be able to compete more effectively with the mega-airlines that had emerged, particularly in the US, during the previous two years.

There were five US airlines bigger than BA, although BA was the largest airline in Europe, and by far the largest in the UK. This demonstrates the problems faced by any competition policy – which *market* should be consi-

The takeover: Lord King (right centre), Chairman of British Airways with the Chairman of British Caledonian, Sir Adam Thomson (left centre)

Table 2.2: Top world airlines (1987) (in terms of number of international and domestic passengers using scheduled services)

Airline	Passengers (000s)
1 United Air Lines	50,372
2 American Airlines	46,072
3 Eastern Air Lines	42,649
4 Continental Airlines	20,384
5 Trans World Airlines	19,842
6 British Airways	16,998*
7 Lufthansa	15,174
8 Japan Air Lines	15,148
9 Iberia	13,593
10 Alitalia	12,968

* British Caledonian ranked 43rd with 2,381,000 passengers. When added to BA, total is 19,379,000 – still ranking sixth.
Source: Lata; *World Air Transport Statistics*, 1987
From: *Financial Times*, 17 July 1987

dered? Lord King, the BA Chairman, talked of the need to create an airline which was 'capable of taking on the world' in an increasingly 'global market place' (refer to Table 2.2). There is undoubtedly considerable choice provided by airlines on many routes (especially inter-continental routes), but BA's already dominant position in the domestic market would be reinforced by a merger with British Caledonian (refer to Table 2.3). The proposed merger called into question Britain's civil aviation policy of the previous twenty years. The Edwards Committee report in 1969 supported the concept of a 'second

Table 2.3: Top UK airlines (1986)

	Output in available tonne-km (millions)†	% of all UK available tonne-km	Passengers (000s)* Scheduled	Non-scheduled	Total
British Airways	8,122	56.77	16,960	445	17,405
British Caledonian	1,942	13.58	2,354	1	2,355
Britannia	959	6.70	57	5,397	5,454
Dan Air	728	5.09	1,080	3,938	5,018
British Airtours	468	3.27	—	2,212	2,212
Monarch	396	2.77	9	1,971	1,980
Virgin Atlantic	316	2.21	290	7	297
Orion	262	1.83	19	1,340	1,359
Air Europe	261	1.82	100	1,054	1,154
Cal Air International	211	1.47	—	959	959
British Midland	132	0.92	1,553	48	1,601
British Island	90	0.63	—	651	651
Air UK	63	0.44	859	5	864

† Available tonne-kilometres (1 tonne of payload carried for 1 km) are the basic measurement of air transport output.
* Rounded to nearest 1,000.
Source: *Civil Aviation Authority Annual Statistics*, 1986
From: *Financial Times*, 30 July 1987

force airline' and 'dual designation' of routes (ie having two British airlines on any given route) and led to the formation of British Caledonian, as a result of a merger of two small independent airlines. British Caledonian had always reminded the general public in its advertising campaign that: 'We never forget you have a choice'.

The 1984 White Paper on Civil Aviation supported the idea of a 'sound and competitive multi-airline industry'. However, there was no significant enforced reduction in BA's route network or market share (in favour of British Caledonian or other British airlines) prior to its privatisation. This must have contributed eventually to the decision of the British Caledonian board reluctantly to consider a merger with the much larger BA. The government referred the bid to the Monopolies and Mergers Commission (MMC) which allowed it to proceed, ruling that it was 'not against the public interest'. This ruling, in effect, accepted the reality of a *global market place*. BA was, however, to be forced to give up some of British Caledonian's route network.

This was followed by an attempt to thwart the deal by Scandinavian Airlines System (SAS), which made a partial bid for 26 per cent of British Caledonian's shares in a proposed deal which also involved a complex financial restructuring package. The key attraction of British Caledonian to SAS was that it was based in Gatwick airport – a key hub airport. Great savings are possible in the airline industry from access to a 'hub and spokes' system of routes. For similar reasons BA, a Heathrow-based airline, was also keen to establish itself at Gatwick, thereby making itself the dominant airline at Britain's two largest airports. Faced with a competing predator, BA raised its bid to a knockout £250 million and this won the day. During the takeover battle, questions were raised about the desirability of allowing a foreign airline to bid for a British airline, providing access to Britain's second largest 'hub'.

The attitude to foreign takeovers is now considered by studying the contested takeover for Rowntree.

THE ATTITUDE TO FOREIGN BIDS

A study of the contested bid between Nestlé and Suchard for Rowntree

During April 1988, Suchard, the Swiss-based chocolate manufacturer, launched a **dawn raid** on Rowntree, the York-based company, quickly scooping up a stake of 14.9 per cent as a 'strategic investment', but claiming that it had no intention of launching a full-scale takeover bid. In response to this, the Swiss conglomerate Nestlé, which is the largest food company in the world, launched a hostile cash bid for Rowntree, which valued the British company at £2.1 billion. The then Secretary of State for Trade and Industry, Lord Young, decided that there were no grounds for referring the bid to the Monopolies and Mergers Commission; nor were there any grounds for referring the Suchard holding in Rowntree, which had, by that time, been increased to 29.9 per cent. This, therefore, set the scene for a three-way takeover battle for the future of Rowntree. Suchard responded with an offer of £2.32 billion, which was countered by a further bid from Nestlé, valuing Rowntree at £2.55 billion. This bid won the approval of the Rowntree Board, which had strenuously opposed the previous bids.

Suchard was unwilling to increase its bid and sold its 29.9 per cent stake to Nestlé, at a profit close to £200 million. This gave rise to speculation that Suchard planned to use these funds to launch another takeover bid, possibly for Cadbury Schweppes. The effect of contested takeover bids on a company's share price may be seen from the 139 per cent increase in the price of Rowntree's shares during the first six months of 1988 – the best performance of any share in the FT-SE 100 index.

The contested takeover for Rowntree came in the wake of a series of other moves in the European chocolate industry. In particular, Nestlé and Suchard had been involved in a similar takeover battle for the ownership of Cote d'Or, the Belgian chocolate company, during 1987. This produced a successful outcome for Suchard, in preference to the much larger Nestlé.

The bid for Rowntree was set in the context of a shift in consumer preference away from 'slab' bars of chocolate towards 'countline' products (individually wrapped chocolate snacks) – an area in which Rowntree had great strength. Rowntree's leading brands included Kit Kat, Smarties, Yorkie and Quality Street and the bids for the company were based on a desire by the Swiss companies to own these brands and to market them globally. It takes a great deal of time and money to establish a brand which explains why predators may be willing, when purchasing a company with strong *brand identification*, to pay far more than the stock market valuation of that company. This appears to be an increasingly important trend. The price paid includes a substantial amount for the *goodwill* that the brands yield. Purchase of *market share* is seen to be less costly than establishing brands – and is quicker too.

The takeover battle produced an outcome, which was, at the time, the largest ever bid for a British based company by a foreign one. But it also raised a number of important questions, which are now addressed:

1 How does the completion of the Single European Market in 1992 and the increasing globalisation of world markets affect takeover bids?

2 Does it matter that the relatively liberal capital laws in Britain allow British companies to be acquired by foreign ones, whereas the acquisition of foreign companies by British ones is more difficult?

3 Does the nationality of firms matter?

The bids for Rowntree may be seen as part of a growing trend towards *globalisation* in world markets. Just as the reduced level of import controls during the post Second World War period saw a substantial increase in world trade, so the increasingly liberal attitude to capital controls during the 1980s has seen a marked increase in cross-border investment – both to establish new factories and to engage in takeovers of existing firms. Furthermore, the intention of the European Community to complete the Single European Market by 1992 was seen as an additional factor behind the bids from the two Swiss companies. A liberalised single market, often referred to as 'Fortress

Europe', could well create obstacles to outsiders – and Switzerland is not a member of the EC.

Factors which affect the concentration of any particular industry are extremely complex. There are some European industries (eg volume car production – see Chapter 4) which are already very concentrated and integrated on a European basis (both in terms of sales and location of production facilities). There are others (eg insurance) which are neither concentrated nor integrated. As far as the *consumer goods industries* are concerned, there are forces pushing for greater concentration and integration. This is evident especially in the food and drinks industries, both of which have seen takeover activity during the 1980s. The breakdown of traditional national markets, in terms of taste and fashion, coupled with the need to cope with a Europe without internal frontiers in 1992 have been the major stimuli towards growing internationalisation. Companies with well-established brands, which are the best vehicles for such expansion, are likely to be increasingly few and far between – this explains the keen interest in and premium price paid for Rowntree.

When Lord Young, the Secretary of State for Trade and Industry (1987–9), decided not to refer the Nestlé bid for Rowntree to the Monopolies and Mergers Commission (MMC), he did so because the effect of the merger on competition would have been negligible. Rowntree supplied 26 per cent of the UK chocolate confectionery market, second only to Cadbury with 30 per cent. Suchard supplied 2 per cent and Nestlé 3 per cent. Mars, Cadbury and Rowntree between them controlled about 80 per cent of the market, and so an addition of 2 or 3 per cent would be unlikely to affect the competitive position (refer to Table 2.4). However, although the effects on market share in the short term were certainly negligible, it is possible to argue, from a dynamic perspective, that the removal of Rowntree from the market place as an independent supplier eliminated a potentially powerful long-term competitor in world markets for the Swiss firms. This is of particular importance in an industry in which it is hard for new entrants to establish themselves, in view of the high costs of entry into the market.

During the takeover battle, it was suggested that Cadbury Schweppes should act as a **white knight** to Rowntree, in order to form a strong British company able to compete effectively with the Swiss. However, this suggestion would have given the combined group a market share in excess of 50 per cent of the British market, which would have fallen foul of the MMC guidelines.

Various other objections to the Nestlé takeover of Rowntree were raised at the time. Great play was made of the **reciprocity** argument. This is based on the comparison between the relative ease with which foreign companies may bid for British ones, due to the liberal capital markets in Britain, whereas Swiss companies are less likely to be the subject of takeover bids from abroad due to the financial structure of Swiss companies.

However, it was argued that, if a foreign predator wishes to place a greater value on a British company than the stock market does, then that is to the benefit of shareholders. Whether the interests of shareholders are the same as the interests of the workers, the company and the country (however 'interests'

Table 2.4: European chocolate confectionery market shares (percentage by sales value) for 1987/88

	UK	Austria	% Belgium	France	Italy
Mars	24	4	6	11	1
Suchard	2	73	82	13	—
Rowntree	26	—	2	17	—
Ferrero	2	—	5	6	34
Cadbury	30	—	—	8	—
Nestlé	3	5	3	10	5

	Netherlands	Swizterland	% W. Germany	Total
Mars	23	9	22	17
Suchard	—	17	15	13
Rowntree	13	—	3	11
Ferrero	—	—	16	10
Cadbury	—	—	—	9
Nestlé	—	17	8	9

Source: Hendersen Crosthwaite
From: *Financial Times*, 29 April 1988

may be defined) is possibly another matter. Such an argument also presupposes that the 'market knows best' (where the term 'market' today often means a limited number of institutional fund managers, whose time horizons may be 'short term') and that the nationality of a firm 'does not matter'. These issues caused great controversy at the time of the takeover battle.

Critics of foreign ownership argue that British plants may become **satellite plants** or **screwdriver plants**, involved in the low value-added parts of the production process, providing jobs that are the first to disappear in times of difficulty. This contrasts with the secure, skilled jobs provided in the 'core activities' of, for example, research and development and product planning. These tend to be located close to the company's headquarters, which, for a foreign-owned multinational company, is unlikely to be in Britiain. This is known as the **headquarters effect**. (The issue is viewed again in Chapter 4, where the effects of the creation of Japanese car plants in this country are considered.) It is, however, worth mentioning that Nestlé subsequently established a special unit based in York responsible for developing the whole group's wordwide confectionery business.

Sir Hector Laing, Chairman of United Biscuits, in a letter to *The Times* (2 June 1988) questioned:

> Do we really want to go down in history as the generation which sold for a mess of pottage the finest British companies, which have successfully built brand names and franchises of high repute over a century or more. . . ? I do not believe the vast majority of people want to see British industry sold abroad for jam today.

However, those who criticize foreign inward investment are accused of possessing a 'Little Englander' mentality, in an environment in which the nationality of companies is becoming 'increasingly irrelevant in modern trading conditions' (Kenneth Clarke, *Hansard*, 8 June 1988). Supporters of the free movement of capital believe it to be of benefit to all countries, as a means of creating a dynamic market structure and determining the optimal use of resources. The free movement is particularly beneficial for Britain, which is itself a major overseas predator, particularly in the US, helping to accummulate overseas assets, the earnings from which contribute to the balance of payments. Lord Young argued that Britain was creating a 'third empire' by her overseas investment. Hence any attempt at national chauvinism, by acting against foreign inward investment, would make it more difficult to argue in favour of British outward investment with foreign governments.

The growth of cross border mergers, the increasingly free capital movements and the completion of the Single European Market in 1992 all make it essential that an effective EC merger policy is devised. Some countries have systems of self-regulation and others rely on legislation; but, in addition to this, there is the problem of definition of 'market share' – should it refer to a particular country or to the EC as a whole?

Some concern has also been expressed about the impact of conglomerate mergers on the economy and it is this issue which is addressed next.

A CHARTER FOR CONGLOMERATES?

Although British merger policy has lacked consistency and coherence, it has been based on the principle that mergers which are deemed to be 'against the public interest' should be prevented. What is 'against the public interest' has, however, never been fully defined, although the emphasis placed on competition as a major theme of economic policy by the Conservative government means that only mergers which reduce competition per se are likely to be investigated. On this basis it would seem that a *conglomerate merger* is unlikely to fall foul of the guidelines. This has led to the claim that British merger policy has potentially represented a *Charter for Conglomerates*, although it should be noted that, as discussed in the next subsection, there has been a move away from diversification and conglomerates, especially after the Stock Market Crash of 1987.

Proposed mergers involving Britain's two largest conglomerate companies will be considered, in an attempt to highlight the issues raised.

A study of the contested bids by Hanson and United Biscuits for Imperial

An agreed merger was proposed in 1985 between Imperial Group, with interests in brewing, tobacco, food and restaurants and United Biscuits (UB), with interests in biscuits, snack foods, frozen foods and restaurants. Imperial would benefit by reducing its dependence on the declining tobacco market and UB would gain access to Imperial's reserve of cash, necessary for further expansion. Imperial and United Biscuits claimed that, although there was relatively little overlap between the two groups (except in crisps and snack food), growth could be more rapid as a combined group as a result of concentrating on complementary activities (eg UB's products could be sold more extensively in Imperial's Courage pubs). It was calculated that the merger could produce £30 million extra profits in 1988, by creating the proposed new 'consumer goods group'. According to Sir Hector Laing, Chairman of United Biscuits: 'In a world where the large food companies are getting larger, backed by the cash resources of very rich large partners, it is not good enough to be a minnow: in order to compete internationally each company has to get bigger.' This is similar to GEC's arguments for taking over Plessey and BA's arguments for taking over British Caledonian. When presented in this way the proposed merger appears to be based on clear industrial logic, although it was considered by some to be partly a defensive move on the part of the companies involved (especially Imperial, which was hoping that, by increasing its own size, it would help to reduce the chance of an unwanted takeover from a third party).

However, the unwanted takeover bid for Imperial did materialise, as had been rumoured, from Hanson Trust (subsequently renamed Hanson), the largest conglomerate company in the UK, which also had substantial interests in the US. Hanson had a wide range of manufacturing and retailing interests containing virtually no product overlap with Imperial. Although the Hanson plans for Imperial were never fully spelled out, it was claimed that Hanson had great experience of digesting major acquisitions and also had the ability to rejuvenate ailing companies, transforming their profitability. On the other hand, it was claimed that Hanson was only interested in short-term profits, rather than long-term investment and that the company was only capable of limited organic growth, thus forcing it to rely on ever larger takeover bids to sustain its expansion.

Faced with the two conflicting bids the Department of Trade and Industry decided that the agreed merger between Imperial and UB should be referred to the Monopolies and Merger Commission (MMC), as the combined company would hold over 40 per cent of the snack food market – this together with a similar share of the market held by Nabisco would create a duopolistic situation in the market. However, the contested takeover of Imperial by Hanson was not referred to the MMC as it did not adversely affect competition or the 'public interest'. The difference of treatment for the two bids gave rise to criticism that the government's merger policy favoured conglomerates.

A revised merger proposal between UB and Imperial, which involved disposing of Imperial's Golden Wonder subsidiary, thus reducing market share in the snack foods market, was not referred to MMC and hence both bids were allowed to proceed. After a closely fought battle Hanson won control of Imperial for £2.8 billion.

Hanson has been built up into one of Britain's leading companies over a period of twenty years based on an acquisition philosophy which involves a reduction in the acquired company's bureacracy, devolution of responsibility to local managers, a tight control of capital expenditure and a disposal of some of the peripheral assets which are not part of the company's 'core activities'. With the aim of keeping only the Imperial Tobacco and Imperial Foods divisions, Hanson within a short period of time sold Imperial's hotels and restaurants interests to Trust House Forte (£190 million), Golden Wonder Crisps to Dalgety (£87 million) and Courage to the Australian company Elders IXL (£1.4 billion). Thus almost £1.7 billion of the £2.8 billion spent on the Imperial takeover was recouped and yet the remaining assets yielded over half the Imperial profit! This confirms Hanson's reputation for being able to spot cheap assets and sell off unwanted parts profitably, but it also gives rise to the charge that Hanson is involved in **asset stripping**.

On the day (19 September 1986) that Hanson sold Courage to Elders, the *Financial Times* leader 'Reshuffling of Assets' (part of which is reproduced below) provided an interesting view of the company, which helps one to consider the effect of such conglomerates on the economy as a whole.

> Hanson Trust has two main roles. It is an industrial company, managing certain assets, and it is a trader in companies, redistributing assets from one owner to another. In its first rôle, it has tended to concentrate on low-technology businesses which are managed with a close eye on reducing costs and generating cash. Its record is entirely respectable, but there is no evidence to suggest that Hanson's skills are appropriate for the really difficult management problems like the rebuilding of the Rover Group or the strengthening of I.C.L.'s position in the world computer market. To the extent that the U.K. needs more internationally competitive companies in research-intensive sectors, Hanson does not offer, or claim to offer, much of a contribution. This is not to denigrate what Hanson does, but the limits to its managerial scope need to be recognised. It is the second role which has recently come into greater prominence. When it attacks companies like S.C.M. and Imperial, it does so with the clear intention of keeping only part of the business for its own portfolio and selling the rest to the highest bidder. The most obvious targets are the unwieldy conglomerates built up in the late 1960's and early 1970's which still represent an area of managerial weakness in the British (and U.S.) economy. Thus Hanson's role in redeploying industrial assets can be helpful.

A study of the failed bid by BTR for Pilkington

In 1987 BTR launched a bid for Pilkington, the world's leading manufacturer of flat and safety glass, which presented the arguments about conglomerate mergers even more starkly than did the Hanson bid for Imperial. BTR was Britain's second largest conglomerate which, like Hanson, had a reputation for spotting companies with undervalued assets. After gaining control of a company, BTR would sell off unwanted divisions and then significantly improve the performance of those remaining. Its share price and profitability improved dramatically during the 1980s (refer to Figure 2.1). BTR had successfully mounted takeover bids for Thomas Tilling in 1983 and for Dunlop in 1985, improving the performances of each company after the merger by improvements in productivity. Although the Secretary of State for Trade and Industry decided not to refer the bid for Pilkington to the Monopolies and Mergers Commission, BTR abandoned its attempt to takeover the company, claiming that this had been motivated, not by adverse public reaction and the political storm created, but by Pilkington's better than expected profits forecast, which indicated that the likely price required to capture the company would be greater than BTR was willing to pay.

Figure 2.1: BTR share price and profitability

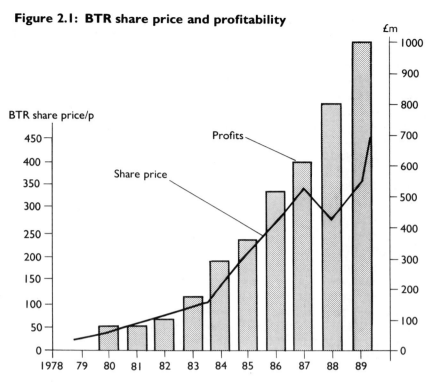

From: *Sunday Times*, 18 March 1990

The BTR/Pilkington takeover battle focused attention on the guidelines for referral of bids to the MMC. As BTR had no stake in the glass industry prior to the bid, the proposed merger did not qualify for referral on the competition yardstick. Questions were also raised about the industrial impact of the merger. The two companies were portrayed as representing totally contrasting management philosophies. On the one hand, Pilkington was represented as a company committed to long term research and development, whereas BTR was seen as a company interested in quick profits, increasing efficiency by **rationalisation** (and job losses) and **asset stripping**. This was contrasted with the 'paternalism' shown by Pilkington, an important employer in the north west of England, concerned to 'buy local' and to protect the local and regional economy. Certainly the local community expressed overwhelming opposition to the BTR bid.

BACK TO THE CORE

Although many firms do continue to diversify, there has been a growing mood against conglomerates and away from the notion that diversification was an automatic virtue and an inescapable trend, views which were accepted by most people in the 1960s and 1970s. This has been replaced by a move which is variously described as a return 'back to basics', an attempt to 'focus on the core' or 'unbundling'. This is made possible either by divestment of subsidiaries (ie a sale from one company to another) or by hostile takeovers from 'break-up specialists', who calculate that the value of the whole company as determined by the Stock Market, is less than the value of the sum of the parts. The break-up specialist may have an interest in retaining certain parts of the company or he may wish to dispose of all of it to other companies. Hanson, Britain's largest break-up specialist retains certain parts of the conglomerates which it has taken over, but has as a result itself became a conglomerate – as discussed in the previous subsection.

A study of the Hoylake bid for BAT

The £13 billion bid for BAT (formerly known as British American Tobacco) in 1989 was the largest bid ever involving a British company. The bid was made by a consortium headed by Sir James Goldsmith through a specially created company called Hoylake.

The background to this bid may be seen in BAT's attempt to diversify out of tobacco, which was a 'mature' industry with relatively limited growth prospects. Diversification centred on three areas: retailing, paper and insurance. This resulted in four different parts of BAT in totally unrelated areas, with relatively little scope for efficiency gains by **economies of scale** or **synergy**. Furthermore, the Stock Market continued to value the diversified BAT as if it were a (lowly-rated) tobacco stock, despite its expensive acquisitions in other

The Hoylake trio: (left to right) Jacob Rothschild, Sir James Goldsmith and Kerry Packer

Figure 2.2: BAT share price during the 1980s relative to the FT-Actuaries All Share Index

FT-Actuaries All Share Index

From: Financial Times, 15 July 1989

Figure 2.3: The unbundling of BAT

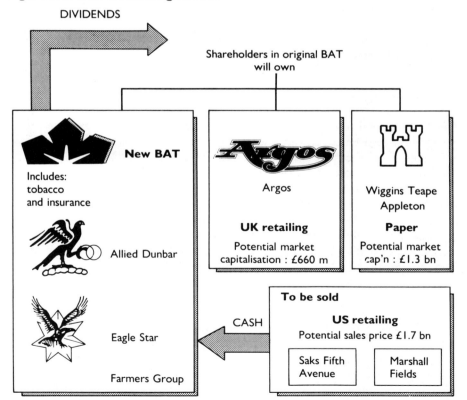

From: Financial Times, 27 September 1989

fields. However, reference to Figure 2.2 indicates that the BAT share price outperformed the market during the 1980s, although this outperformance was concentrated in the first half of the decade. Hoylake's bid was intended to 'unbundle' BAT's tobacco core, disposing of the other divisions of the company and retaining the original tobacco interests. Hoylake claimed that: 'BAT's urge to conglomerate has diverted its attention from the traditional core business, tobacco towards "ill-conceived diversification"'.

The bid and the general shift in mood against diversification highlights a fundamental problem which faces a company which is based on one product with limited growth prospects. Diversification may at the time appear to be the only way that the company can maintain its profits growth and defend the value of its shares. (This can be seen most clearly in the case of a company involved in mining natural resources which are in finite supply. In the long term, failure to diversify would mean that the company would disappear.)

Break-up bids are often financed by means of a *leveraged buyout*. Shareholders of the company under attack are generally offered relatively little cash or equity, but instead high yielding bonds (referred to as 'junk-bonds'). This debt is settled when the company is 'unbundled' and parts are sold off.

During 1990 Hoylake withdrew its bid for BAT, partly because of problems encountered with the US regulatory authorities when it tried to arrange a buyer for BAT's US insurance business. However, far more significant in explaining the failure of the bid was the decision of BAT to 'unbundle' itself by selling off its paper and retailing interests (refer to Figure 2.3). Although its bid failed, Hoylake's objective of maximising shareholder value had been realised.

THE GUINNESS AFFAIR

The Guinness takeover of Distillers is studied, not just as an example of a keenly contested takeover, but also as it demonstrated what many saw as the unacceptable sides of takeover activity and the City of London.

Distillers, the Scotch whisky firm, when faced with an unwanted takeover bid from Argyll, the supermarket chain, in December 1985, attempted to merge with Guinness, using it as a **white knight** (ie a friendly rescuer) in an attempt to thwart this move. Guinness, in addition to its traditional brewing interests, had acquired Bell's whisky after an acrimonious takeover battle in 1985. As a consequence the bid for Distillers was referred to the Monopolies and Mergers Commission because the combined Guinness/Distillers share of the whisky market was in excess of 35 per cent, which was considered to confer too much market-power on the combined company. The government was criticized for referring an agreed bid, while leaving a hostile bid free to proceed. In addition, questions were again raised about the criteria used to judge whether or not a bid should be referred – the Guinness bid was referred on grounds of reduced competition, but, again, this allows companies in unrelated industries to make bids unhindered. The Guinness bid was subsequently revamped to include the sale of a small number of minor whisky brands, which was designed to reduce the combined market share of Guinness and Distillers to below 25 per cent.

This second bid avoided reference to the MMC and thus the way was open for a contested takeover battle between Guinness and Argyll for control of Distillers.

According to the Argyll offer documents:

> with Argyll's management and substantial experience in the food and drink markets, both nationally and internationally, we can restore Distillers to the pre-eminent position it once occupied at home and abroad, and that we have the opportunity to build Distillers and Argyll into Scotland's greatest company . . . based in Edinburgh and directed from there.

On the other hand Mr Ernest Saunders, Chief Executive of Guinness, claimed that: 'The important thing is that we are going to create a major new international brands business in Britain – the first since Beecham's in the 1950s'. Distillers claimed that 'Argyll is unsuited for the stewardship of the Scotch whisky industry, because the majority of its business is as a UK discount supermarket operator'.

After an acrimonious and close battle, Guinness emerged narrowly as the victor. Part of the reason for victory was that the value of the Guinness offer was higher than that of Argyll, aided by the rise of the Guinness share price before the offer closed. (Although there is usually a cash offer for the shares of the company being taken over, a share alternative is generally on offer. The predator company will offer x of its own shares in exchange for y shares of the target company and thus the value of the offer will depend on the relative share prices of the two companies. Any increase in the share price of the predator company will therefore enhance the value of its offer).

In an attempt to sway Scottish shareholders of Distillers and to influence Scottish public opinion (which was anxious that a merger with Guinness might reduce Distillers' involvement in Scotland), Guinness promised during the campaign that the 'largest part of our business will be Scottish-based', that Scotland would be the 'decision-making centre' of the company and that Sir Thomas Risk, Governor of the Bank of Scotland, would be appointed as Non-Executive Chairman of the combined group. However, in July 1986 Guinness announced that 'it has not been possible to reach agreement with Sir Thomas Risk and he will not now be invited to join the board, nor therefore be nominated as Non-Executive Chairman'. Furthermore, the company also seemed to be reneging on some of the assurances given to placate Scottish interests during the takeover battle.

Guinness was accused of bad faith, in particular for failing to adhere to promises made in the official offer documents. In addition, there were fears that, if undertakings made during a takeover bid could be put aside subsequently, then there would be calls to replace the present takeover system, based to a great extent on a voluntary code of conduct and self-regulation, by a statutory system. On the other hand, Risk was seen as being a possible focus for dissent on the Board, as someone who would interfere with hard decisions that might have to be made about Distillers, and who would, therefore, behave in a more executive role than had been envisaged, rather than as a figurehead. Thus the decision not to appoint Risk could be seen as an attempt by the Board to carry out its *fiduciary duty* to the shareholders (ie to act in their best interests). In the end Saunders achieved overwhelming support when the issue was put to shareholders and he himself was confirmed as Chairman and Chief Executive and the new structure of the Board was accepted.

As has been explained previously, the value of the Guinness offer for Distillers depended on the relative share prices of the two shares and the Guinness share price proved to be strong during the final lap of the campaign. However, this was achieved partly by the creation of a false market in Guinness shares. Money, paid allegedly for takeover fees and consultancy advice, was channelled to various associates of Guinness for the purpose of buying Guinness shares, thereby increasing the share price – this is known as a *share-support operation*. Amid the growing City scandal, Ernest Saunders temporarily stepped down as Chairman and Chief Executive of Guinness and was subsequently dismissed. Saunders and three others were found guilty (in a trial in 1990) on charges of conspiracy, theft and false accounting. In what became known as the 'City trial of the century', Saunders received the longest prison sentence of five years.

The Guinness Affair aroused serious public concern specifically about the government's competition policy, but more generally about self-regulation in the City, leading to calls for statutory framework.

COMMENT

The case studies considered in this chapter indicate how difficult it is to formulate a coherent policy for mergers. In addition traditional views on the need to maintain competition within an economy have been influenced not only by the existence of large foreign companies, but also by the increasing globalisation of world trade and the completion of the Single European Market by 1992.

Attention has also focused on British merger policy which has operated in a self-regulatory framework, rather than a statutory one. Furthermore, Britain's liberal capital market has allowed easier access for foreigners to British firms than vice versa and this has caused some to claim that British industry is vulnerable.

3 *Privatisation*

■ Nationalisation: development, performance and disenchantment
■ The meaning of privatisation
■ Arguments for privatisation
■ Privatisation in practice
■ Comment

During the second term (1983–7) of the Conservative government privatisation became one of its main economic policies. In order to understand privatisation fully, since it may be viewed as a reaction to what went before, it is necessary to consider the nationalisation and state enterprise of the post-war period. The arguments for nationalisation, the performance of nationalised industries and the disenchantment that developed with them in some quarters are studied.

The meaning of 'privatisation' and arguments put forward in favour of it are then considered. The chapter finishes with a section on 'Privatisation in Practice'.

NATIONALISATION: DEVELOPMENT, PERFORMANCE AND DISENCHANTMENT

The state had been involved in the running of publicly-owned enterprises before the Second World War, but it was not until the post-war Labour governments of 1945 to 1951 that there was an attempt to extend public ownership to any significant degree. The Labour government was elected at a time when Keynesian economics was moving towards being accepted as economic orthodoxy. Keynesian policies were directed at ensuring full employment and involved government intervention in the running of the economy using **demand management** techniques (refer also to Chapter 1, page 13). It was believed that this intervention would be aided if the state had control of certain key industries (eg coal, railways, gas, electricity distribution), which were crucial to post-war economic recovery and which were in such a rundown state that it was unlikely that sufficient private capital would materialise to rejuvenate them. Many industries had suffered from a lack of investment during the depression in the 1930s and had been further weakened by the effects of the Second World War.

Thus nationalisation could assist the government's macroeconomic management and planning of the economy. In addition the government would be more able to pursue policies designed to rescue collapsing firms and to reduce regional disparities of income. This was all the more important as many nationalised industries were operating in markets which were affected by long-term decline, where contraction and a low rate of return on capital were probably inevitable. Thus the Labour government's nationalisation programme was intended also to facilitate post-war regional policy.

There are certain costs and benefits which are not taken into account by the price system. Such costs and benefits (termed *social costs* and *social benefits*) are external to the firm and are not measured in a firm's costs or revenue accounts. A firm is often able to ignore the social costs imposed by pollution, congestion or noise associated with its operations. However, it may also be unable to reap the benefits by charging the community for the advantages gained by improved amenities installed close to its factory (eg an approach road), which benefit local people. In situations where the price system does not take into account all the costs and benefits to the whole community, nationalised industries operating in the 'national interest' were directed to take into account the *externalities* discussed above. These arguments have been used to justify the continued operation of branch railway lines and low productivity coal pits, where the costs of closure to the local economy were deemed to be too high, even if the operations themselves were unviable. Furthermore as nationalised industries were intended to operate in the 'national interest', it was claimed that this should lead to improved industrial relations, as the strife between labour and capital, associated with capitalist ownership, was reduced.

Labour was attempting to control what were known as the *commanding heights* of the economy. In addition to the economic arguments put forward for nationalisation, there was also a strong political impetus, as the Labour party attempted to achieve a 'fairer, more egalitarian' society, in which social priorities and the 'national interest' took precedence over the desire to maximise profits. This policy was an attempt to satisfy Clause 4 of the Labour Party's Constitution, which committed the party to 'the common ownership of the means of production, distribution and exchange, and the best possible system of popular administration and control of each industry or service'. There were, in addition, further arguments put forward to support and justify the policy of nationalisation and public ownership.

In some industries, competition is considered to raise the costs of production rather than, as is usually expected, to reduce them. This is because smaller competing firms lose the benefits of size – **economies of scale** – which would have accrued to a single, large firm. This describes a situation in which a monopoly appears to be the best structure for an industry, and is called a **natural monopoly**. Public utilities such as electricity, gas, water and telecommunications provided the best examples of what were considered to be natural monopolies, although when technological advances are made, certain industries formerly classed as natural monopolies may cease to be so (eg telecommunications). The possibility that a natural monopoly under private ownership might abuse its dominant position led to arguments in favour of nationalisation and public ownership, so that the state could operate the nationalised industry in the 'public interest'. The benefits of scale, coupled with the end of 'wasteful' competition (eg duplicated research and development expenditure) should also lead to a more efficient industry.

After the initial nationalisation programme carried out by the post-war Labour government, there was relatively little change in the frontiers between the state sector and the private sector. Both the Conservative and Labour parties accepted the existence of a **mixed economy** (an economy with both private and public sectors) and a welfare state. This period of time has been described as a period of *consensus*. Although politicians at the time would certainly not have viewed it in the same light, with the benefit of hindsight, we can claim that, as both of the main political parties broadly supported Keynesian economics and the existence of the mixed economy, the differences between them were, in today's terms, relatively small. This contrasts with Mrs Thatcher's Conservative government, which has rejected Keynesian economics and has questioned the whole role of the state and the very existence of the mixed economy.

The changes in the state sector before the 1980s have occurred in a relatively piecemeal fashion. Rolls-Royce collapsed in 1971 under the strains of developing the RB 211 aero engine, and was nationalised by Edward Heath's Conservative government, unwilling to see such an important part of British industry going bankrupt. This happened despite the government's claims that it was injecting market discipline into the private sector by not 'bailing out lame ducks'. In 1975 the Labour government was equally unwilling to see British Leyland collapse and this company too was nationalised (see Chapter 4, page 63). It would be true to say that, when the Conservatives were elected in 1979, the composition of the nationalised industry sector had certainly not been arrived at by any clear sets of principles or criteria.

Nationalised industries have been accused of inefficiency for a variety of reasons. It is claimed that the lack of competition and market discipline induces a complacent attitude in both management and the workforce. In addition the possible abuse of monopoly power in any nationalised industry which is a monopoly may also lead to inefficiency. Such a firm will have little need to respond to consumer requirements, either in terms of the price of the product or its quality. This will result in limited choice for the consumer and a lack of innovation (eg British Telecom phone equipment, which for many years was severely limited whilst it was part of the public sector). Whether or not these criticisms of inefficiency are valid is extremely difficult to assess, and the situation is complicated by repeated political interference by governments of both parties in the pricing, investment and employment decisions of nationalised industries, thereby concealing their real performance.

The traditional theory of the firm assumes that profit maximisation is the objective of all firms and, on this basis, in competitive markets, high profits are a sign of success and efficiency. Realistically, perfectly competitive markets rarely exist (ie there is some monopolistic tendency in most markets). Furthermore, firms may set themselves several targets and not simply restrict themselves to the sole target of profit maximisation. Therefore, even for a private company, high profits do not necessarily imply efficiency. (A further discussion of the possible efficiency gains from privatisation follows later in the chapter.)

The problems faced when assessing the performance of a nationalised industry are even more serious. When established during the 1940s, nationalised industries were instructed to operate in the 'public interest' and to break even over a period of years. It is, of course, possible for a monopoly, to break even at a whole series of different outcomes, at different pricing, output, employment and investment levels. When taken with the latitude allowed by the instruction to 'operate in the public interest', it is easy to see that, with such imprecise targets, it was bound to be extremely difficult to assess the performance of nationalised industries. Government interference, whether for political or economic reasons, is likely to make this assessment even more difficult.

In order to counter concern about the lack of guidance for nationalised industries, there were two government White Papers during the 1960s, which attempted to produce financial targets for nationalised industries and, at the same time, guidelines for pricing and investment decisions.

The attempts to improve the performances of nationalised industries were not allowed to run their course, because in the 1970s governments of both major parties used nationalised industries in order to achieve wider macroeconomic targets. The increasing concern for inflation, felt during the 1970s, meant that governments restricted the price rises of nationalised industries in an attempt to moderate inflation in the economy as a whole. During the latter part of the 1970s, cash limits, known as *External Financing Limits* (EFLs), were introduced as governments tried to control public spending. Limits on the deficits of loss-making industries (eg British Rail) and profit targets for the profitable industries (eg British Gas) were set. However, although an EFL appeared to set a clear target for a nationalised industry, it was not unambiguous. Unlike in the private sector, borrowing for investment was treated in the same way as borrowing to finance current spending (on labour or raw materials). Hence an EFL target may be achieved by cutting investment rather than improving efficiency by cutting costs. Similarly in those nationalised industries which are monopolies, the EFL may be met simply by raising prices.

During the 1970s increasing concern was expressed about the performance of nationalised industries, many of which were monopolies, insulated from the pressures of the market and, therefore able to charge high prices. In addition they were perceived to be inefficient, measured in terms of productivity, and also unprofitable, causing a drain on public finances. The disenchantment with nationalised industries and moves by the Conservative government towards denationalisation, or 'privatisation', must be seen in this context.

THE MEANING OF PRIVATISATION

The term *privatisation* is a new one and is hard to define precisely. There are three main strands to the policy of privatisation:

1   *A transfer of ownership from the public sector to the private sector*

This is achieved either through the sale of a public sector firm directly to a private sector firm or, more commonly, by the sale of at least 51 per cent of the shares in the company to the general public. Although this could be termed *denationalisation*, the fact that it is not (instead the word 'privatisation' is now more commonly used) is an indication of the extent of the change in thinking brought about by Thatcherism.

2   *The provision of goods and services by the private sector, which were previously supplied by the public sector*

This is achieved when local authorities replace directly employed labour with a private sector firm (eg street cleaning, hospital laundry and catering services) and is known as *contracting out*. It is hoped that, by putting the contract out to **competitive tender**, efficiency will rise and costs will fall. Competitive tendering is a system whereby contracts are awarded to the supplier who offers the best deal.

Contracting out by local authorities has increased under the Conservative government – partly voluntarily and partly as a response to changes in the law requiring them to do so for certain activities. However, opposition from Labour local authorities to privatisation measures, in principle, has been coupled, in practice, with a fear that job losses and a decline in the standard of services will occur as a result of contracting out.

3   *Liberalisation or deregulation*

This occurs when markets, previously served by the public sector monopolies and governed by regulations, are opened up to competition from the private sector. (In fact the benefits of competition could be gained without the private sector acquiring public sector assets, ie competition could be created between different parts of the public sector.)

Liberalisation and deregulation measures are designed to stimulate competition, to improve the working of the market mechanism and to remove unnecessary regulations or controls. Long distance coach travel was deregulated in 1979 and the results of competition were beneficial, in terms of reduced prices and a higher level of service on most routes. The success of this measure led to the deregulation of local bus services in 1986, involving the break up of the National Bus Company and the introduction of private sector competition. The effects have yet to be fully assessed, but there is some concern that, as bus companies are no longer allowed to engage in **cross-subsidisation** (ie direct profits from profitable routes towards subsidising unprofitable ones), unprofitable routes and evening and weekend services may be forced to close. On the other hand, the service provided is more likely to be responsive to customer demand.

The most prominent aspect of privatisation, as practised by the Conservative government, has been the transfer of ownership of assets from the public sector to the private sector (as in definition 1), and it is the arguments for this that are now considered.

ARGUMENTS FOR PRIVATISATION

Improved efficiency and greater choice for the consumer

> A company which has to satisfy its customers and compete to survive is more likely to be efficient, alert to innovation, and genuinely accountable to the public (1983 Conservative Election Manifesto).

Thus, using arguments which are, in effect, the same as the criticisms levelled against nationalised industries, it is claimed that privatisation leads to greater competition and efficiency, by exposing the privatised firms to market forces. This responsiveness to consumer demand is also likely to lead to greater choice. It is hoped that the managers, spurred on by the profit motive, will have an incentive to improve efficiency, as will the workforce, aware that the state will not be there to bail out loss-making enterprises.

Three aspects of efficiency are now considered.

1 'Product Market' discipline

The increased discipline of competition in the *product market* (ie the market in which goods and services are sold) ensures that firms will be more responsive to consumer demand, providing better quality goods at lower prices than previously. In addition, firms will be more able to respond to changes in demand by innovating and providing new products, once they are released from the bureaucratic requirements of state control. How significant the product market discipline will be depends on the situation in that particular market. In an industry in which there already exists a large number of competing firms, privatisation is unlikely to increase competition significantly. There will be no effect on competition if a **natural monopoly** is privatised intact.

However, it is possible in both instances that efficiency may be improved, notwithstanding the reservations listed above, as a result of improved managerial decision making (see 'Managerial Efficiency' below). It is generally accepted that privatisation will have the most favourable effect on competition when monopolies are broken up or when new competition is introduced. On the other hand, it is also true to say that the benefits of scale may be lost (especially for a natural monopoly) and also that **oligopolistic pricing** may not always produce a desirable outcome.

2 'Capital Market' discipline

It is also hoped that the introduction of the *capital market* discipline, which is largely absent from nationalised industries (as previously mentioned), will help to improve efficiency of companies after privatisation in several ways:

(a) by providing the threat of bankruptcy, spurring both the management and workforce on to strive for improved productivity and greater efficiency. However, for this to act as an effective discipline, the market must believe that the government would not rescue the firm if bankruptcy actually did occur. Whether a government, even as market-orientated as Mrs Thatcher's Conservative government, would allow an important firm, such as British Gas, to collapse is debatable;

(*b*) by creating a possible threat of takeover which, by forcing the manage-ment to take note of the company's share price, would force action to improve efficiency and profitability in the hope of raising the share price. This assumes that companies will respond to a weakening share price by improving efficiency in the long term, rather than by making short-term savings which might help the company's performance in the short term (known as **short termism**), to the detriment of long-term performance. (Refer also to Chapter 2, pages 24–5). This threat of takeover may act as an effective discipline in some cases, although it is hard to prove. However, even in an era of *megamergers* and *leveraged buyouts*, it is questionable whether large companies such as BT and British Gas are really likely to face predators. Moreover, if the predator was foreign, it is debatable whether the government would be willing to allow the takeover to succeed – such sentiments were behind the enforced reduction of the Kuwaiti Investment Office's stake in BP in 1988;

(*c*) by creating a need to satisfy the capital market (ie by making good profits) in order to gain access to funds for borrowing. In a competitive situation, this would act as an effective discipline. However, as has previously been stated, a natural monopoly, if privatised intact, may achieve high profits by exploiting its monopoly position, rather than by increasing its efficiency. The performance of the industry might then satisfy the capital market, even though efficiency has not been raised.

3 *Managerial efficiency*

It has been argued that corporate efficiency in privatised industries has improved, not just by an exposure to market forces and an acceptance of the profit motive, but by the extra freedom given to managers. (Critics argue that the most obvious signs of this freedom are the huge pay rises awarded by the directors of many privatised companies to themselves. Refer to Table 3.1.)

Privatisation removes day-to-day government interference in corporate decision-making. When in the state sector, firms may be subjected to the imposition of economic and social objectives and, in particular, interference in

Table 3.1: Changes in top executives salaries in first year after privatisation

Company	% increase
Cable & Wireless	114
Amersham	61
Britoil	23
Associated British Ports	23
Enterprise Oil	167
Jaguar	100
British Telecom	32
British Gas	68
British Airways	126
Rolls Royce	31
BAA	110
average	78

From: *Does Privatisation Work?*, M. Bishop and J. Kay 1988 (London Business School)

pricing and investment decisions. Privatisation removes these constraints and also allows managers to improve the speed of decision-making, essential in a rapidly changing market – decisions may now be made by managers rather than by lengthy referral to government departments. Diversification into dynamic fast-growing industries is also made possible, as are moves to expand internationally.

In conclusion, there are wide-ranging claims made that privatisation improves efficiency, although critics argue that increasing competition has not played a sufficiently large part in the government's privatisation programme. The behaviour of privatised industries will have to be studied over a number of years before it is possible to conclude whether the *ownership* of the company (ie private or public) or the *market structure* (ie competitive or monopolistic) is the major determinant of corporate behaviour. If the latter is the more important, then privatisation of large nationalised industries intact will have little beneficial impact.

Other arguments for privatisation are now considered.

Wider share ownership

'A free and independent society is one in which the ownership of property is spread as widely as possible' according to the 1983 Conservative Election Manifesto. The Conservative government has set out to achieve this by selling council houses and also by attempting to widen share ownership. There has been a long-term decline in the number of private shareholders since the Second World War, matched by a rise in the importance of the institutional investor (eg insurance companies and pension funds). The government has been keen to encourage employees to buy shares in their privatised companies, in an attempt to improve industrial relations and productivity and to eradicate the 'them and us' attitude in industry, by improving employee identification with their company.

Great effort has also been made to sell shares in privatised companies to the general public, many of whom have never owned shares before. Favourable treatment has been given to the small shareholder, when allocating over-subscribed issues, in some of the privatisation issues. However, although there has been a substantial rise in the number of private shareholders in the UK, many investors have sold their shares immediately after the purchase. As most of the privatisation issues are sold at a discount, there is usually a substantial capital gain to be made. If individuals restrict their share purchases to a limited number of privatised companies, selling soon after purchase, and not extending their purchases to other companies already quoted on the Stock Exchange, then the government's plan to widen share ownership and extend **popular capitalism** in any meaningful sense is open to doubt.

An article, critical of privatisation, in *Marxism Today* (January 1987) comments:

> The idea of popular capitalism envisages a world where most people are active shareholders – it is vibrant, energetic, risky. In contrast the style of shareholding encouraged by privatisation is secure, self-satisfied. There is little accumulation

Last minute applications for shares in British Gas, 3 December 1986

because many people sell the shares soon after the flotation, and most of those that hang on do not accumulate others. There is little short-term risk because underpricing ensures a handsome short term profit. In the longer run risk is minimised because BT and British Gas have been privatised as monopolies, with a secure position to generate profits. As a consequence they are safe investments.

Although it is certainly true that individuals can gain a false idea about the ease of making money on the Stock Market, there is also no doubt that privatisation has generated substantial interest in the Stock Market, much of it from new investors. This interest was encouraged by the **bull market** which dominated

Figure 3.1: Shareholders as a percentage of UK adult population

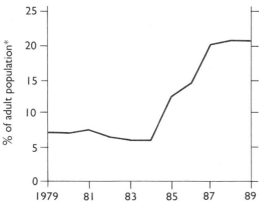

From: Social Trends 20, 1990, (HMSO)   * Aged 16 and over

the Stock Market during the 1980s, until the Crash of October 1987. The number of shareholders, as a percentage of the adult population, rose from 7 per cent in 1979 to 20 per cent in 1989 (see Figure 3.1).

By building up an army of individual shareholders the Conservatives may well have expected to gain political support. The evidence for this is mixed, showing that a great number of those who bought shares were already Conservative supporters anyway. Threats by the Labour party to renationalise privatised firms or to introduce 'social ownership' dented the share prices of privatised companies, whenever the Labour party appeared to be doing well in the opinion polls prior to the 1987 election. However, in its 1989 Economic Policy Review Labour committed itself only to renationalising British Telecom and the water industry, as well as tightening regulations on privatised monopolies.

Budgetary benefits

A reduction in the role of the state in the running of the economy is, as has been outlined above, a major driving force behind the whole privatisation programme. Yet, increasingly, arguments about the effects of privatisation on the state's finances, rather than discussion about the appropriate role of the state, have come to the fore as the revenue gained from asset sales has become sizeable.

The Medium Term Financial Strategy (MTFS) introduced in 1980 provided the basis of the government's monetarist economic strategy. The strategy involved controlling the money supply and also achieving progressively smaller budget deficits, as measured by the public sector borrowing requirement (PSBR). However, the government found it more difficult than expected to cut public expenditure and this, coupled with a desire to reduce taxation in order to increase incentives, meant that the PSBR targets could not be met without an extra source of revenue. Asset sales helped to provide this. Therefore the government was able to meet its borrowing target without resorting to raising taxation or cutting public expenditure (or, if these two options were politically unpalatable, abandoning the borrowing target).

The government treats asset receipts not as a means of financing the budget deficit, but instead as *negative public expenditure*. This has the effect of reducing both public expenditure and the budget deficit below what they would otherwise have been. Critics of privatisation extend their concern about the government's accounting procedures, seen as a 'cooking of the books', to the whole principle of selling assets (ie capital) to finance current spending. This concern was voiced most publicly in November 1985 by Lord Stockton, the former Conservative Prime Minister, Harold Macmillan, who complained that selling off state assets was similar to a family 'selling off its silver', and questioned what would happen when none was left. The government response was swift. Peter Walker, the then Secretary of State for Energy, claimed:

> The suggestion that privatisation is selling off the family silver is nonsense. The reality is that both public and private sector companies are part of the nation's assets. . . . There is a great myth that the government, in conveying from the state to the people an asset, is selling the family silver. It is not in fact selling the silver; it is transferring the silver from the politicians and civil servants to the family.

However, although the sale of a nationalised industry will provide a once-off boost for government finance, it should not be forgotten that the profits of the company, once privatised, will thereafter accrue to the private shareholders and not to the government, thereby reducing government revenues in the future. (On the other hand, if the profit of the company rises after privatisation, whether due to efficiency gains or due to abuses of a **natural monopoly** position, the tax levied by the government on the company's profits might actually rise.) Furthermore, once the profitable state enterprises have been sold, the state will be left with unprofitable 'rump', which will still require state funding, no longer offset by the profits made by other state enterprises. It has been argued that, as newly privatised companies will be responsible for obtaining their investment from the market rather than from the government, the PSBR will fall. This is certainly true, but it underlines what many consider has been the undue emphasis placed on the PSBR in the government's policy making. Private borrowing is likely to rise by the same amount and may rise by even more if the privatised company is able to borrow freely from the market rather than relying on the government. Hence overall borrowing for the country as a whole is unlikely to fall.

PRIVATISATION IN PRACTICE

The word *privatisation* was not mentioned in the 1979 Conservative Election Manifesto. There were plans to 'sell back to private ownership the recently nationalised aerospace and shipbuilding concerns' and to 'sell shares in the National Freight Corporation to the general public'. (In fact, shares were not offered to the public, but instead the management were offered the chance to organise a **management buyout**.) In addition the powers of the National Enterprise Board, which operated various state-owned businesses, were to be restricted.

During its first term (1979–83) the government's main public sector policies involved achieving reductions in the public sector borrowing requirement (PSBR) and improving the profitability of nationalised industries. Although a number of companies were privatised (some were fully transferred to the private sector, whereas in other cases only a partial stake was sold), the scale of the programme and the sums of money raised were relatively small when compared to privatisation during the second and third terms. The companies involved included BP, ICL, Ferranti, Fairey, British Aerospace, British Sugar, Cable & Wireless, Amersham International, Britoil, Associated British Ports and National Freight Corporation. None of these companies was a *natural monopoly* and hence the concerns about competition, described above, did not apply, although there was opposition to the privatisation proposals from the Labour Party and the trade unions on grounds of principle.

Surprisingly, the 1983 Conservative Election Manifesto again failed to mention the word *privatisation*, but under a lengthy section on 'the nationalised industries' it was claimed:

reform of the nationalised industries is central to economic recovery ... We shall transfer more state-owned businesses to independent ownership. Our aim is that British Telecom, Rolls-Royce, British Airways and substantial parts of British Steel, of British Shipbuilders and British Leyland, as well as many as possible of Britain's airports, shall become private sector companies.

The plan was to sell £2 billion of assets per annum, but, as a result of the success of the British Telecom privatisation of December 1984, the figure to be raised was more than doubled (to £4.75 billion per annum) – by this time the revenue-raising implications of privatisation had become more apparent. Privatisation during the second term of the Conservative government (1983–7) was dominated by the sell-off of monopolies and public utilities.

The sale to the public of 50 per cent of British Telecom (BT) in December 1984 was, at the time, the largest privatisation issue and it provided a major spur to the whole programme. The sale was aimed particularly at small investors in accordance with the government's commitment to wider share-ownership and was preceded by heavy advertising. In addition, potential shareholders were offered telephone vouchers or a bonus share issue if the shares were held for a period of three years, in order to try to prevent the immediate sale of shares after the issue. Generous offers were also made to BT employees in order to encourage them to subscribe to shares in their own company.

In a further move to stimulate demand for the shares, only 50p of the £1.30 share price was required as an initial payment. The huge interest generated in the share issue meant that on the first day of trading, the partially paid price of 50p immediately increased to 93p, which emphasised the extent of the undervaluation of the company; the share price subsequently increased by even more.

Although there was an attempt to introduce some competition for BT, this has been limited due to the **natural monopoly** position of parts of the telecommunications industry. However, Mercury Communications was licensed as the sole competitor to BT under the 1981 Telecommunications Act, with the initial aim of providing a business communications system. Thus BT has been provided with competition in part of the market, although the bulk of its services still face no competition.

The Office of Telecommunications (OFTEL) was created to act as the regulatory body for the telecommunications industry in order to ensure that BT did not abuse its dominant position. In particular, the government imposed maximum permitted price rises on BT, in accordance with the formula $(n - 3)$ per cent, where n is a measure of inflation, as measured by the Retail Price Index. Thus, for example, for an inflation of 5 per cent, BT's prices were allowed to rise by 2 per cent. This was an attempt to force BT to pass on productivity gains to the consumer. The $(n - 3)$ formula was fixed for a 5 year period of time and was subsequently tightened to $(n - 4\frac{1}{2})$ per cent, reflecting BT's high profits and the further likely gains in productivity expected. However, although the overall price rise permitted has been fixed, this does not prevent BT from increasing different tariffs at different rates (provided it does not engage in **predatory pricing**). BT chose, however, to alter its charging structure, so that the domestic customer (previously subsidised by the business user) paid relatively more, whereas business users (facing competition from Mercury) paid relatively less. This, together with what was seen as its neglect of its social function as a provider of services (eg public phone boxes), led to public disquiet about the operation of BT. However, the consumer has certainly gained by the liberalisation of the supply and maintenance of telephone equipment, introduced by the 1981 Telecommunications Act, which has resulted in lower prices, wider choice and improved products.

The British Gas flotation, in November 1986, raised almost £6 billion and, like the BT offer, was directed at the private shareholders. The minimum investment was for 100 shares at a price of £1 per share, but, as the initial payment was only 50p per share, members of the public could become shareholders of British Gas for a down-payment as low as £50. During the years prior to the flotation, British Gas had been forced by the government to sell both its North Sea oil interests and also its half share in the onshore Wytch Farm oilfield in Dorset. However, Sir Denis Rooke, the Chairman of British Gas, successfully opposed moves to force it to sell off its showrooms and other component parts of the business. The possibility of breaking up British Gas into competing units was also successfully opposed by Sir Denis, who argued that it was impossible to achieve competition in a **natural monopoly**. Thus the monopoly was preserved intact and British Gas was privatised as a single entity, with no attempt to introduce competition (unlike BT where one competitor – albeit a small one – was introduced). A regulatory body, OFGAS, was set up with similar responsibilities to OFTEL.

Amongst the other companies to have been privatised during the Conservative second term are Jaguar (1984), British Airways (1987) and Rolls-Royce (1987). The privatisation of Jaguar, formerly part of British Leyland, was deemed to be a great success (although the company ran into difficulties later – refer to Chapter 4, page 76). The 1987 Conservative Election Manifesto claimed:

> In 1980 Jaguar made 14,000 cars a year, losing well over £3,000 on each car sold. Now the company is hard put to keep up with overseas demand and last year sold over 40,000 cars, making a pre-tax profit of over £120m.

No monopoly issues were raised by this privatisation, nor were there any raised by the privatisation of Rolls-Royce. Despite the fact that Rolls-Royce is the only UK aero engine manufacturer, international competition is intense.

However, monopoly questions were raised by the sale of British Airways (BA). Although there were limited route transfers to British Caledonian before privatisation, BA was left as the dominant carrier and, at the time of privatisation, provided over three-quarters of British scheduled airline services. British Caledonian (BCal), the 'second force' British airline, unable to compete effectively with its giant competitor, was forced to seek a merger with BA (as discussed in Chapter 2, pages 28–30). Many observers believe that this outcome would not have happened if BA had not been privatised as such a dominant carrier in the UK, but others argue that this claim is irrelevant and that world competition is what matters; BA and BCal were both relatively small on the world stage, but might have been able to compete effectively in a merged form.

The privatisation of the British Airports Authority (BAA), postponed for several weeks by the 1987 election, also raised worries of monopoly – no attempt was made to privatise the airports controlled by the BAA as separate competing companies. The arguments for promoting competition were rejected in favour of the argument that an *integrated airports' policy* was necessary and that this was best achieved by one company. Critics supported this point of view, but argued that the public interest would have been best served by a company which had remained in the public sector.

The sale in October 1987 of the government's remaining 31.7 per cent shareholding in BP, Britain's largest company, showed that the purchase of shares in privatised companies need not always be the risk-free investment that its opponents allege. The world stock market crash during the period of privatisation ensured that almost all of the BP stock was left with the underwriters. In order to try and give the market some confidence the government organised a temporary 'buy-back' scheme, which provided, in effect, a minimum support price for the shares (only 2 per cent of the shares issued were in fact returned). However the BP debacle was a major setback for the privatisation programme.

The privatisation of British Steel and Rover during 1988 were probably the privatisations which gave government ministers the most satisfaction, particularly in the aftermath of the disappointments of the BP flotation. For many years both companies had been associated in the public's mind as loss-making nationalised industries. Both companies were subjected to a drastic **rationalisation** programme. As a result British Steel produced profits of over £400 million in the year 1987/88 and was privatised by means of a share sale to the general public. Rover, although in a far healthier financial state than before, was not considered suitable for a similar sale of shares to the public. However, the company was bought by British Aerospace (as described in Chapter 4, pages 72–4). Thus, within a period of a year, two of the government's notorious former loss-makers had been privatised. To this was added the promise to privatise British Coal if the Conservatives were re-elected for a fourth term.

The privatisation of water during 1989 created a great deal of controversy because the water industry probably provides the best example of a **natural monopoly**, and the likelihood of any competition is almost non-existent. (This contrasts with the two large energy privatisations of gas and electricity where there are at least some areas of direct competition between the two industries – the privatisation of electricity is considered next.) In addition, domestic water is generally charged at a flat-rate, which does not depend on consumption, and, in the absence of meters, there is no incentive for customers to conserve water – nor is there any indication to the consumer of the price of the water.

It was proposed initially that the ten water authorities should be privatised intact, but these proposals were abandoned. The revised scheme proposed that the water authorities, now with only the functions of water supply and sewage disposal, should be privatised, but that a new National Rivers Authority should be created (in the public sector) to take over from the water authorities the regulatory functions of pollution control, water conservation, land drainage and flood protection, conservation, recreation, fisheries and navigation. Thus the government abandoned its earlier proposal to transfer to the new private sector companies the powers of regulation over river basin management, previously exercised by the water authorities. The concept of an *integrated river basin management approach*, controlled by one authority in each area, was therefore destroyed by the proposals.

The need for proper regulation is greater in the water industry than in almost any other. The problems of choosing an appropriate framework for any privatised natural monopoly have already been considered. Any regulatory system will be judged not just by its ability to provide a 'fair' rate of return for investors and 'fair' prices for consumers, but on its ability to avoid under-investment. Vast sums of money will be needed to replace Victorian sewerage systems and, under pressure from environmentalists and the EC, to improve the quality of water.

The government's proposals for regulation of the water industry, announced in August 1989, provided a £4.9 billion debt write-off and an injection of new funds to the tune of £1 billion, referred to as a *Green Dowry*, to help pay for environmental improvements. In addition, in order to fund the water industry's capital investment programme, a complex system of price regulation was announced. This became known as the *retail price index (RPI) plus K factor*, where K varied for different water authorities between 3 per cent and 7 per cent. The positive K factor was intended to allow water prices to rise by more than the rate of inflation, in order to help finance a £18.65 billion investment programme over ten years.

A consideration of the movement of the partly-paid share prices of the ten privatised water companies during the three days after the issue shows the size of the gains made and supports the view that the companies were undervalued (see Figure 3.2).

The electricity industry had always been considered to be a **natural monopoly** and plans to privatise it were preceded by lengthy discussions about the ideal structure for the industry. These were designed to ensure that consumers were protected, but at the same time companies earned a fair rate of return on their investment. Public concern about the privatisation of another energy supplier, British Gas, as a monopoly, coupled with a relatively weak regulatory framework, put pressure on ministers to ensure that this situation was not repeated. As part of the state sector, the Central Electricity Generating Board (CEGB) owned and operated all the power stations in England and Wales and controlled the transmission grid. Twelve area boards were responsible for distributing and selling the electricity to both industrial and domestic users.

The CEGB argued that the whole electricity industry should be 'privatised intact' and cited the benefits of an integrated generation and transmission system, based on the benefits of 'tight margins of spare generating capacity (amongst the lowest in the industrial countries)' and 'unified control in emergencies'. The then Secretary of State for Energy, Cecil Parkinson, ruled out the creation of a private monopoly. He also rejected the radical free market view, which proposed that each part of the electricity industry (generation, transmission and distribution) should be broken up into a large number of

Figure 3.2: **Share price movements of the partly-paid shares (in pence) of the ten privatised water companies during the three days after privatisation**

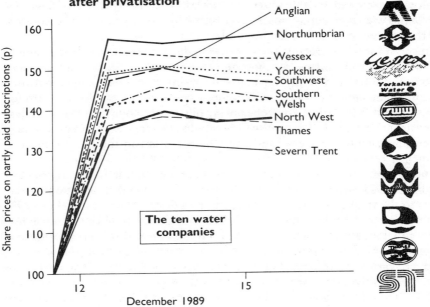

From: *Financial Times*, 16 December 1989

competing companies. This was partly due to the timescale involved (the commitment to privatise during the Conservatives' third term ruled out any complex break-up), but was also due to the problems involved with the nuclear industry. It was felt that small companies would be less willing to take on the responsibilities of nuclear power plants. The South of Scotland Electricity Board was, however, to be maintained after privatisation, as both a generator and distributor of power (ie as a regional integrated monopoly).

The details of the privatisation, announced in February 1988, involved the break-up of the CEGB into three parts – generation, transmission and distribution. Two companies were to be formed from the CEGB's generating activities. National Power was allocated 70 per cent of the power plant, but was given control of the nuclear programme. PowerGen was created out of the remaining 30 per cent of the power plant, thereby forming a competitor to the dominant supplier. In addition independent generating companies were to be encouraged to enter the market as competitors for the duopoly created.

Crucially, the CEGB was to lose the ownership of the national transmission grid. This was to be jointly owned by twelve area distribution companies, which were to be created to take on the distribution role of the existing twelve area boards. The control of the grid is vital to the operation of the electricity industry, and the decision was also seen as being a good indication of the government's views on competition in the industry. If the grid had remained under the control of the generating companies, it would have meant that the government had accepted the CEGB's view that an integrated network was the key to efficiency and lower prices. Instead, by separating transmission from both generation and transmission, the government showed that it had rejected the dangers of efficiency losses due to *fragmentation* in favour of the potential benefits of competition.

The National Grid was to be responsible for ensuring that sufficient power was provided by the generating companies to the distribution companies at all times. The demand for electricity is uneven throughout the day, involving certain periods of peak demand. The National Grid was charged with adopting a 'merit order' of power stations, based on efficiency, in order to fix which power stations were to be used at which times. This was seen as being a major spur to improving efficiency for the generating companies.

Despite the moves outlined above, the need for regulation in the electricity industry remains of crucial importance. The construction of an appropriate regulatory framework is extremely complex and this has been borne out by the US experience. At the time of writing, full proposals have yet to be announced. It would be possible to institute a 'retail price index minus x' formula, designed to encourage efficiency and to ensure that productivity gains are passed on to the consumer. The questions of whether to allow increases in the industry's import fuel bills to be passed on to the consumer and how to treat investment need to be addressed. If the regulatory framework permits the transfer to customers of the whole cost of rising fuel bills, but makes no allowance for investment, generating companies would have an incentive to build the cheapest possible power plants, which are likely to be costly and inefficient in the use of fuel.

In an embarrassing retreat, the government was forced to withdraw the nuclear power stations from its proposed electricity privatisation during 1989, in a blow both to its privatisation and nuclear power programmes. For years the economics of the nuclear power industry were concealed within the overall accounts of the public sector electricity industry. However, during the run up to privatisation, it was established that the running costs of the nuclear power stations were higher than was previously believed and that, in addition, the costs of decommissioning these power stations and reprocessing the spent fuel were both high and uncertain. The costs and risks involved indicated that it would have been very difficult to convince investors to invest in the generating company National Power if it had been responsible for the nuclear power stations, even though it had been given control of the majority of the generating capacity in order to compensate for this. Nuclear Electric, a third generating company, was to be established to take control of the nuclear power stations and to remain in the public sector.

A list of privatisations between 1979 and 1990, together with the proceeds from privatisation, are contained in Table 3.2.

COMMENT

Privatisation has become a major plank of the Conservative government's programme. Supporters argue that privatisation increases efficiency, widens

Table 3.2: Privatisation proceeds from 1979/80 to 1989/90

	1979–80 outturn	1980–81 outturn	1981–82 outturn	1982–83 outturn
Amersham International			64	
Associated British Ports Holdings plc				46
British Airports Authority				
British Aerospace plc – sale of shares		43		
British Airways plc – sale of shares				
British Gas plc – sale of shares				
British Gas plc – redemption of debt				
British Petroleum plc – sale of shares	276		8	
British Steel plc – sale of shares				
British Sugar Corporation			44	
British Telecommunications plc – sale of shares				
British Telecommunications plc – loan stock				
British Telecommunications plc – redemption of preference shares				
Britoil plc – sale of shares				334[4]
Cable and Wireless plc – sale of shares			181	
Enterprise Oil plc – sale of shares				
Forestry Commission				14
General Practice Finance Corporation				
Land Settlement				
Motorway Service leases				4
National Enterprise Board Holdings	37	83	2	
Plant Breeding Institute				
Rolls-Royce				
Royal Ordnance				
Water plcs-sale of shares				
Miscellaneous[6]	64	84	194	57
Total	377[7]	210[7]	493[7]	455

(1) The figures do not include the proceeds of sales after 31 December 1989

(2) Net of the cost of acquiring partly-paid shares under the support arrangements announced by the Chancellor on 29 October 1987

(3) Includes some third instalments of approximately £87 million paid early

(4) Includes repayments of debentures of £88 million with interests

(5) The central government sector received £65 million but only £27 million was paid to the Consolidated Fund

share ownership and increases consumer choice. Opponents argue that it is a cynical way of both raising extra government revenues and also buying votes. In addition, whenever a **natural monopoly** is transferred intact to the private sector, there is a danger that the consumer will suffer. In order to meet this danger, the government has introduced a regulatory framework in some cases.

It is extremely difficult to provide a clear conclusion about the success of privatisation. For example, British Telecom's service has received heavy criticism since privatisation; but how much of this failure to provide an 'adequate' service is due to post-privatisation behaviour as opposed to decisions (perhaps inadequate investment) made beforehand?

However, if success can be measured by the number of governments in all

1983–84 outturn	1984–85 outturn	1985–86 outturn	1986–87 outturn	1987–88 outturn	1988–89 outturn	£ million 1989–90 estimated outturn[1]
	51					
				534	689	
		347				
			435	419		
			1,820	1,758	1,555	
			750		250	400
543				863[2]	3,030[2]	1,370
					1,138	1,280
	1,358	1,246[3]	1,081			
	44	61	53	23	85	
			250	250	250	
293		426				
263		577				
	384					
21	28	17	18	15	15	10
					67	
2	12	5	2			
1				2	1	
	168	30	34			
				65[5]		
				1,028	3	
				186		
						500
15	4	−2	15	−2	−7	20
1,139	2,050	2,707	4,460	5,140	7,073	3,580

(6) Includes expenses which cannot be netted off the associated sale because they arose in a financial year in which there were no proceeds from that sale

(7) Excludes certain advance oil payments which net out to zero 1979–80 (£622 million) 1980–1 (−£49 million) and 1981–2 (−£573 million)

Source: Public Expenditure White Paper, January 1990 (HMSO)

parts of the world now privatising their state-owned assets, then privatisation can be seen as a great success.

4 *An Industrial Case Study: The Motor Industry*

■ Background

■ The Japanese connection: a Trojan horse?

■ The Rover sell-off

■ Restructuring the Italian and Spanish car industries

■ The drive for quality

■ Comment

BACKGROUND

The motor industry has been chosen as a case study to consider various industrial issues that have affected the British economy during the period of Conservative government. In order to do this, the background to this period is also briefly considered.

The chapter investigates:

(*a*) the reasons for the decline of the British motor industry;
(*b*) the government's response to the decline and prospects for the future;
(*c*) the need to exploit **economies of scale**;
(*d*) the role of foreign investment and the implications of foreign ownership (with particular reference to Japan);
(*e*) the trend towards greater collaboration and cross-border mergers;
(*f*) the privatisation of Leyland/Rover;
(*g*) the implications of the EC completion of the *Internal Market* in 1992.

The British car industry

Encouraged by the Labour government's attempts to **restructure** parts of British manufacturing industry (see Chapter 2, pages 25–6 concerning the formation of GEC), the British Leyland Motor Corporation (BLMC) was formed in 1968 as a result of the merger of BMC and Leyland. This followed a succession of smaller mergers during the previous decade as the once dominant, but then struggling, independent British car makers joined together in an attempt to gain **economies of scale** and to maintain their market share in the face of fierce international competition. (In 1930 the combined UK market share obtained by Austin and Morris – later both to be parts of BLMC – was approximately 60 per cent.)

However, throughout the 1960s and 1970s the company was plagued by poor industrial relations and inadequate investment. In addition there was no serious attempt to **rationalise** the model range; thus too many different, mainly outdated, models were produced and insufficient profit was generated to develop new products. For many, the performance of the company epitomised the problems faced by British industry.

On the verge of bankruptcy in December 1974, Leyland approached the recently elected Labour government for assistance. This was provided as a consequence of the Ryder Report, which recommended a substantial injection of public funds in April 1975. At that time Mr Tony Benn was Industry Secretary and the Labour government was attempting to increase state involvement in private industry by means of the National Enterprise Board (NEB). However, it became increasingly obvious during the next two years that the Ryder Report had been over optimistic about the market share of Leyland, and that even large injections of capital were insufficient to overcome the problems of poor labour relations, low productivity and entrenched attitudes. Critics of the report saw it as an old-style socialist attempt to plan the future of an industry, without due regard to market forces.

Sir Michael Edwardes was appointed to the task of rescuing the company in 1977 and in the next five years attempted to reduce excessive centralisation in the company and to improve efficiency, which involved many plant closures and redundancies. Although appointed under a Labour government, he was in every sense a Thatcherite manager. The drive to increase productivity resulted in a series of conflicts with the unions as Sir Michael sought the **right to manage**. He often went over the head of union officials, appealing directly to the workforce, and, to a great extent, the workforce accepted his proposals, thereby improving productivity and dramatically reducing the days lost through industrial disputes.

After unsuccessful attempts to merge or collaborate with Renault and certain other European manufacturers in 1978–9, Leyland announced proposals to collaborate with Honda in 1979. The management of the company had concluded it was too small to survive on its own.

The European car industry

The European car industry has increasingly become dominated by a small number of large companies. The main reason for this is that large production runs are necessary in order to cover the massive **fixed costs** involved in developing new cars or major components (eg engines and gearboxes). Smaller companies, unable to compete effectively and unable to generate the profits necessary for future investment, have tended to stagnate, sometimes propped up by national governments. Mergers and collaborative ventures with one of the larger companies have been common. The 'Big Six' companies in Europe comprise General Motors (Opel/Vauxhall) and Ford (both US-owned multinationals), Fiat, Volkswagen, Renault and Peugeot. No British-owned company is in this list, although General Motors, Ford and Peugeot have car assembly facilities in the UK. At the other extreme a number of specialist car producers have come to dominate the luxury end of the car market. The main companies are Daimler-Benz, BMW, Porsche, Jaguar, Volvo and Saab. In this sector of the market profits per car sold are generally considerably higher than in the mass-produced car market.

Companies such as Rover, Alfa-Romeo and Seat became increasingly caught in no man's land, insufficiently large to compete on effective terms with the Big Six and yet unable to gain a secure niche in the market which would enable them to compete with the luxury car makers. (After a complex series of name changes, Rover had replaced Leyland as the name of the whole company.) All three companies mentioned above were involved during 1986 in merger negotiations with one or other of the Big Six. Such moves, some between private companies and others inspired by governments, can be seen as a further **restructuring** of the European car industry, faced with the increasing challenge of Japanese and other Far Eastern competition. Both Alfa-Romeo and Seat found 'European solutions' to their problems with Fiat and Volkswagen respectively. These solutions, together with the unsuccessful moves to sell various parts of Rover to US multinationals and Rover's subsequent return to the private sector, are considered later in the chapter. West European car sales for 1989 indicate the gap between the production level of Rover and the Big Six: (see Table 4.1).

Table 4.1: West European new car regisitrations in 1989

Company	Market share (%)
VW/Audi/Seat	15.0
Fiat/Lancia/Alfa Romeo	14.8
Peugeot/Citroen	12.7
Ford	11.6
General Motors	11.0
Renault	10.4
Daimler Benz	3.2
Rover	3.1
Nissan	2.9
BMW	2.8
Toyota	2.6
Volvo	2.0
Total Japanese (including European made)	10.9

Note: Only companies gaining more than 2.0% are recorded
Source: Industry estimates
From: *Financial Times*, 22 January 1990

THE JAPANESE CONNECTION: A TROJAN HORSE?

The Japanese motor industry achieved spectacular export growth during the 1960s and 1970s, but has started to locate production facilities abroad in recent years. This has been prompted by the increasing value of the yen, which has squeezed profit margins on cars exported, and also by the growing threat of protectionism in many countries. The UK negotiated a *Voluntary Export Restraint* (VER) (sometimes known as *Voluntary Restraint Agreement* – VRA) with Japan, limiting Japan's share of the UK market to 11 per cent and some other European countries (eg France and Italy) have even more stringent controls. VERs are designed to protect the domestic car industry, but critics argue that consumers suffer, as some are prevented from buying the car of their choice, and that the prices of Japanese cars are higher than they would otherwise have been, thus raising Japanese profit margins (ie profit per car sold). In the absence of keen pricing from the Japanese, the competitive element in the UK market is reduced and therefore car prices are generally higher than they would be if market forces were allowed to operate freely.

Japan's three largest car companies – Toyota, Nissan and Honda – have each announced plans to establish assembly plants in Britain, with Honda having a collaborative agreement and other close links with Rover (see Figure 4.1). The effects of Japanese involvement in the British car industry are now considered.

Figure 4.1: Japanese investment in the UK motor industry

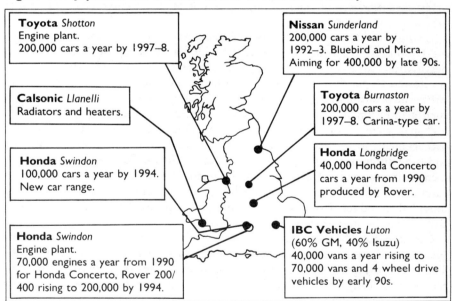

> **Toyota** *Shotton*
> Engine plant.
> 200,000 cars a year by 1997–8.

> **Calsonic** *Llanelli*
> Radiators and heaters.

> **Honda** *Swindon*
> 100,000 cars a year by 1994.
> New car range.

> **Honda** *Swindon*
> Engine plant.
> 70,000 engines a year from 1990
> for Honda Concerto, Rover 200/
> 400 rising to 200,000 by 1994.

> **Nissan** *Sunderland*
> 200,000 cars a year by
> 1992–3. Bluebird and Micra.
> Aiming for 400,000 by late 90s.

> **Toyota** *Burnaston*
> 200,000 cars a year by
> 1997–8. Carina-type car.

> **Honda** *Longbridge*
> 40,000 Honda Concerto
> cars a year from 1990
> produced by Rover.

> **IBC Vehicles** *Luton*
> (60% GM, 40% Isuzu)
> 40,000 vans a year rising to
> 70,000 vans and 4 wheel drive
> vehicles by early 90s.

Source: Industry estimates
From: Financial Times, 22 January 1990

Nissan and Toyota

Nissan, Japan's second largest car manufacturer, put forward proposals in 1981 to establish a plant capable of producing 200,000 cars a year by 1986. However, after doubts had been expressed by certain of Nissan's executives, this proposal was drastically scaled-down. The factory which opened in 1986 at Washington, Tyne and Wear was capable of assembling 24,000 cars only and these were to be constructed from 'kits' imported from Japan. The *local content* of those cars (where 'local' means 'European', not necessarily 'British') was approximately 20 per cent and only 500 jobs were created. Under Phase 2 of the scheme, Nissan proposed to increase output to 100,000 cars a year by 1991, with local content rising above 60 per cent during 1988 and subsequently rising to 80 per cent. As a result, an additional 2,200 jobs would follow. Plans to start exporting the Nissan Bluebird to continental Europe were announced in 1988 and the production target was raised to 200,000 cars a year for 1992/93. These plans were opposed by the French and Italians who questioned the 'European credentials' of the cars.

The Nissan plant, although smaller than the one originally envisaged, was welcomed by the depressed North East of England. Not only would jobs be provided directly, but there would also be additional employment generated in the components industry and in ancillary services. Although the amount of employment created by Nissan was relatively small compared to the huge loss of manufacturing jobs caused by de-industrialisation in the North East, the investment was seen as a sign of hope, possibly leading to involvement by other Japanese companies.

A **single-union agreement** was negotiated with the Amalgamated Engineering Union (AEU), which effectively provided a **no-strike deal** for Nissan. If negotiation fails to provide an agreement acceptable to both sides then a dispute is referred to **pendulum arbitration**. In this case the arbitrator has to accept either the position of the management or that of the workforce – the purpose of such arbitration is to encourage moderation, by discouraging unrealistically high pay claims from the workforce and unrealistically low offers from the management, in the expectation that a traditional arbitrator would eventually 'split the difference' between the two positions. In view of the high unemployment existing in the North East of England, Nissan has been able to select carefully whom to recruit. Job flexibility was an important feature and was intended to reduce **demarcation disputes** (ie disputes about 'who does what') and add to the smooth running of the plant.

Concern has, however, been expressed about the overall impact of the Nissan plant on the rest of the motor industry and on the economy as a whole. The effect of Japanese competition in some industries in the past has been to reduce drastically the size of those industries and in some cases (eg motor cycles) virtually eliminate the industries altogether. Thus it is argued that, in order to provide protection for the UK car industry, the VER negotiated with the Japanese to limit car imports into the UK should be tightened and the Japanese should certainly not be allowed to establish production facilities in Britain, whereby the VER might be avoided.

However, assurances have been received that the level of the local content of the Nissan cars would rise to 80 per cent and this would appear to convert the existing 'kit' assembly plant into a full scale production facility. Nonetheless, there is still concern about exactly how the 80 per cent is to be measured. If the high technology components continue to be produced in Japan, there will be relatively little scope for research and development in the UK and the plant will remain a **satellite** or **screwdriver plant**.

Although the Nissan investment will undoubtedly create employment there is argument about the *net* employment effect – this involves a consideration of the jobs lost indirectly as a consequence of the establishment of the factory. This analysis falls into two parts. Firstly there are fears for the UK components industry and worries that, even when the 80 per cent 'local' (ie European) content has been reached, Nissan will be less willing to 'buy British' components than other established carmakers. Secondly it is necessary to consider the effect on the other car-producing manufacturers in the UK. This will depend whether (*a*) the Nissan cars are for export to the EC, (*b*) they are sold in the UK to customers who would otherwise have purchased an imported car or (*c*) they are sold in the UK to customers who would otherwise have bought a car produced in the UK by one of the other UK manufacturers.

In the first two cases ((*a* and (*b*)) there will be a beneficial effect on output, employment and balance of payments, whereas in the third case there will be no overall positive effect on any of those variables; it may even result in a negative effect if Nissan's components are 'less British' than those of other UK-based manufacturers. Thus, if Nissan gains market share at the expense of cars which would have been manufactured in the UK anyway, problems may be caused for other companies, especially Rover which relies principally on the UK market for its sales.

These concerns clearly were not shared by Mrs Thatcher who welcomed the announcement of the second phase of the Washington development in September 1986: 'This is good news for the North East and for Britain and makes Nissan a fully-fledged UK car manufacturer and a major exporter.'

When Toyota, Japan's largest automative group, announced in 1989 its intention to construct a plant at Burnaston, near Derby, the reaction to it was far more favourable than that received by Nissan eight years previously. This was largely a result of the widely-perceived success of the Nissan plant. The £700 million investment was the largest single investment by a Japanese company in Europe. Plans were announced to produce 100,000 cars a year by 1995, rising to 200,000 cars a year by 1997/8.

The high subsidies offered by the UK government to Nissan and by other European governments to encourage Japanese investment gave rise to fears that the Europeans were engaging in 'beggar-my-neighbour' subsidy policies, which would benefit the Japanese and give them an unfair competitive advantage when compared to existing producers. However, unlike Nissan, Toyota received no state aid towards its investment, as Derbyshire was not an eligible area. Under 1989 EC guidelines, state aid provided to the motor industry has to be cleared by the European Commission and the generous level of aid provided to Nissan in Tyne and Wear would not have been available, had Toyota decided to invest there instead. Shortly afterwards Toyota announced plans to establish an engine plant in Shotton, North Wales and this was seen as a further sign of confidence in the British economy.

Honda

Cooperation between Rover and Honda has become increasingly close since links were forged in 1979. The initial agreement made was a licensing agreement whereby Rover (then known as BL) assembled the Honda Ballade from 1981 onwards with limited alterations and sold it as the Triumph Acclaim. This served as a stop-gap measure intended to fill the gap in Rover's range before the introduction of the Maestro and Montego models. The Acclaim proved so successful that production was continued after the introduction of these cars, although a restyled model was named the Rover 200 as part of Rover's plan to improve the image of the company by concentrating on fewer marques.

Whereas the Triumph Acclaim/Rover 200 was a Japanese car built under licence in the UK, the second venture between Rover and Honda involved the joint development of a luxury car. The two models, the Rover 800 and the Honda Legend share basic design but have slightly different exteriors and interiors. Further collaboration involved the joint development of a medium-sized car, the Rover 200/Honda Concerto, launched in 1989.

The deals announced allowed Rover to share research and development costs with Honda. It was also hoped that Honda's management philosophy and production techniques would improve working practices at Rover. There was lengthy speculation that Honda might take an *equity stake* (ie a shareholding) in Rover, but there appeared to be little enthusiasm for that from Honda. It was hard to see what extra benefit would accrue to Honda from such a stake, especially when, in addition to the ventures already discussed, an agreement had been reached to assemble Honda cars in Rover factories on spare production lines in order to provide jobs for Rover workers. In seemed that Honda was therefore able to get the benefits from the relationship between the companies, without becoming involved with the responsibilities of ownership.

In the light of this, the announcement in 1989 that Honda was to take a 20 per cent stake in Rover, was seen as a further cementing of ties between the two companies and a long term commitment to Rover's development by Honda. Previously the possibility that Honda viewed the links as only short-term could not be ruled out.

At the same time, Honda announced a £300 million investment for an assembly plant at Swindon, capable of producing 100,000 cars a year by 1994. This announcement meant that the three biggest Japanese car makers had all selected the UK as the site for their first European car assembly plant, in preparation for the completion of the Single European Market in 1992. However, the UK willingness to accept inward investment by Japanese car firms has been criticised by other European car makers as an attempt to export unemployment to other countries. Thus these plants can be seen as creating a 'Trojan Horse', whereby Japanese firms attempt to evade protectionist measures against imports from Japan by locating production facilities within the EC.

At the time of writing, doubt still exists over two important issues relating to Japanese cars. Britain, France, Italy, Spain and Portugal all have different VERs – all negotiated bilaterally – on Japanese cars. How these restrictions are to be handled post-1992 has yet to be fixed. This is of crucial importance, because restrictions on trade between EC countries will not be permitted post-1992; hence with the present system of VERs, Japanese cars would be imported into one EC country without a VER and then moved to another EC country with a VER. Furthermore, it has yet to be decided whether or not Japanese cars produced in Britain should be part of an overall fixed limit. Mr Calvert, President of Peugeot and highly critical of Britain's stance on Japanese investment, insisted: 'Even if Nissan had 100 per cent local content as well as local design, they would go in the overall quota'. The resolution of these issues is clearly crucial for the future of the Japanese car industry investment in Britain.

THE ROVER SELL-OFF

Returning Rover to the private sector had been an aim of the Conservative government for several years. However, continuing financial uncertainty meant that privatisation by means of a share issue to the public was out of the question. The government therefore turned to multinational companies as potential suitors for Rover. When details of its plan to split up and sell off parts of Rover became public in 1986, however, the government faced a political storm. It followed shortly after the 'Westland Affair' – a dispute about whether Westland, a manufacturer of helicopters, should become involved with European or American collaboration which resulted in the resignations of two cabinet ministers (Leon Brittan and Michael Heseltine).

The government proposed (*a*) that Austin Rover cars should be sold to Ford, (*b*) that Leyland Vehicles (including Land Rover) should be sold to General Motors, which manufactured Bedford trucks in the UK and (*c*) that Leyland Bus should be sold to the other major UK-based bus manufacturer, the Laird Group. Each part of these proposals is now considered.

The Austin Rover/Ford proposal

Despite substantial state investment, drastic **rationalisation**, increased productivity and the agreement with Honda, Austin Rover had been unable to increase its market share or return to economic viability. In an industry dominated by much larger producers who were able to benefit from **economies of scale**, the government therefore concluded that the sale to Ford was preferable to continued state subsidy and/or ever closer links with Honda. Since Ford would dominate the UK car market, it was hoped that the company would have a major interest in ensuring that this market was successful and that this might involve the expansion of research and development in the UK.

Many objections were voiced against the proposed deal which caused such a storm that it was dropped within days of the news breaking. It was not at all clear exactly what the proposed Austin Rover/Ford operation would entail. Critics argued that it was merely an attempt by Ford to purchase market share in the UK and that rationalisation would inevitably cause massive job losses. There was added concern that Ford would use its position to increase its *tied imports* of cars – cars assembled overseas but indistinguishable from those assembled in Britain. Concern was also expressed for the future of the British components industry if Ford showed less willingness to purchase British components than Austin Rover traditionally had done – thus any job losses could extend beyond the two firms engaged in the merger.

There were worries that the combined Austin Rover/Ford operation would develop merely into an assembly plant for cars designed abroad. It was also feared that the British car industry would lose its research and development facilities, together with its high technology capability, with employees finishing up as 'metal bashers' for overseas companies, performing low 'value added' jobs. Such concerns have already been voiced earlier in this chapter when considering the impact of Japanese plants.

These arguments led critics to claim that the position the company found itself in underlined the flaws of Thatcherism, highlighted the weakness of the government's policy towards industry and emphasised the need for a clear **industrial strategy** (refer also to Chapter 1, pages 12–13). It was argued that the government's policy towards Austin Rover could be viewed as an attempt to slim down the company through **rationalisation** and privatise parts as they became profitable (eg Jaguar), finishing up with an unprofitable rump which had very little chance of long-term viability on its own.

There was also concern that, as the combined market shares of the two companies approached 50 per cent, this could lead to an abuse of monopoly power. Although there were many existing and potential foreign competitors in the car industry, car prices in Britain were already significantly higher than in other EC countries and such a dominant company could have made matters worse. (The Monopolies and Mergers Commission announced in May 1990 that it was to investigate car pricing in Britain.) Finally there were those who argued that it was essential to keep British control over at least part of the British car industry and that, after all the taxpayers money invested in Austin Rover, the company should not be turned over to Ford, a US multinational.

The Leyland Vehicles/General Motors proposal

The proposal to sell Leyland Vehicles including Land Rover to General Motors, manufacturer of Bedford trucks, caused as much disquiet as the mooted sale of Austin Rover to Ford and was eventually thwarted after much public argument, when General Motors withdrew from the deal. Faced with a much reduced market for heavy trucks in Europe (including the UK) in the early part of the 1980s, talks were began between Leyland Vehicles and GM's Bedford Trucks in 1984 to see if there was scope for collaboration between the two companies. Talks between GM and other European truck manufacturers had failed to produce the collaboration that GM wanted. The benefits of a merger to GM would be to gain access to Leyland Vehicles' recently introduced product range, whereas Leyland Vehicles would have access to GM's financial muscle and foreign dealer network. Although there would undoubtedly have been job losses after the merger, the proposal can be viewed as a relatively straightforward attempt to **restructure** and then **rationalise** an industry with excess capacity, with firms which were insufficiently large to exploit **economies of scale** and thus unable to make a profit. If this argument is accepted, some job losses in the short term would be preferable to both companies remaining in an unviable position with the possibility of complete closure for both in the long run.

The merger failed because, in the post-Westland environment it was seen as yet another sop to the United States, and more specifically, because GM insisted that Land Rover should be included in the package with Leyland Vehicles. Critics argued that Land Rover was being offered as a sweetener to offset the lossmaking Leyland Trucks part of the business, whereas GM claimed that access to its US dealership network would be beneficial to Land Rover. Despite assurances from GM that it would maintain the British content of Land Rover vehicles at existing levels, considerable unease was felt by many politicians.

After the news of the secret negotiations between the government, Leyland Vehicles and GM broke in February 1986, the government allowed alternative bids to be put in for the different parts of the firm. Although there were several offers made for Land Rover, there were no serious contenders for Leyland Trucks. Despite press speculation that GM might be offered a modified deal on Land Rover (49 per cent of the shares), the government eventually made it clear to GM that Land Rover was not part of the Leyland Vehicles deal, and as a result GM withdrew its offer. The government subsequently decided not to accept any of the bids for Land Rover during April 1986 amid considerable political embarrassment.

When in August 1986 GM announced that it was merging its North American heavy truck operations with Volvo, under Volvo's control, the future of Bedford looked bleak. It was in the context of this merger and GM's failure to find a partner for Bedford in the UK that it announced the ending of medium and heavy truck production in September 1986.

It would appear that this closure and the consequent employment effects can be attributed to the government's failure to sanction the deal with Leyland Vehicles earlier in the year, as a result of the political pressure imposed. However, the position is not as simple as this because, if the merger had taken place, **rationalisation** and **restructuring** would have happened anyway and it is likely that certain plants in any combined GM/Leyland group would have closed. Moreover, the lack of success of many previous mergers in the UK motor industry between struggling groups does not fill one with confidence for the long-term success of that proposed venture.

The government continued to explore other possibilities during 1987, engaging in talks with Paccar of the US, which owns the British lorry maker Foden, and DAF of the Netherlands, which already had a distribution deal with Leyland. The European solution prevailed and a joint company, Leyland DAF, was formed, in which Rover had 40 per cent of the equity. Both Leyland Trucks and Freight Rover, the profitable Sherpa Van subsidiary, were included in the deal. The restructuring involved plant closures and the loss of 2,200 jobs, but it was hoped that the future of the firm would be more secure as part of a larger organisation, able to secure the benefits of DAF's distribution network in Europe. A £750 million grant from the British government to 'write-off accumulated debt' was cut by £70 million by the European Commission. The deal fell foul of the Commission which, during the run up to the elimination of European trade barriers and the completion of the Internal Market in 1992, had begun to play an increasingly important role in competition policy. EC rules ban subsidies which are likely to distort competition. As a consequence of the write-off of debt by the government and the upturn in the European truck industry, the merger proved successful and was profitable from the start, with output at Leyland increasing.

The Leyland Bus/Laird Group proposal

After the initial failure to sell Austin Rover and Leyland Vehicles the government continued to negotiate for the sale of Leyland Bus, which was to have been sold to the Laird Group, the second largest UK bus manufacturer. The demand for buses has dropped dramatically since the late 1970s and this process has been accelerated by the ending of both the bus grant and revenue support for bus services. Furthermore, the deregulation of bus services has shifted demand away from traditional large buses towards smaller ones, the demand for which has been met to a great extent by importers.

The proposal was, however, rejected in favour of a **management buyout** which valued the company at £4 million in January 1987. Thus the government rejected the argument that the best way to improve the long-run viability of the industry would be to restructure it by merging the two leading manufacturers. Instead both firms were to compete in the market against one another and against foreign competition. Yet in 1988, the management confortium sold the company to Volvo of Sweden for £15 million claiming that the business had been restructured during the previous two years, but that the 'key to success in this business is to be a world player'. Volvo promised to create extra work for the two plants and to provide 'substantial investment'. It is possible that the increase in the value of the company was justified, but it is also possible to understand accusations that this represented yet another privatised company sold at less than its real value.

The Rover/BAe deal

Despite signs of renewed interest from both Ford and Volkswagen (keen to re-establish itself as the largest car manufacturer in Europe), the British government announced in March 1988 that it intended to pursue a wholly British solution for the remaining parts of Rover by selling it to British Aerospace (BAe). Although Rover had reported an operating profit of £27 million for 1987, after years of heavy losses, covered by government handouts, the chances of privatising the company by an issue of shares to the public still seemed remote. The political storm generated in 1986 by the proposals to sell various parts of Rover to foreign competition had not been forgotten and the government was keen to avoid a repetition of this, particularly if unpopular rationalisation and plant closures were involved. In those circumstances the only option open to a government, determined to return Rover to the private sector, was to sell it to a British company which was not involved in the car industry. When the BAe/Rover deal was first announced, surprise was expressed and questions were raised about the reasons for BAe's interest in Rover.

Bryan Gould, the Labour Trade and Industry spokesman, questioned: 'Is this not a further example of the sort of conglomerate merger that has served British industry so ill in the past?' The Chairman of Aerospatiale, the French aerospace group, commented that the proposed merger (together with that between Daimler Benz and Messerschmitt under consideration at the same time) risked setting a trend towards diversified national groupings, which would make the task of creating a European aerospace industry, capable of competing with the US, more difficult. Questions were raised about the 'industrial logic' of a merger between an aerospace company and a car company, although there are several foreign combined aerospace/car groupings (eg General Motors, Daimler Benz, Fiat and Saab). Indeed Saab has run an advertising campaign specifically linking the two activities in the hope of raising car sales, by transferring an up-market high-technology image from aeroplanes to cars. The benefits of **synergy** or *cross-fertilisation* were claimed to be one of the main reasons for the link-up. Professor Smith, Chairman of BAe, claimed that synergy existed between the two companies in terms of 'engineering technology, marketing, purchasing and quality standards'. Others see little sign of overlap between the two and, moreover, claim that any benefits will take time to accrue. The long-term nature of the potential benefits is, however, supported by Graham Day, Chairman of Rover: 'This is long-term and strategic. To spot the synergy you must focus on the manufacturing process, not the product.' He also claimed 'everyone is looking at new materials to bring down the weight of vehicles.' BAe was keen to diversify, in order to protect itself from the cyclical swings of both civil and military aerospace manufacturing.

In addition, the Rover link would bring BAe into contact with Honda, a link which was welcomed by BAe, both in terms of potential collaboration in manufacturing and also as a means of facilitating sales in the Far East. (As stated earlier in this chapter, Rover's links with Honda were further cemented when Honda acquired a 20 per cent stake in Rover.) The Rover link gave BAe minority stakes in several companies previously hived off from Rover – in particular the 40 per cent stake in Leyland DAF. (The flotation of Leyland DAF on the Stock Market in 1989 yielded BAe £100 million for the sale of part of its 40 per cent stake in the company; this compares with £150 million paid by BAe to the government for the whole of the Rover Group, including the Leyland DAF stake!)

It is hard to put a value on a company which has large assets and turnover, but which is barely profitable, and it could be that BAe found the price it had to pay for Rover just too good to refuse. The terms agreed with the British government valued the company at £150 million, but there would be an £800 million cash injection by the government in order to wipe out 'past indebtedness'.

However, this deal, like the Leyland DAF deal, fell foul of the European Commission's rules banning subsidies which are likely to distort competition,

Figure 4.2: The Rover Group – making more from less

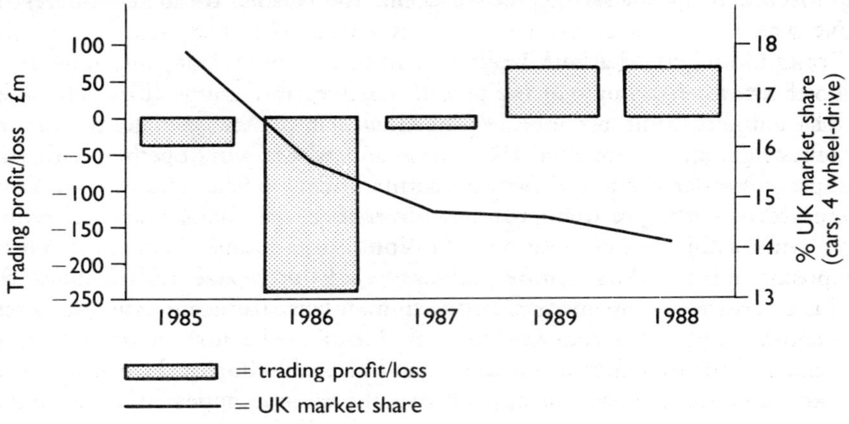

Trading profit/loss £m

% UK market share (cars, 4 wheel-drive)

☐ = trading profit/loss
—— = UK market share

From: Independent on Sunday, 1 April 1990

and the EC judged that £253 million should be reduced from the cash injection and that there should be no further government aid for Rover. The revised deal was accepted by BAe. The EC also insisted on a biannual monitoring of Rover's hitherto secret five-year corporate plan, in order to confirm that the money allocated for restructuring was being spent on that. The plan involved proposals to reduce excess capacity and to transform Rover from being a volume car producer to a specialist producer in an 'up-market move' with the aim of increasing profit per car sold (see Figure 4.2). The disclosure of these plans forced a premature announcement that two plants – Cowley South and Llanelli Pressings – were to be run down and closed in the early 1990s with the loss of about 3,400 jobs. Although BAe was blamed, it was correct to point out that the corporate plan had been drawn up before the proposed merger. Small comfort was gained from the fact that had a competitor taken over Rover instead, job losses might have been considerably greater.

RESTRUCTURING THE ITALIAN AND SPANISH CAR INDUSTRIES

In order to try and place the problems faced by the British car industry into an international perspective, the car industries of Italy and Spain are briefly considered.

In 1985 Ford failed in its attempt to merge its European car production facilities with those of Fiat, largely on the issue of which company would be dominant in the partnership. The very fact that two of the Big Six European companies were even considering merging indicates the growing emphasis on scale in the car industry, and highlights the difficulties that a company such as Rover faces in the world market. This abortive merger was followed for Ford in 1986 by the suspension of the preliminary discussions with the British government on the sale of Austin Rover. Twice thwarted Ford then turned its attention to the loss making, state-owned, Alfa Romeo company of Italy, in what was seen as a continuation of its battle with Fiat, which was also interested in acquiring Alfa Romeo.

Ford claimed that 'an association with another company is not essential for Ford's continued success in Europe'. However, the move was seen as one which would boost Ford's market share and which would also provide the company with a prestigious marque with a sporty image. The Ford bid can, therefore, be seen as an attempt to establish Alfa in relation to Ford in the same way as the Audi cars complement the Volkswagen range. Fiat countered by proposing to merge Alfa with its own Lancia subsidiary and claimed that: 'Our aim is to create a company specialising in high performance prestige cars with the sporty, aggressive characteristics of Alfa and the luxurious comfort of Lancia; a company which can put itself and Fiat at the top of the European car market.' On the face of it the motives of Ford and Fiat appeared to be similar, but the key difference was that Ford's share of the Italian car market was minimal, whereas Fiat's was in excess of 55 per cent. Thus the merger of Fiat/Lancia and Alfa would increase Fiat's existing dominance of the Italian car market and be liable to lead to an increase in monopoly power. Critics of Fiat therefore argued that its bid could be seen as a defensive move to improve its domestic position and, perhaps more importantly, to prevent a competitor from obtaining Italian production facilities, which in the long run could pose a threat to Fiat.

Although there was opposition to the Fiat-Alfa deal from some trade unionists who were concerned at the possible job losses caused by rationalisation after a merger, the Italian government was subjected to considerable political pressure of a nationalistic nature to support the Fiat bid – pressure similar to that which forced the British government to cancel the talks between Ford and Austin Rover – and eventually rejected the Ford overtures in favour of an 'all Italian solution'. Thus the Italian government increased the dominant position of Fiat and rejected the chance of increase competition in its home market.

The Spanish government too was faced with questions concerning the **restructuring** of the car industry during 1986. (Spain joined the European Community together with Portugal in 1986.) These questions arose largely as a consequence of EC membership, which necessitated a phased withdrawal of 'protection' from the Spanish home market. The Spanish government, keen to maintain Spain's position as a major producer of small cars, made various agreements with Peugeot, Citroen and Renault to guarantee continuation of existing production capacity and sold loss-making state-owned Seat, the only Spanish-owned car company, to Volkswagen. The Spanish car industry is dominated by five multinational companies: Peugeot/Citroen, Renault, Ford, General Motors and Volkswagen. Spain is the fourth largest manufacturer of cars in the EC – ahead of the UK. The strategy of the Spanish government (ie to encourage multinational firms to establish car plants in Spain) may be contrasted with the Italian government's approach, considered above.

THE DRIVE FOR QUALITY

The huge costs of model development and the increasingly competitive environment for luxury cars forced both Jaguar, privatised in 1984, and Saab to seek collaboration with other companies during 1989. Jaguar initially favoured a deal with General Motors (GM), whereby the American company would acquire a partial stake in Jaguar – in other words Jaguar's independence would be maintained. GM would provide funds which would have led to the joint development of a new product range.

However, Ford, GM's main US rival, launched a bid for Jaguar, which valued it at £1.6 billion. Jaguar had felt itself to be protected from such a takeover by a **golden share** (a mechanism whereby the government provides protection from takeover to recently privatised companies for a finite period of time). However, the government removed the golden share protection in response to the Ford bid, 14 months before it was due to expire, and the Ford offer was finally recommended to shareholders by the Jaguar board. The removal of the golden share protection, followed by similar action when BP acquired Britoil in 1988, questioned the government's whole commitment to the concept of golden shares for recently privatised companies. GM did not put in a counterbid, as it considered that the company was being overvalued. When one notes that Jaguar's pre-tax profits for the first half of 1989 had slumped to £1.4 million, it is easy to see that a company valuation of £1.6 billion might be considered rather high.

However, the value of a company is based on more than just short-term profitability. There are very few independent luxury car firms with the reputation of Jaguar, and volume manufacturers have found it hard to develop luxury cars of their own, considered to be competitive with specialists such as Daimler Benz and BMW. In addition, the move may be seen as partly defensive – in order to prevent Jaguar from falling into the hands of one of Ford's competitors.

From Figure 4.3 it can be seen that shareholders of Jaguar have done very well since privatisation – especially as a result of the bid from Ford. However, although the dramatic progress, in terms of productivity, made by Jaguar since privatisation is acknowledged, critics claim that it was bound to be a takover candidate before too long, as it was a small player in a market which was becoming increasingly concentrated.

Saab faced problems similar to those confronting Jaguar. It too was involved in talks with Ford, GM and, in addition, Fiat. A deal was struck with GM, in which GM acquired a 50 per cent stake in Saab for $600 million. This deal provided GM with the entry to the luxury car market that it had sought – Saab was promised access to GM's resources and dealership network. The option of a 'Swedish solution', by means of a merger with Volvo, was not seriously considered in view of the restructuring and job losses considered to be inevitable from the merger of two specialist car manufacturers. Volvo itself, shortly after the Saab/GM deal, announced an extensive cooperation deal with Renault, accompanied by an exchange of equity stakes. The link between the

Figure 4.3: Jaguar share price between the company's privatisation and its purchase by Ford

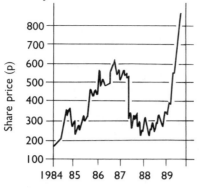

Source: Datastream
From: *Guardian*, 1 November 1989

two companies resulted in the creation of the world's largest bus and truck manufacturer, overtaking Daimler Benz of West Germany.

COMMENT

It is hard to say whether any conclusions may be draw for the British car industry by considering the car industries of other countries. It might be argued that for years Britain unsuccessfully attempted the 'Italian approach', trying to establish an independent, strong domestic producer and that now an approach, in some respects similar to the 'Spanish approach' (welcoming foreign investment) is being adopted. This can be seen in the attitude adopted towards Nissan, Toyota and Honda, although the 'national solution approach' prevailed in the sale of Rover to British Aerospace rather than to a US multinational. It is certainly true that the huge costs of new model development, including the cost of meeting higher environmental standards, have forced many European car manufacturers to collaborate or merge. This process is being accelerated by the competition provided by Japanese firms.

The trade balance of the motor industry has been in deficit since 1982 and in 1989, at £6.55 billion, accounted for 28 per cent of the UK visible trade deficit of £23.1 billion. From this it may be seen that the health of the motor industry is critical to the health of the British economy. An examination of Figure 4.4 shows that it is expected that UK car production will increase in the next ten years (largely as a result of Japanese investment) and that consequently the share of car imports in the British market will decline, as will the motor industry trade deficit.

Whilst the Conservative government was delighted to have sold back to the private sector one of its most difficult privatisation candidates, the impact of recent changes in the car industry have yet to be fully assessed. In a sense the motor industry can be seen as a test case for the Thatcherite medicine for industry.

Figure 4.4: UK motor industry

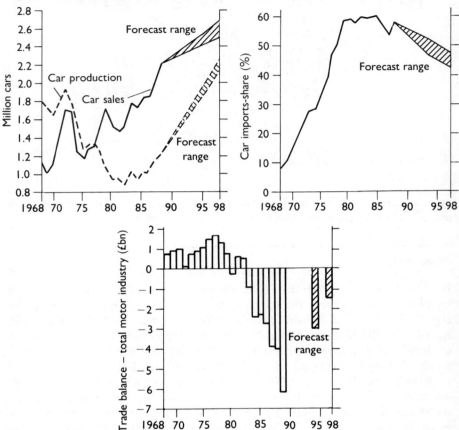

Source: historical figures; Society of Motor Manufacturers and Traders; forecasts; industry estimates
From: Financial Times, 1 August 1989

PART 2

WHITHER THE WELFARE STATE?

5 A Welfare State or Dependency Culture?

- ■ Background
- ■ The operation of the Welfare State
- ■ Comment

BACKGROUND

It is not surprising that, as a major part of public expenditure, the finances of the Welfare State should have received attention from a government, which has been keen to reduce the rate of growth of public expenditure and to limit the role of the state. However, the concern with the cost and scope of the Welfare State has been ideological as well as purely economic. Although many measures have been introduced, some of them extremely controversial, the basic structure of the Welfare State has remained intact and the Conservative government has appeared to be more reluctant to legislate in this area than in most others, content with modification rather than substantial revision.

The Welfare State was set up after the Second World War as a means of providing universal 'freedom from want', according to **Sir William Beveridge**, and 'care from cradle to grave' for the whole population according to Sir Winston Churchill. The Welfare State includes the provision of health care by means of the National Health Service, state education and council housing. Furthermore, an insurance against loss of income due to unemployment, old age or illness is provided by means of the social security system, which also provides support for those on low pay or in poverty. The Welfare State was intended to eliminate *want, waste, ignorance, disease* and *squalor*, the 'five giants' identified by Beveridge as barriers to both prosperity and participation in society. Consideration is given in subsequent chapters to aspects of poverty, to health and to housing (Chapters 6, 7 and 8 respectively), but this chapter deals with the social security system and attempts to reform it.

The social security system was, at first, principally intended to support pensioners and, although the numbers have increased during the last forty years, the main increases in those claiming *supplementary benefit* (now

Figure 5.1: Who gets supplementary benefit in Great Britain

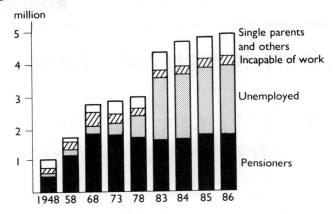

From: Financial Times : A Balanced Appraisal, 1987
Source: DHSS (1987)

renamed *income support*) have been the unemployed and single parents (see Figure 5.1). This point emphasises why it has been so difficult to control the overall cost of benefits, which depends on both the level of benefits provided and the number of people claiming them. This will be affected not just by economic factors, but by demographic and social factors as well.

THE OPERATION OF THE WELFARE STATE

Many right-wing economists have criticised the big-spending programmes of the Welfare State which were rapidly built up, especially during the 1960s. They argue that the tax burden required to finance the Welfare State has reduced incentives and thereby curbed initiative and enterprise, leading to an adverse effect on economic growth. Many of the benefits of the Welfare State were provided at no direct cost to the consumer (ie they were **free at the point of use**) although, of course, the cost was met by the taxpayer. (This concept is considered again when discussing the NHS – refer to Chapter 7, pages 90–7.) These economists argue that, by being insulated from market forces, the consumer has no realistic assessment of cost and is therefore liable to overconsume. If this is true, then the Welfare State may always have difficulty satisfying the expectations of the public, even though the resources devoted to it since its inception have increased rapidly. Critics point out that poverty, homelessness and poor standards in both health and education still exist and that the only remedy offered by supporters of the Welfare State is to 'spend more money', with no assurance that demand will ever be met.

According to Charles Murray of the Manhattan Institute for Policy Research, it is essential to 'move away from the language of entitlement'. By providing welfare benefits, recipients may become less reliant on self-help and more dependent on the state, entering what has become known as a **depen dency culture** or **benefit culture**. This may lead to a *cycle of dependency*, from which it is hard to break loose. This is likely to be particularly serious if either the **poverty trap** or the **unemployment trap** is encountered.

The *poverty trap* exists when a low paid worker receives a pay increase, but then, as a result of the higher income level attained, not only has to pay tax, but also loses various **means-tested benefits** previously received. ('Means-tested' benefits are benefits which are not automatically given, but which are dependent on the recipient's income or wealth, ie his 'means'.) As a result, the individual may retain only a very small percentage of the extra income earned and, in some cases, may actually lose more than the extra income earned. Hence, there may be little or no incentive for a low paid worker to strive for a higher income, whether by gaining promotion or by working overtime, if the welfare benefits previously received disappear rapidly as income rises.

Similarly, the *unemployment trap* exists when an unemployed worker, receiving benefit, may be less well off, or only marginally better off, in low-paid employment. In both instances a worker, acting in his own self-interest, may choose to retain his benefits (by refusing extra pay or a job), thereby perpetuating his dependency on the Welfare State. (See Chapter 6, pages 86–7 for details of the Conservative government's 1988 Welfare Reforms.)

This highlights the twin difficulties faced when investigating welfare economics: the problems of **targeting** and whether to apply means-testing or not. It is not just a case of directing sufficient welfare benefits towards those in 'need' to induce a state of 'well-being' (in which needs are satisfied). 'Need' does not end suddenly; instead there is a continuous spectrum between the two states. If benefit ceases to be paid completely when an individual reaches a certain level of income, then there will be an anomaly at that point, as someone earning £1 less will still be eligible for the benefit.

This leads to the question of targeting, which has concerned the Conservative government in its social security reforms. If benefits are targeted at those most in need as assessed by a means test, then the poverty and unemployment traps may be encountered. However, if the benefits are spread more widely, then either the value of benefits per person will be diminished or an increase in the resources to fund the benefit will be necessary.

In the UK some benefits are automatic (eg child benefit, which is received by all families with children) and others are means-tested (eg family credit, which is received only by those families with low incomes). Separate systems for income tax, national insurance and welfare benefits in Britain mean that people on low incomes may be required to pay income tax and national insurance contributions, whilst at the same time receiving welfare benefits.

An ideal programme to help those in poverty (which is probably impossible to attain in reality) may be defined as one which meets the needs of the people concerned, without adversely affecting their incentive to self-help, by which means the individuals might reduce or eliminate reliance (or dependency) on the state.

COMMENT

The Conservative government has attempted to replace what it sees as a **dependency culture** by an **enterprise culture**. It has sought to do this by fostering **popular capitalism** in the hope of reintroducing the entrepreneurial streak into the British economy and revitalising British industry, through the introduction of incentives to both management and workforce. Moves to return to management the **right to manage**, increasingly eroded by trade unions and governments during the post-war period, have been encouraged. Popular capitalism necessitates a belief in the power of market forces, a reduction in the role of the state, an increasing reliance on self-help and moves towards extending the property-owning democracy. The Conservative government has emphasized the notion of *self-help*. It has stressed the need for personal and family responsibility within a framework of the local community or neighbourhood. The role of the state was to be changed so that it would offer help in the last rather than in the first resort.

Critics of popular capitalism argue that it is a programme for increasing inequality and poverty. To back this up they claim that a reliance on market forces has widened pay inequalities and also significantly increased unemployment. Tax cuts have been directed primarily at the 'better-off' and welfare benefits have been restricted. The long-term trend towards greater equality of income and wealth has been reversed under the Conservative governments of 1979 onwards and it is argued that this 'strategy of inequality' (Child Poverty Action Group), which is seen as a direct consequence of the drive towards popular capitalism, has led to a major increase in poverty in the UK and to the possible emergence of an *underclass*, who lack any stake in popular capitalism and who are caught in the dependency culture.

The argument about equality is, of course, at the heart of economic/political debate. Socialists believe in greater equality in society: 'A more equal society will be a more prosperous society and a more peaceful society' (Roy Hattersley, *Hansard* 16 April, 1987), but they are criticised for favouring policies of distribution rather than production – 'Someone has to create wealth before the politicians fall to sharing that wealth out' (Kenneth Clarke, *Hansard* 6 April 1987). Conservatives are less concerned about equality and more concerned with generating production and income, believing that the benefits will 'trickle down' through society to benefit all.

6 Poverty in the Midst of Plenty?

■ Measurements of poverty
■ Aspects of poverty
■ Three views on poverty
■ Comment: The moral high ground

The Conservative government has been accused of presiding over an economy in which the benefits of economic growth have not been distributed fairly. Furthermore, it has been argued that, during the Conservative terms of office, there has been an increase in the number of those living in poverty. These points are now considered.

MEASUREMENTS OF POVERTY

The most serious difficulty faced when trying to assess the extent of poverty in any society is to find a clear definition which is easily understood and universally accepted. Whereas most people find it relatively easy, when faced with inflation or unemployment figures, to decide whether those economic problems are improving or getting worse, it is not so easy in the case of poverty, in the absence of a clear, widely accepted measure.

Some definitions of poverty have sought to define it in terms of **absolute deprivation**, where some measure is made of subsistence requirements based on physical needs. This represents an attempt to assess a level of income below which it is impossible to ensure survival. In a speech, shortly before leaving his position as Secretary of State for Social Security in 1989, John Moore claimed that poverty in the 'old, absolute sense of hunger and want' had been eliminated. Certainly, if one compares living standards today with those experienced in this country one hundred years ago or, to make an even more stark comparison, with those experienced in many Less Developed Countries (LDCs) today, then it is true that poverty in the UK in the 1980s is relatively insignificant.

However, most definitions of poverty are based in terms of **relative deprivation** (ie deprivation relative to others in the community, rather than a comparison over time or between countries). These measures present a rather different picture. Such measures take into account society's expectations of steadily rising standards of living, which also affect those living in poverty. Thus according to the Child Poverty Action Group (CPAG) 'poverty is viewed in relation to a generally accepted standard of living in a particular society that goes beyond basic physical needs' to include 'broader social and cultural needs' as well. More starkly, Fran Bennett, director of CPAG says: 'Our contention is that you have to judge poverty by referring it to culture, society, and the times you live in, not just to what you need to avoid dying'. The EC defines people in poverty as those whose 'resources are so small as to exclude them from the minimum acceptable way of life of the member state in which they live'.

Many economists have used the *supplementary benefit* (SB) level (now renamed *income support*) to define poverty. However, a consideration of this measure reveals the problems faced when trying to assess the extent of poverty. Any increase in the SB level increases the number of those eligible to claim benefit. Hence any increase in the provision for those in poverty is likely to result in a perceived increase in the problem. Although the SB level increased by 5 per cent in real terms between November 1978 and April 1987, this compares with an average increase of 14 per cent in real terms for personal disposable income. As a result the SB level for a couple on the ordinary rate has fallen from 61 per cent of personal disposable income per capita in 1978 to 53 per cent in 1987. The number claiming SB has risen over the same period from three million to just under five million (figures from CPAG). The CPAG itself has chosen to define those earning less than 140 per cent of SB as 'living in poverty or at the margins of poverty'.

ASPECTS OF POVERTY

Evidence produced in *Social Trends 1987* (CSO), after studying the composition of the lowest income group, suggested that changes have occurred in the nature of poverty. Significant increases in those claiming supplementary benefit were recorded from both the unemployed and from single-parent families, whereas the number of pensioners claiming had decreased (see Figure 5.1, page 80).

The number of those affected by poverty in any society will, however, be influenced not only by the level of unemployment, but also by what happens to the incomes of those on low pay. In addition, government policies on taxation and welfare benefits will have a significant influence. These aspects of poverty will now be considered.

Low pay

During the period of the Conservative government there has been a marked growth in pay inequality. If all incomes rise by the same percentage amount, then those at the lower end of the income scale will, of course, receive a lower extra sum of money compared to those at the higher end of the income scale. In this case pay differentials and inequality in society would be unaltered. However, the figures in Table 6.1 indicate that not only have the amounts of

Table 6.1: Gross weekly earnings per week of full-time males at constant (1986) prices

	April 1979 £	April 1989 £	Change %
Lowest decile	115.5	117.9	+5.7
Median	169.2	201.5	+19.1
Highest decile	265.4	362.6	+36.6

Notes: (a) The data for women are similar.

(b) 'Constant' prices means that the figures are expressed in 'real terms' (ie inflation has been taken into account.

Source: New Earnings Survey

From: *Living Faith in the City* (1990), General Synod of the Church of England

extra income received by those on higher incomes been greater than those on lower incomes, but so too have been the percentages.

Between 1979 and 1989 those at the highest decile (ie those earning more than 90 per cent and less than 10 per cent of the population) increased their real income by 36.6 per cent whereas those at the lowest decile (ie those earning more than 10 per cent and less than 90 per cent of the population) who increased their real income by only 5.7 per cent. Based on these figures it is clear that income inequality has increased and that the benefits of economic growth have not been evenly distributed. Critics of the government have argued that, although the need for incentives throughout the economy has been stressed, at the lowest end of the income scale there is greater emphasis on the need for workers 'to price themselves into employment' by accepting less than the 'going rate' of pay increases. The fear of unemployment, the imposition of public sector cash limits and the reduction (and, in some cases, removal) of minimum wage protection provided to millions of low paid workers by Wages Councils has contributed to this.

It is correct to say that, under the Conservative government, pay inequalities have widened. Whether or not these can be said to have caused an increase in poverty depends, of course, on the definition of poverty chosen, as has been described above. However, there are also other factors which determine whether the low paid have slipped into poverty. These include the government's policy on taxation and welfare benefits and are considered below.

Taxation and welfare benefits

The Conservative party was elected in 1979 on a promise to reduce the overall level of taxation and, in addition, to shift the burden of tax to some extent from income (**direct tax**) to expenditure (**indirect tax**). Both policies are in accordance with the principle of allowing the individual to have control over more of his own income.

In the 1979 'Incentive Budget', the basic rate of income tax was cut from 33 per cent to 30 per cent, whilst the top rate was cut from 83 per cent to 60 per cent. At the same time the standard rate of VAT was raised from 8 per cent to 15 per cent. The basic rate of income tax was then reduced from 30 per cent to

29 per cent in 1986 and, thereafter, to 27 per cent in 1987 and 25 per cent in 1988, thereby achieving the Chancellor's longstanding commitment. In addition, the top rate of tax was reduced from 60 per cent to 40 per cent in the 1988 Budget and all intermediate tax rates were abolished.

Cuts in the rates of taxation may be justified in terms of improved incentives and (at the top rate of taxation) a reduction in the 'brain drain' abroad. However, no direct benefit accrues to individuals who do not pay taxation. Further dispute centres on the 'trickle-down' effect of tax cuts. Conservatives believe that tax cuts will lead to greater incentives and initiative, thereby creating an **enterprise culture** in which the benefits of growth will ultimately spread to everyone. However, Dr Robert Runcie, the then Archbishop of Canterbury, claimed in the House of Lords (2 February, 1987) that 'there is no automatic trickling down process that ensures that increased wealth will benefit the poor.'

Although statistics show that many benefits paid to the old, poor and unemployed have maintained their real value (ie kept pace with inflation) under the Conservative government during the 1980s, these calculations are based on the rate of inflation for the average person. However, rising prices affect different groups in different ways. The low-income groups and pensioners spend a higher proportion of their money on food and fuel, whose prices have risen by more than other items, and so the inflation index for these groups has risen faster than inflation for the average person.

An example of the way in which the government has 'pared back welfare' without affecting its actual structure, may be seen by considering the provision of pensions. Although the state retirement pension remains linked to prices and, subject to the proviso noted above, retains its 'real' value, the commitment to raise pensions in line with earnings (in years when earnings rose by more than prices) was abolished in 1980. Hence the position of those relying on pensions has deteriorated relative to those in employment with rising real incomes. Although linking pensions to prices rather than incomes may not produce a great difference in one year, after twenty-five years, assuming incomes rise by 2 per cent per annum faster than prices, the *price-linked* pension will be worth only approximately 60 per cent of the *earnings-linked* pension.

Less than a month after the 1988 budget (providing tax cuts for all income earners, but especially for those on high income), the government's social security reforms came into force amid great controversy, with a revised scheme of welfare benefits. The aims of the reform were: simplification, improved **targeting** of benefits and a reduction in the impact of both the **unemployment trap** and the **poverty trap**. (The reforms were based on the principles discussed in Chapter 5, pages 80–1.) The rules relating to **means-tested benefits** for *housing benefit, family credit* (family income supplement) and *income support* (supplementary benefit) were redesigned and simplified. However, according to calculations produced by the Policy Studies Institutes and noted in *The Economist* (12 March 1988) 'the overall impact of the reforms will simply be to redistribute from one group of the very poor to another'.

Two of the social security reforms proved to be particularly controversial.

Firstly, the rules which sharply reduced those eligible for *housing benefit*, thereby removing benefits from pensioners with limited savings, were opposed by many Conservative MPs. Secondly, the *Social Fund* was introduced. This was designed to replace the former system of emergency grants for special needs for such items as cookers and clothing, which were dispensed under a variety of rules. In its place the Social Fund removed the right to a grant and instituted instead a system of discretionary loans. However, critics claimed that this scheme did not provide sufficient funds to those in real need.

The widespread unease with several of the measures proposed in the welfare reforms felt by many Conservative MPs, demonstrates how difficult it is for any government (even one with a large parliamentary majority) to reform the Welfare State. Although great controversy was generated, the proposed reforms were really only dealing with the margins of the Welfare State rather than with any fundamental alterations in its structure.

An examination of Figure 6.1 reveals that, whilst each of the groups considered has gained over the period 1979–89 (due to the tax and benefit changes discussed above), the greatest gain was made by the richest tenth of the population. At the same time there were large numbers of losers within the poorest groups.

Figure 6.1: **Average gain in income 1979–89, by tenths of population, showing the effect after tax and social security changes**

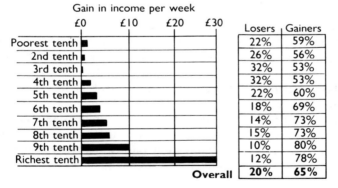

	Losers	Gainers
Poorest tenth	22%	59%
2nd tenth	26%	56%
3rd tenth	32%	53%
4th tenth	32%	53%
5th tenth	22%	60%
6th tenth	18%	69%
7th tenth	14%	73%
8th tenth	15%	73%
9th tenth	10%	80%
Richest tenth	12%	78%
Overall	**20%**	**65%**

Source: Institute of Fiscal Studies
From: Independent, 13 May 1989

THREE VIEWS ON POVERTY

Although more recent documents have been produced, a study of the main political parties' policies on tax, the social security system and poverty during the 1987 General Election campaign summarises clearly the different strands of opinion expressed during the 1980s. In their Election manifestos both the Labour and Alliance parties produced specific programmes to deal with poverty: *The Anti-Poverty Programme* and *Ending Poverty* respectively. The Conservative party did not have a programme as such, but included two sections: *Lower Taxes* and *Social Security – a fair deal for those in need*, which addressed the same problems, albeit with different solutions.

> Lower taxation coupled with lower inflation makes everyone better off ... It promotes a climate of enterprise and initiative.

This clearly sums up the Conservative attitude to taxation and, most importantly, it views the alleviation of poverty as part of an overall policy to improve prosperity for everyone. It was hoped that people would not be made worse off by taking a job (the **unemployment trap**), nor would they lose money when their gross pay rose (the **poverty trap**), due to the loss of **means-tested benefits** in each case. The Conservatives also promised to:

> reform the tangled web of income-related benefits which had grown up piecemeal over forty years. Success in social policy depends on growth in national prosperity. Labour's economic failure led to damaging cuts in health care and benefits. Our increasing economic strength means that resources for care have grown and are growing.

The Labour party promised in its Manifesto:

> For the first two years in government we will concentrate resources on the essential tasks of combating unemployment and poverty ... The spread of poverty in the eight years has strained the whole nation, and widened misery and disadvantage amongst the old and young. Much of it is the result of deliberate government policy.

As a first step pensions and child benefit were to be raised and long-term supplementary benefit extended to the long-term unemployed. The recovery programme was to be paid for by reversing the tax gains made by the top 5 per cent of earners under the Conservatives, although specific details were not published, and by reversing the 2p cut in the basic rate of income tax proposed in the 1987 Conservative Budget.

The Labour party promised to introduce a 'comprehensive strategy for ending low pay, notably by the introduction of a statutory national minimum wage'. This, of course, runs counter to the Conservative view that workers should be allowed to 'price themselves into employment' by accepting wage cuts if necessary.

According to the SDP/Liberal Alliance Election Manifesto:

> Poverty in Britain is getting worse. The Conservatives' taxation and benefit policies have redistributed income from the poor to the rich.

The Alliance proposals for combating poverty fell into two parts. Firstly, in proposals similar to those put forward by the Labour party, benefits for 'pensioners, families with children, the unemployed, disabled and carers' were to be raised. Secondly, in proposals which caused considerable controversy between the two parties comprising the Alliance before the election, a radical 'restructuring of the tax and benefits systems to create one integrated system', intended to be simpler and fairer, was suggested.

COMMENT: THE MORAL HIGH GROUND

The Conservative government's policies on taxation and welfare have brought it into increasing conflict with the Church of England. The Church has criticised the great emphasis placed on *individualism* rather than *collectivism*, and has complained about the government's over-reliance on market forces. The Conservative emphasis on incentives, initiative and the spirit of enterprise may well improve average living standards, but there is a danger that not all people will participate in the general prosperity. This gives rise to the danger of what has become known as the *two-thirds, one-third society* in which the majority obtains secure well-paid full-time 'core' jobs and the minority become 'marginalised', obtaining less well-paid, part-time, temporary, 'peripheral' jobs and hovering on the verge of poverty. Often concentrations of such people are located either in depressed regions or in run-down inner-city areas. The Bishop of Gloucester claimed in June 1988 that 'wealth gained regardless of the welfare of the rest of the community is difficult to justify'. Dr Robert Runcie, the then Archbishop of Canterbury, claimed in October 1989 that Britain risked becoming a 'Pharisee society' of self-interest.

As discussed earlier in this chapter, the Conservatives counter with the argument that the generation of wealth is the pre-requisite for increasing social spending programmes. They also claim that poverty is not alleviated by providing ever-increasing welfare benefits, but rather by providing an appropriate economic and social environment, in which individuals have the incentive and the ability to raise themselves out of poverty, without encountering the **poverty** or **unemployment traps**.

7 *Health*

BACKGROUND

The National Health Service (NHS) was created in 1948 as a service designed to provide every citizen in post-war Britain with 'whatever medical treatment he requires, in whatever form he requires it' (**Sir William Beveridge**). Aneurin Bevan who, as Minister of Health in the Labour government, pioneered the introduction of the NHS, claimed: 'Medical treatment and care should be made available to rich and poor alike in accordance with medical need and by no other criteria.'

The NHS was created at a time of post-war reconstruction, when large sections of British industry were being nationalised by the Labour government. This nationalisation was an attempt to achieve the socialist objective of common ownership of the means of production and also to facilitate government intervention in the running of the economy. At the same time the Welfare State, designed to provide a safety net for those incapable of fending for themselves, was being rapidly expanded, and the NHS can be seen as its greatest and most enduring feature.

Britain was the first country to offer health care to the entire population **free at the point of use**. The NHS, of course, did use resources and was not 'free' to the extent that it had to be funded. However, it was funded from taxes collected by central government rather than from direct payments by members of the public in exchange for the medical services received. The pioneers of the NHS accepted that it would initially be necessary to increase the resources devoted to the service, but that this would level off as medical needs were satisfied. However, early budgets were rapidly broken as demand for medical services increased relentlessly and the need to make choices with scarce resources soon became apparent, thereby straining the original promise of the NHS that all medical needs should be met.

Yet, despite an increase of spending on health in the UK from 3¼ per cent of national income in 1948 to over 6 per cent (of a much larger national income)

Figure 7.1: Health spending as a percentage of GDP

i. **1970–86**   ii. **1986**

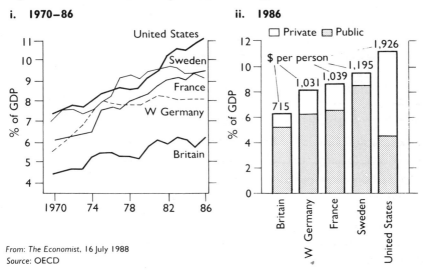

From: *The Economist*, 16 July 1988
Source: OECD

forty years later, it is alleged that the NHS is underfunded and periodically in a state of near collapse. On the other hand despite the increase in funding during the last forty years, the UK spending on health as a proportion of national income is lower than that in most West European countries and considerably lower than in the USA (see Figure 7.1).

Higher spending need not of course necessarily imply an improvement in the standard of health care provided. This will be affected not just by the amount of resources devoted to health, but also by the efficiency of the service. Hence it is not possible to claim conclusively by observation of expenditure figures that

Table 7.1: Health compared

	Sweden	West Germany	France	Britain	United States
Doctors per 10,000 population	26	26	24	14	23
Acute hospital beds per 10,000 population	138	109	107	77	58
Average length of hospital stay (days)	22	17	9	11	7
Infant mortality rate per 1,000 live births	5.9	8.6	7.7	9.5	10.4
Life expectancy for men (years)	74.0	71.2	72.0	71.5	71.3

Source: OECD (1988)
From: *The Economist*, 16 July 1988

standards of health care today have improved compared to forty years ago, nor that the standards in the UK today are worse than those in other industrialised countries. Table 7.1, which compares five countries, indicates that the US (the highest spender on health as a percentage of GDP) has the highest infant mortality rate and the second lowest life expectancy, whereas Sweden, another high-spending country, has the lowest infant mortality rate and the highest life expectancy. This demonstrates the difficulties in proving that higher expenditure leads to better health. The claim that the NHS is 'underfunded', despite the huge increase in resources devoted to it, will be examined in this chapter.

The NHS today

The Conservative government has been committed to increasing the role of market forces generally and reducing the role of the state in the economy. This has been shown by its programme of privatising nationalised industries and by its desire to maintain a firm control on public expenditure. There have also been moves to reduce reliance on the Welfare State and to change the **dependency culture** by increasing self-reliance (see Chapter 5). The 'Thatcher revolution' has affected most areas of British life so it is perhaps surprising how little it seems to have impinged on the NHS.

Although there has been a radical management shake-up and there have been improvements in organisation and efficiency, the fundamental ethos of the NHS – provision of medical service **free at the point of use** – has remained unchanged. Indeed in the Conservatives' 1987 Election Manifesto, there was ample support for the NHS and no mention of an enhanced role for the private sector. It was claimed that money spent on the NHS between 1979 and 1987 had increased in real terms by a third, that more patients were receiving treatment than ever before and that the numbers of doctors, dentists and nurses had increased substantially. When faced with complaints about hospitals, and especially about unacceptable waiting lists, the government made an emergency payment of £100 million for 1987/88 and commissioned a review of the NHS.

In order to make any meaningful assessment of whether the present tax-funded NHS is preferable to schemes involving greater private sector involvement, it is necessary to consider the meaning of the words: *'underfunding'*, *'demand'* and *'efficiency'* and to answer the following questions:

1 How is it that, despite large increases of spending on the NHS in real terms, there are continuing claims about 'underfunding'?

2 As there is no direct charge for health care, is demand really 'infinite'? If this is so, then however many resources are devoted to the NHS, demand will never be satisfied. What is the nature of demand for health care and does it differ from demand for other services?

3 What is the meaning of 'efficiency' when applied to health care?

1 Funding and the NHS

Although the resources allocated to the NHS have increased in real terms, there are a number of factors working against this. For example, the NHS is 'labour intensive' and 70 per cent of its costs are accounted for by wages. Thus, if wages in the NHS are linked to price increases (as measured by the Retail Price Index), real wages of NHS employees will be maintained, but they will fall behind the increases awarded to other workers, if earnings are rising faster than prices in the rest of the economy. If, as is likely, NHS employees then seek and obtain wage increases in line with other increases in earnings, then a greater amount of resources will be needed to fund them. However, at the same time there will be no increase in the standard of services provided. Hence it may be said that 'health service inflation' has risen faster than inflation in the rest of the economy. The funds of the NHS have been put under further strain, in addition to the pressures of rising demand, by a number of other factors.

The government has not always fully funded the nationally agreed pay awards, leaving health authorities to fund part of the increase from existing budgets. Furthermore, during the 1980s there has also been shift of resources away from hospitals towards the family practioner services in order to build up 'primary care'. Problems with the hospital sector come most readily to the general public's attention, contributing to a belief that the NHS is *underfunded*, and this has been exacerbated in parts of the South East by moves to distribute resources away from London and the South East (based on the teaching hospitals) in favour of the regions.

(Note: 'underfunding', of course, is a word that only means something when 'funding' (ie resources available) is matched against demand. The nature of demand for health care is considered below.)

2 Demand for health care

The demand for health care has risen for many reasons. As personal income and wealth rise, consumers increase their demand for most goods. It is therefore not surprising that this should also be reflected in a rise in demand for health care. Moreover, to a great extent the health service is a victim of its own success. New technology has allowed doctors to perform previously unheard of operations such as hip replacements and open-heart surgery, thereby creating a demand which had not appeared before. In addition, greater life-expectancy, for which better health care is partly responsible, has resulted in a greater number of old people, which has created further demands on the NHS. Rising expectations about the standards of health can therefore be seen as fuelling further demand for health care. In fact, in some ways it can be seen that the more capable the NHS is of meeting demand, the greater the demand is likely to be.

Health care is an unusual 'commodity' and the demand for it may not be particularly responsive to price. The vast majority of consultations are handled by General Practitioners (GPs), with no need for referral for expensive hospital treatment. In those cases where the patient is referred to a hospital for further treatment, it is the doctor who makes the decision, as the patient will generally possess insufficient information. Therefore it is, in effect, the doctor who is deciding on the level of *demand*. Other demand is made purely by force of circumstances (eg after a car crash). In both situations demand is determined not by price but by clinical judgement.

Demand for health care is clearly not 'infinite', but it is difficult to meet rapidly rising demand in an affluent society. This problem is not helped by the provision of health care **free at the point of use**, which prevents the patient from knowing the cost of the treatment. In conclusion, the *demand* for health care differs from the demand for other services and its responsiveness to market forces is open to question.

3 Efficiency and health care

What is the meaning of *efficiency*, when applied to health care? When considering the number of units of output produced per worker in a factory, it is relatively easy to consider efficiency over a period of time. However, in health care the concept is more difficult to explain. For example, a doctor may be able to see more patients each hour and he may be being more efficient by seeing more people in a fixed period of time. However, he could achieve the same result by giving less attention to each patient. Similarly the efficiency of a hospital should not be judged just by the number of operations completed, but perhaps also by the effectiveness of the operations.

Whilst the introduction of competition will undoubtedly benefit some aspects of efficiency, additional costs might also be incurred. In particular the costs of administration involved in valuing various aspects of medical care (essential if a free market is to be created) might be considerable. In addition, in order for the price mechanism to be an effective way of allocating resources, the consumer (ie the patient) must possess good information and it is doubtful whether this is so in most cases. Critics of the government's drive for efficiency claim that it is motivated more by considerations of cost rather than of value for money or quality of service provided.

PROPOSALS FOR INCREASING RESOURCES DEVOTED TO THE NHS

Those supporting the continuation of an NHS based on its initial principles, funded centrally by tax finance, claim that any alternative system based on private health insurance would be bureaucratic, involving high administrative costs. NHS costs may be kept under control because of both the NHS's ability to act as a bulk buyer of medicine supplies and the unlikelihood of competitive upward pressure on wage costs for health workers. Moreover, patients are more likely to receive the 'appropriate' treatment from the NHS, whereas in private schemes, unnecessary treatment might be given, when doctors are paid a rate for the job. Advocates of funding by tax finance therefore claim that 'underfunding' of the NHS may be remedied by increasing government expenditure on the service. However, it would be fair to say that they do not have a long-term answer to the question: 'What is the appropriate level of funding?', except that of adding on an amount, based on the estimated shortfall, to existing expenditure.

It would also be possible, although it would contravene the fundamental principles of the NHS as originally conceived, to introduce charges for NHS treatment – for example, a small charge for every visit to a GP or a 'hotel charge' to cover the cost of food consumed in hospital as a means of raising additional funds. The pressures of funding have already encouraged many hospitals to generate revenue raising schemes from non-medical activities. Such commercial schemes include cafeteria services and newsagents. However, although there is clearly scope for raising revenue in this way, the amounts likely to be raised (in the context of overall health spending) are likely to be fairly limited.

An alternative scheme for financing the NHS involves the removing of finance from general taxation and the introduction of a *health stamp* or *hypothecated tax*. This 'stamp' would emphasise to users the cost of the health service since it would appear as a separate tax item on the pay slip, and would therefore increase in line with earnings and not prices.

There are many who believe that the NHS, by providing care **free at the point of use**, is facing an impossible task in which demand can never be satisfied. Various schemes of reform have been proposed involving the private sector in an attempt to introduce market forces to some extent into health care. These schemes may be divided into two: those advocating that the service provided by the NHS may best be improved by increasing its efficiency through the introduction of more commercial criteria; and those claiming that the greatest improvements would come from changing the funding arrangements by introducing some form of health insurance.

PROPOSALS FOR REFORM: IMPROVING THE EFFICIENCY OF THE NHS

Competitive tendering (see also Chapter 3, page 47) has already been introduced for many ancillary services (eg cleaning, catering) and has reduced costs, although some health authorities have found that quality of service has also suffered. Competitive tendering could be extended to certain medical services as well.

Improvements could also be made to the management structure, with the introduction of more commercially-minded managers with clear financial objectives, in addition to the fiercely resisted management changes already made in the NHS. What has attracted great attention recently are moves towards an **internal market** in the NHS, which would allow health authorities to buy and sell services to and from one another. Not only would this permit the benefits of specialisation and **economies of scale** (ie lower average cost) to be felt, but would also avoid expensive duplication. It could also be used as a means of overcoming excessively long waiting lists in some areas. The service would still be free to patients and the financial transaction would take place between the two authorities. However, most health authorities are not used to pricing their services on a commercial basis and an efficient allocation of resources would require costs to be calculated as a pre-condition.

Further moves could also be made towards increasing the two-way interaction between public and private health care sectors. Such links do exist at the present time, but they are the exception rather than the norm. The NHS could purchase services from the private sector in order to clear waiting lists for particular ailments or to obtain access to specialised equipment possibly not available in NHS hospitals. Similarly the NHS could hire out spare capacity to the private sector (eg pay beds) and sell support services (eg X-rays).

PROPOSALS FOR REFORM: RADICAL SCHEMES BASED ON HEALTH INSURANCE

More radical moves to reform the NHS are based on a belief that individuals should take more responsibility for their health care and that this can be achieved by extending the choice of different suppliers of medical services. There is, of course, already a private sector in this country (incorporating companies such as BUPA and PPP) and radical policies on the health service involve extending the health insurance principle in some way. A large number of schemes have emerged from various right-wing 'think-tanks'.

Tax relief on premiums paid to private insurance schemes could be introduced. Subscribers to private schemes at present pay twice and tax relief would be a way of compensating subscribers for relieving pressure on the NHS. However, the granting of additional tax relief runs against recent trends in fiscal policy, which has aimed to simplify the tax system, and, from an economic point of view, represents a *deadweight cost*, because those who are already members of private schemes have chosen to be so without the incentive of tax relief. The purpose of tax relief would be to encourage more people to join private schemes, but this, in view of the deadweight cost, would be expensive.

Alternative schemes involve giving individuals vouchers, to be used as payment for health care, on condition that they *opt out* of the NHS. This requires the individual to give up his right to free use of some or all NHS services and instead to look after his own health needs, either in the private sector or by paying the NHS. There are certain problems with opting out. For example, the private sector at present only provides a limited range of services and therefore no one would be able to opt out entirely from the NHS. There would also be arguments concerning which ailments should be covered by the terms of private schemes. However, the greatest problem is that those opting out would tend to be the relatively young, affluent, low-risk groups. This would create a great strain on the NHS, which would be dominated by the high-risk groups who would not be particularly welcomed by the private insurance companies. Such strains would be exacerbated if a trend developed in which young and middle-aged people opted out, only to return to the NHS when they were unable to afford the private premiums in later life. The NHS relies on **cross-subsidisation**, not just between high-risk and low-risk groups but also for every individual between their low-risk years (young and middle aged) and high-risk years (old age). The danger of allowing opting out would be that the NHS would finish up as a rump and would provide very much a second class service.

THE 1989 CONSERVATIVE NHS REFORMS

The Conservative government's proposals to reform the health service published in the White Paper *Working for Patients*, were designed to improve the efficiency of the NHS and, at the same time, increase the patient's choice. Conservative philosophy has relied on competition to improve efficiency in other areas of the economy and the same principles were applied to the NHS.

The criteria, whereby resources were to be allocated, were shifted from decisions based on assessment of need by doctors and managers towards outcomes based on competition and market forces. This radical change of emphasis proved to be extremely unpopular with doctors both in primary care and the hospital service. However, the fundamental nature of the NHS was maintained in the sense that it remained a service funded from general taxation, **free at the point of use**.

In order to stimulate competition, large hospitals were encouraged to become *self-governing*. These hospitals would remain as part of the NHS, but would be given the freedom to run themselves. Furthermore, district health authorities were obliged to become traders rather than simply suppliers of hospital services. This means that, as part of an **internal market**, hospitals would trade with one another, with self-governing hospitals or with the private sector in order to provide their patients with the best treatment available.

In the primary care sector of the NHS, general practitioners (GPs) with large practices are to be offered the chance to control their own budgets and to buy hospital services on behalf of their patients. In addition it was proposed that payment to GPs should be based far more on the size of the doctor's patient list, as this was seen as a good proxy for assessing how hard doctors work. Although alternative plans to finance the NHS were rejected – ie the service continued to be funded from general taxation – tax relief was offered on health insurance premiums for retired people.

The 1989 NHS Reforms were greeted with great hostility by much of the medical profession, partly because they were seen as part of possible moves towards dismantling the NHS, but also because of the changed emphasis brought about by the consideration of terms such as: 'efficiency', 'internal market', and 'payment by results' in areas where the role of the market had previously been much less prominent.

Critics also considered that the emphasis on efficiency did not give sufficient importance to the quality of health care provided. They also argued that, although the whole system of competition and pricing would possibly be appropriate for specific items of surgery based on short periods of acute illness, it ignored the nature of health care generally. Health care cannot be conveniently packaged and priced into such things as health problems of the 'elderly' or 'mentally ill'.

COMMENT

All countries are faced with the problem of how to respond to the rapidly growing demand for health care from their populations. This is true whichever of the many varied methods of finance is used – all systems experience problems with managing resources. This is partly because it is hard to identify true costs in any health system, but also because the market for health care does not operate as a normal market – particularly with respect to the nature of demand. Any proposed alterations to a health care system have to weigh up the obligation of society to those who are old and sick against the preferences of those who wish to determine their own health care provision.

8 *Housing*

BACKGROUND

The main economic and social themes which have already been considered in many of the chapters of this book reappear as the dominant themes in any discussion on housing policy. On the one hand, the Conservative government has sought to improve the workings of the market for housing by *deregulation*. Allied to this is a belief in the primacy of the private sector and owner-occupation, together with a rebuttal of public-sector municipal spending (mostly associated with the 1960s), which is alleged to have 'thrown money at problems', without any consideration for the real housing needs of the people involved. On the other hand, critics claim that the government has allocated too few resources to housing and has given too little emphasis to the needs of those 'at the bottom of the pile' in the housing market – the homeless and those on low incomes. Critics also argue that this has been compounded by a policy which has unfairly favoured the private sector in preference to the public sector.

According to the 1983 Conservative Election Manifesto:

> A free and independent society is one in which the ownership of property is spread as widely as possible ... Under this government the property-owning democracy is growing fast. And the basic foundation of it is the family home.

From these statements it is clear where the emphasis of the Conservative government lies. Families are to be encouraged to live in their own homes rather than to rely on the state (in the form of local authorities) for the provision of council housing.

The *Right to Buy* scheme, introduced by the government in 1980, gave council tenants the legal right to buy their homes, often at big discounts. A

Figure 8.1: Sales of dwellings owned by local authorities and new towns in England and Wales (excluding transfers to housing associations)

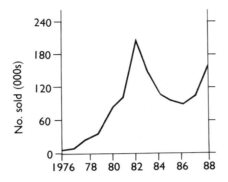

Source: Department of the Environment
From: Social Trends 20, 1990 (HMSO)

million homes were sold by the public sector to the private sector during the Conservative government's first two terms (1979–87) (see Figure 8.1). This spread of home ownership may be seen as part of the drive towards establishing a *capital-owning democracy* or **popular capitalism** (refer to Chapter 5). According to the 1987 Conservative Election Manifesto: 'Home-ownership has been the great success story of housing policy in the last eight years.' However, promises were made to shift the emphasis of policy during the Conservatives' third term towards reforming the private rented sector of the housing market.

The Royal Institution of Chartered Surveyors has stated that:

> The principle aims of national housing policy should be to ensure that, as far as possible, every household shall be able to occupy a dwelling of a size, standard and location suitable to its needs, free from nuisance, harassment or arbitrary eviction and should have a free choice of tenure (ie freehold, leasehold or other).

There has been much criticism of the government's housing policy, much of it from organisations outside parliament. By neglecting the public sector, the government is accused of lacking an effective long-term housing policy which will meet the needs of future generations. The criticisms made are very similar to some of those made of the government's programme for privatising nationalised industries, namely, the government may have a clear policy on transferring firms from the public sector to the private sector, but lacks a real industrial policy. Similarly the government may have a clear policy on transferring houses from the public sector to the private sector, but it lacks a real housing policy. In other words, according to its critics, the Conservative government has been too concerned with ownership and not concerned enough with the quantity and quality of the housing stock.

Figure 8.2 shows that the decline of the private rented sector and the growth of owner-occupation have been long-term phenomena. However, the decline in resources directed to the public sector and the encouragement of moves

Figure 8.2: Stock of dwellings by tenure in the UK

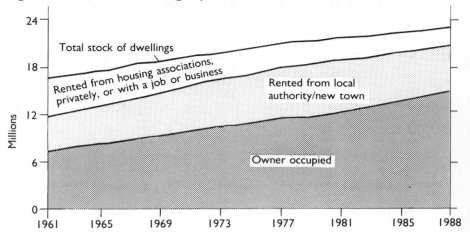

Source: Department of the Environment
From: *Social Trends 20*, 1990 (HMSO)

towards owner-occupation under the Conservative government have prompted criticism that the three main forms of tenure (owner-occupation, private-rented and public-rented) are not treated even handedly. These sentiments are summed up by comments from the Church report, *Faith in the City*:

> The promotion of home ownership is a deliberate policy decision, encouraged directly by central government subsidy and indirectly by withdrawal of subsidy from local authority housing, and the pushing up of rents. The cost of choice for the majority is the absence of choice for the minority who will never afford to buy, ... 'the Right to Buy' and growth of owner-occupation are effectively carried out on the backs of poor people.

Such sentiments have been strongly rejected by the Conservative government, which considers its drive towards **popular capitalism** to be open to all members of society. The report further claims that:

> One of the many misconceptions about housing finance is that home-owners are self-reliant, buying their houses with no resort to the state, while public sector tenants are the recipients of huge hand-outs.

These claims are now examined by considering the position of each sector in turn.

OWNER-OCCUPATION

An owner-occupier is allowed to claim tax relief on the interest paid on a loan to purchase his house (up to a maximum loan of £30,000). This relief cost the Exchequer £1.1 billion in 1978/79, but is estimated to have reached £7 billion in 1989/90 (see Figure 8.3). The existence of such substantial relief to owner-

Figure 8.3: The cost to the Treasury of mortgage interest tax relief (at 1989/90 prices)

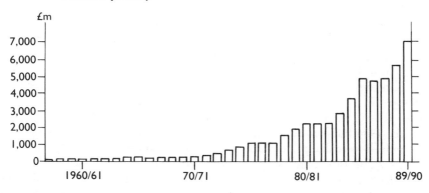

Source: Inland Revenue
From: Guardian, 14 February 1990

occupiers produces a major vested interest which political parties will find hard to ignore, particularly as the ranks of the owner-occupiers are swelling all the time. Mrs Thatcher pledged that the relief would remain for as long as she was Prime Minister and the opposition parties appear unwilling to commit themselves to abolishing it. The existence of mortgage interest tax relief (*MITR*), is now examined critically in view of its rapidly escalating cost.

(*a*) MITR is effectively an open-ended tax relief, the cost of which will be determined by the number of people obtaining mortgages and the rate of interest prevailing. This contrasts with the cash limits imposed on public sector housing subsidies and other government expenditure.

(*b*) The system is of greater benefit to those with large mortgages than to those with small mortgages and, of course, is of no help at all to those without a mortgage. Moreover, it is of greatest benefit to the top-rate taxpayers, as the relief granted is based on the taxpayer's marginal (ie highest) rate of taxation. (Income tax is levied at a basic rate of 25 per cent and a higher rate of 40 per cent – correct as of 1990 budget.) Thus, the relief may be termed 'regressive'.

Table 8.1: Mortgage interest tax relief

Mortgage £	Interest rate (per annum) %	Interest paid (per annum) £	Marginal tax rate %	MITR £
15,000	10	1,500	25	375
30,000	10	3,000	25	750
30,000	10	3,000	40	1,200

Note: Assuming a 10% interest rate and a constant rate of repayment of interest over the term of the mortgage.

(c)   Some tax reformers have argued that the abolition of MITR and other tax reliefs, such as that provided for pension fund contributions, would allow further cuts in income tax to take place. (The basic rate of income tax was cut from 33 per cent to 30 per cent in the 1979 Conservative Budget – the 'Incentive Budget' – but further cuts were not made until 1986 when the rate was cut to 29 per cent, and thereafter to 27 per cent in 1987 and 25 per cent in 1988). Others have argued that, whatever resources are available to housing, they could be used more effectively than is the case with the present system of MITR.

Â Â Â Â Â Â The Chancellor abolished tax relief on (new) Life Assurance Policies in the 1984 budget, but has made no move to abolish, or phase-out MITR – indeed speculation in some parts of the Conservative party before the 1987 Election centred not on whether there would be a reduction, but whether there would be an increase in the maximum level of relief permitted (the previous increase was in 1983, also a general election year). However, in the 1988 Budget, the Chancellor abolished tax relief on home improvements and also limited tax relief to only one mortgage per home. (Previously two or more people purchasing a property were each able to claim tax relief up to the £30,000 limit.) No other changes were made to the structure of the system.

(d)   It has been shown above that those with larger mortgages and those on higher incomes benefit most from MITR, but one of the main arguments originally put forward to justify its existence was that it benefited first-time buyers, enabling them to purchase a house which would otherwise have been beyond their means. However, there is no clear evidence that this is true. It may even be possible that house prices have merely adjusted upwards to meet the extra spending power of those obtaining mortgages with tax relief attached. This is likely to be the case not just for the first-time buyer, but also higher up the housing market. If this argument is correct, then MITR merely boosts the capital value of all property rather than aiding first-time buyers.

(e)   There is no clear evidence that the MITR has helped to contribute to the nation's stock of housing.

(f)   Although it is difficult to measure accurately, a certain amount of money borrowed from the building society or bank, based on the security of the house, may be spent on general household expenditure to finance, for example, a new car or holiday. If the mortgage is eligible for MITR the borrower is in fact taking advantage of subsidised credit. (The Bank of England, in its *Quarterly Bulletin* (March 1985), has estimated that this 'leakage' from the housing market amounted to £7.26 billion in 1984.)

In conclusion, these arguments claim that the MITR is an expensive subsidy which distorts the market, is regressive in its effect, produces minimal help for first-time buyers and does little to enhance the housing stock. However, the political problems of abolishing it outright would be huge and so some have advocated phasing it out over a period of time. For example, the ceiling for relief could be reduced from £30,000 to zero in ten equal steps over a ten-year period of time. If even this measure were deemed politically unacceptable, then by maintaining the £30,000 limit over time, the real value of the relief would, of course, decline. Assuming a constant rate of inflation of 5 per cent per annum, the real value of the relief would decline by a compounded figure of 39 per cent over 10 years and, if inflation were at a constant 10 per cent per annum, the corresponding decline would be 61 per cent.

In addition to the tax advantages gained from MITR, the owner-occupier gains from the tax system in two additional ways. Firstly, no tax is levied on the capital gains realised on the sale of an owner-occupier's house. (This applies to one house only.) Thus the capital invested in house purchase is treated differently to other forms of investment. It is true that since 1982 allowance has been made for inflation – *indexation* – when calculating capital gains generally (and gains made before 1982 are no longer eligible for any tax). However, even if the price of the house rises by more than the rate of inflation (ie a real capital gain has been made) capital gains tax (CGT) is not levied. Secondly, there is no tax levied on **imputed income**. This represents a notional calculation of the benefit gained by living in one's own house or, in other words, the rent which one would consider paying for the use of the house. This benefit is taxed in several other European countries, but was abolished in this country in 1963.

Figure 8.4 indicates that, although private sector construction increased steadily from the depths of the recession in 1981, the number of dwellings completed in 1988 was still below completions achieved during the 1960s. This was the case despite the great shift towards preference for owner-occupation that had occurred subsequently and, as described above, a favourable tax regime towards such housing. Although there has been some fluctuation in private sector figures, this is nothing compared with the dramatic decline shown in the public sector figures.

Figure 8.4: Housebuilding completions in the UK (by sector)

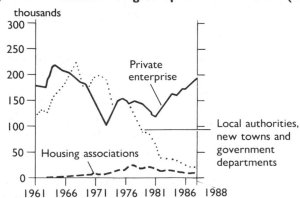

Source: Department of the Environment
From: *Social Trends 20*, 1990 (HMSO)

PUBLIC RENTED SECTOR

Local authorities constructed only 21,000 dwellings in 1988, compared with an average of 152,000 per annum during the 1960s. It should be pointed out that the decline has not just been in evidence under the Conservative government, but was also apparent before 1979, although it has accelerated subsequently. The main reason for the decline in housebuilding in the public sector is the strict control of local authorities' capital spending by the central government, as part of the government's attempt to control overall public expenditure. Furthermore local authorities are also allowed to spend only 20 per cent of the money raised from the sale of council houses to tenants. This limitation, of course, does not allow for full replacement of the council housing stock.

The decline in public sector housebuilding and the rise in council house rents, together with the transfer of many council houses to the private sector, has resulted in an increase in the number of homeless people, most of whom come from groups who are unable to afford to become owner-occupiers. Local authorities have a statutory duty to provide accommodation for homeless households in 'priority need' (eg households with dependent children or where a member of the household is vulnerable due to mental illness or old age). In addition, however, they secure accommodation for some homeless households who do not fall within this category. Numbers overall for those homeless have increased from 97,000 in 1984 to 135,000 in 1988.

The rise in homelessness has given rise to a vast increase in the amount of bed

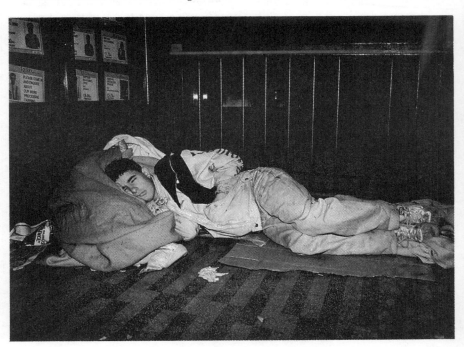

London's homeless

and breakfast accommodation used, particularly in the London area. The expenditure required is borne by the local authorities and occurs because they do not have sufficient suitable housing in a state of good repair. Local authorities claim that investment is needed not only to build new homes and replace dilapidated housing, but also to renovate deteriorating buildings, and thus improve the existing housing stock. Investment is also needed to reduce the backlog of repairs. The calculation of this amount is, again, extremely difficult, but estimates have ranged up to £35 billion (National Economic Development Council).

Based on the forecasts of the Labour government's Green Paper of 1977, 550,000 fewer houses were built during the period 1976–86 than were envisaged as being necessary in order to satisfy the anticipated need.

PRIVATE RENTED SECTOR

The private sector of rented accommodation has become a relatively minor part of the housing market and its long-term decline certainly stretches back to the First World War. At that time about 90 per cent of households lived in privately-rented accommodation; the figure has since dropped to 8 per cent. Thus individuals are only presented with a limited choice of tenure and, according to the Nationwide Building Society

> the prime weakness of the UK housing market is the near absence of provision of private-renting which would meet the demands of lower income households, a very different situation to that which prevails in many European countries.

The reasons for the decline in this sector of the housing market may be seen in terms of simple demand and supply analysis: the letting of accommodation has become less desirable for landlords and other forms of tenure have become more attractive for potential tenants. Rent control and **security of tenure** were first introduced in 1915 as a wartime measure to control rents and have remained ever since, albeit in amended form. It was intended that these measures should provide the tenant with a defence against the unscrupulous landlord, both in terms of protection against unfair eviction and also as a guarantee of 'fair' rents, especially for those on low incomes. However, the attempts to improve the position of the tenant have interfered with the market mechanism, which has led to a decline in the supply of accommodation on offer. Rent control leads to a decline in the rate of return on the rented accommodation, when compared to what could be earned if the capital value of the house were invested elsewhere. *Security of tenure* also means that a landlord may be unable to regain his house, if he wishes to. A residence with *sitting tenants* will sell at a discount to its open market value, so there is a strong disincentive for landlords to relet any accommodation which becomes vacant.

Whilst some of this housing stock may be left empty, other landlords may sell to the private sector (ie to individuals who wish to use the building as owner-occupiers). At the same time, there is no incentive to construct new dwellings for the sector owing to the existence of controlled rents, below the market rate. Furthermore a drop in maintenance spending is also likely as both the landlord's means and incentive to spend money on the property are reduced.

There have also been cases of deliberate neglect of property in order to force tenants out of the building. This has become known as *Rachmanism* after the exploits of an infamous landlord in the 1950s, following the 1957 Rent Act, which attempted to de-control private rented accommodation. Thus there will be a decline in the quality of the housing stock available to this sector, and a corresponding increase in both empty houses and the number of those who are homeless. For these reasons critics of rent control and security of tenure argue that, if the market mechanism were allowed to operate, the supply of rented accommodation would increase and its quality improve. If this analysis is accepted, then it is clear that the attempt over a long period of time to protect the position of those living in privately rented accommodation has failed and has, in fact, made the position worse.

VARIOUS PROPOSALS ON HOUSING AND HOMELESSNESS

The 'Inquiry into British Housing' (1985), chaired by the Duke of Edinburgh, under the auspices of the National Federation of Housing Associations, was a report produced one hundred years after the 'Royal Commission on the Housing of the Working Classes', which inquired into housing provision in urban areas during the Industrial Revolution. The report made a number of recommendations which 'add up to proposals for restructuring the way we organise housing provision in this country'. The report called for:

> radical changes in the current fiscal arrangement, both between tenures and within tenures, and a sorting out of local government finance and housing subsidy assistance. We are anxious to see the urgent problem tackled at once.

The report also recommended the introduction of a needs-related *housing allowance* which would be available to people based on their means and their housing requirements. It would replace all

> existing forms of personal support, that is, housing benefit for tenants, mortgage interest tax relief for owner-occupiers, and the housing ingredient in supplementary benefit.

This would create a fairer system in which those in need of help would gain the most and in which a fairer balance would be struck between different forms of tenure.

Secondly the establishment of a new basis for rents was recommended: 'Rents should be related to the capital value of the property, thereby reflecting its popularity in market terms'. This is, in effect, recommending that most rents should rise in order to provide an inducement for landlords to relet empty property. Also it was hoped that investors (eg pension funds) would put their money into property for letting, assured of a reasonable return. The report points out that, in order for those on low incomes to be able to afford a rent based on the capital value of the property, the proposal for the creation of a housing allowance would be a pre-requisite. Similar conclusions were reached in *Faith in the City*.

The charity, Shelter, has produced various reports proposing that greater resources should be directed towards a public sector new housing programme of 100,000 units a year. They have also highlighted the need for increased spending on repair, for improvement of existing public sector housing and also for greater public sector support for private sector improvements.

The Conservative government's 1988 housing reforms contained several proposals aimed at rejuvenating the private rented sector, after the years in which the promotion of home-ownership was at the forefront of housing policy. Rent controls on all new lettings were to be lifted, in an attempt to allow landlords to charge a market rent, in the hope that this would increase the supply of rented accommodation.

In a further attempt to restrict the role of local authorities in housing, council house tenants were given the right to switch to an alternative landlord – either in the form of a *housing association* or an approved private sector landlord – in other words, they were allowed to opt out of local authority control. In addition Housing Action Trusts were proposed in order to take over the operation of specific run-down council estates, with the intention of changing their tenure to the private sector or housing associations.

Critics argue that the proposals to raise rents will have relatively little effect on the supply of rented accommodation, as the balance of advantage is still tilted far too much in favour of owner-occupation. However, the increase in rents will cause hardship to many on low incomes – all the more so after the £600 million cuts in housing benefit which formed part of the 1988 social security reforms (refer to Chapter 6, pages 86–7).

THE CONNECTION BETWEEN THE HOUSING MARKET AND THE REST OF THE ECONOMY

The wide disparity that has emerged between house prices in different regions provides a major obstacle to **geographical mobility of labour**. People in regions with low house prices are usually unable to afford to purchase a house in a higher priced area, whereas those in the higher priced areas are unwilling to move out in view of the lower capital gains to be made. The waiting list system for council housing also inhibits council tenants' mobility. The provision made for those moving from region to region is limited and most have to rejoin the waiting list. As discussed in Chapter 9, this is a feature of the *North-South divide*, where the problem of high house prices is particularly associated with the South East. (Data for house prices is provided in that chapter.) The shortage of land for development has caused the price of land to rise. In order to increase the supply of land, and thereby moderate further upward moves in house prices, the government could allow (controversial) development in the *green belt* or could release public sector land not at present being used.

The housing market is characterised by an (irregular) cyclical pattern of house price movements. To some extent this is due to the relative inelasticity of supply for housing. New houses take time to complete and, hence, increases in demand for houses are reflected in an increase in the price of both existing and new houses. A limited supply of land for building in certain areas will contribute further to price rises.

However, the house price cycle may also be explained by the changing nature of the demand for housing, which is no longer just for *consumption* purposes (ie to provide a roof over one's head), but is also for *investment* reasons. The (tax free) capital gains made by owner-occupiers generally far exceed any possible savings that they might make from their income. The rising trend of house prices (albeit with a cyclical pattern) has, on occasions, given rise to an 'upward sloping demand curve'. This indicates an increase in demand for housing based on the expectation of future price rises. During times when house prices are rising, house purchasers often feel that the upward trend will continue for ever. This encourages first-time buyers into the market, believing that it is 'now or never', and also encourages existing home owners to 'trade up' to larger accommodation. As long as property prices continue to increase, both will feel vindicated and will be able to point to capital gains (albeit paper gains) made. The capital gains to be made exaggerate house price movements. This is because capital gain on the whole value of the house accrues to the owner, whereas he only has to repay a relatively small proportion of the mortgage each year. Thus the percentage gain on the investment made is likely to be large during periods of rapid house price increases.

Owner-occupation, or home-ownership, accounts for a greater proportion of the housing stock in the UK than in any other EC country. The desire to own property has been advanced by the Conservative government's 'Right to Buy' scheme, but the moves towards home ownership have been accelerated by the benefits of mortage interest tax relief and the absence of capital gains tax (as discussed earlier in the chapter) which mean that house purchase is perceived as being an attractive subsidised investment.

We now need to consider the effect of rapidly rising property prices on individual behaviour. The effect is similar to a situation in which share prices rapidly increase – a **bull market**. Rising property prices or share prices cause homeowners and shareholders to feel more wealthy – this is known as the *wealth effect*. Individuals feel that they need to save less than before, as they have property or shares to 'fall back on', and as a consequence they raise consumption. A falling **savings ratio** and rapidly rising consumer expenditure were certainly significant features of the second half of the 1980s. For this reason fears have been expressed that rising house prices pose a major threat to price stability generally.

The consumer boom was fuelled not just by the falling savings ratio at a time when economic growth allowed incomes to rise strongly, but also by (*a*) tax cuts, especially in the budgets of 1987 and 1988 and (*b*) readily available credit – particularly in the aftermath of the deregulation of the City in 1986, known as **Big Bang**. When the Stock Market crashed in October 1987, many economists thought that it would be followed by an end to the property boom and a downturn in the 'real' economy. Monetary policy was eased in order to avoid a downturn or recession. This helped to avoid a recession and the 'real' economy continued to grow strongly. In addition property prices continued to boom, rising at a rate in excess of 20 per cent during 1988 (in some areas, the increase was even more rapid; the rise in East Anglia was approximately 40 per cent).

However, the consumer boom caused a rapid deterioration in the current account of the balance of payments and an upturn in the rate of inflation. Both exerted downward pressure on the sterling exchange rate. Interest rates were raised in response to these problems (refer to Chapter 12) – bank base rates were raised in steps from 7½ per cent in May 1988 to 15 per cent in October 1989 – and mortgage rates followed the interest rate trend. This put an end to the *national* house price explosion, although the effect varied significantly between regions. Average prices decreased by 13.3 per cent in the South East during the twelve months prior to March 1990, whereas the corresponding figure for the North of England was an increase of 25.2 per cent. Those areas which had shown the greatest price increasing during the boom tended to suffer most when the boom ended.

Although for long established homeowners, falling property prices represent merely a paper loss (likely to be relatively small compared to paper gains made in preceding years), those who bought at, or close to, the peak of the boom, will suffer an absolute drop in the price of their homes. In particular, those who borrowed more than was perhaps prudent, based on the expectation of a continuing rise in the price of property, may find themselves facing the twin problems of a capital loss and higher mortgage repayments.

The attractions of home-ownership in times when property prices are falling and also when interest rates are high are that much less, and the Conservative government, which had strongly promoted home-ownership was faced with considerable public disquiet. The increase in the cost of repaying mortgages (the greatest component of the average family's budget) caused a reduction in the amount of money available for general consumption and hence a reduction in living standards.

At the very time when householders were facing high mortgage repayments and declining house prices, the government introduced reforms to the local taxation system which imposed additional financial burdens on many people. The changes made, discussed below, furthermore removed the only remaining form of 'property tax' in the UK.

A POLL TAX OR A ROOF TAX?

The system of raising local authorities' revenue by means of the *rating system* (where the *rateable value* of property served as the basis for payment) had been unpopular for many years. However, as there was no agreement on an alternative, the system survived. During the 1980s, the Conservative government was able to make a great deal of political capital from the activities of high spending Labour councils, many of which were branded 'Loony Left' councils. However, despite attempts to curb the spending power of various councils by *rate-capping*, local authority finances remained a thorn in the flesh of the government. The rating system was criticised for being unaccountable – only householders paid rates and, moreover, local authorities relied on grants from central government for the majority of their funds. This was very complicated and, in the view of the Conservatives, allowed excessive local authority expenditure, without subjecting councils to local accountability.

The *community charge*, referred to by many people as the *poll tax*, was introduced when rates were abolished in April 1989 (Scotland) and in April 1990 (England and Wales). The community charge was intended to be a simple and visible system of raising revenue in which the behaviour of profligate (assumed to be Labour) councils would be evident to the electorate. Each adult would be liable to pay a flat-rate personal community charge. This covered all adults over the age of eighteen (with certain limited exceptions) and was, therefore, more broadly based than rates, in an attempt to improve democratic accountability. The flat-rate system of payment was, by definition, independent of the ability to pay and this caused great controversy. (The previous attempt to introduce a poll tax in England provoked the Peasants' Revolt in the fourteenth century.) As stated above, exceptions were introduced for those with very limited means, but these did not prevent a huge storm of protest at the time of the introduction of the new system. (At the same time, the government reformed the rating system as it applied to companies by introducing a *uniform business rate* – set at the same rate throughout the country.) It should, however, be pointed out that even after the introduction of the community charge, local authorities would still be raising only about one-quarter of their own revenue, the remainder coming from central government grant and the uniform business rate.

Although there were wide variations between local authorities, the government predicted that the average community charge for England and Wales for 1990/91 would be £278. The outcome of £365 was significantly higher than predicted for two reasons. Firstly, in the government's calculations, it had allowed only an increase of 4 per cent in the spending of local authorities over the expenditure under the last year of the rating system, whereas inflation turned out to be in excess of 7 per cent. Hence an increase of 7 per cent would have been required to maintain the real level of spending. Secondly many local authorities took the opportunity to raise expenditure, relying on the complexities of the system to confuse the electorate, by blaming high poll tax bills on the new system itself, and hence on the government, rather than on their own spending plans. Faced with a public outcry at the levels of poll tax, the government announced plans in April 1990 to 'charge cap' twenty-one (mainly Labour) authorities. However, this not only removed local accountability (the original motive for introducing the new system) but it also did not affect many areas of the country which were faced with high community charges.

In the short term, there are various measures that would be open to the government if it wished to reduce the impact of the community charge. Widespread 'charge capping' would be possible, but would reduce accountability. So too would proposals to transfer certain local authority services (eg education, fire, police) from local to central government responsibility. Such a scheme would add to the central government's tax burden and also increase centralisation of power still further. Increased grants from central to local government would allow councils to reduce poll tax demands. However, there would be no guarantee that they would do so – they might use the money for additional spending on services. Moreover, such a trend would be counter to government action during the 1980s, when central government grants to local government were progressively reduced. Another possibility open to the government would be to increase exemptions from the charge for those on low pay, but this would only really operate 'at the margin'.

Various alternative schemes for raising local authority revenue have been proposed and are in operation in other countries. Local authority revenue could be obtained through either a local income tax and/or a local sales tax – in other words, through methods similar to those used in raising central government revenues. The old rating system was of course one form of property tax and various proposals based on the taxation of property, often referred to as a *roof tax*, have been put forward. Taxation of property could be based on the capital value of the house, or its land or rateable value. A great advantage is that taxation of property, which is geographically immobile, is easier to collect than a taxation on individuals, who may be mobile. In addition, those who favour the return of a property tax point out (as described earlier in this chapter) that there are many financial advantages involved in purchasing a house and that a property tax might serve to dampen down the overheating of the housing market evident during much of the 1980s.

It should, however, be pointed out that there is a major difference between theoretical ideas and specific proposals. The major opposition to the poll tax came to the fore only when people realised how much they would have to pay. The theoretical proposal had been public for several years.

COMMENT

The Conservative government has encouraged moves towards owner-occupation, or home-ownership, in Britain. It has obliged local authorities to sell off council houses and has reduced the importance given to municipal housing. Critics claim this has contributed to a significant rise in homelessness and that the government's policy on tenure has not contributed much to housebuilding. Some moves have been made to deregulate the private rented sector, but this still accounts for a relatively insignificant part of the housing stock.

Whilst cutting subsidies to the public sector, tax relief to the private sector has grown enormously. This, together with easy access to credit after deregulation and the political drive towards owner-occupation under the Conservative government, has contributed to a house price boom. This has given large capital gains to many people, but also a misleading picture about the 'ease of making money'. Often capital gains from unproductive assets have been easier to come by than profit from investment or from working. In addition individuals' savings have been directed into house purchase, rather than into productive investment opportunities.

The political spin offs of a stagnant property market for the 'party of home ownership' have yet to be assessed.

PART 3

STILL ONE NATION?

9 The North-South Divide

- What is the North-South divide?
- Does the North-South divide exist?
- Has the North-South divide widened?
- Political implications
- Comment

WHAT IS THE 'NORTH-SOUTH DIVIDE'?

The Conservative government under Mrs Thatcher has been accused of abandoning the *One Nation* style of Toryism and of widening the *North-South divide.*

During the 1980s the discussion about disparities of prosperity between different regions in the UK has focused increasingly on the issue of the North-South divide. The popular conception of this phenomenon is that, if one divides the country into two, there are different characteristics appertaining to the two areas. Prosperity is concentrated in the 'South', which is expanding fast, thereby creating rising real incomes and new employment, particularly in high-technology industries and the service sector. On the other hand, the 'North' remains depressed, containing stagnant industries and high unemployment, with many areas in decline, particularly in the inner cities and the longstanding **assisted areas**. However, before even considering the data and evidence required in a discussion of the North-South divide, there are two points which need to be made.

Firstly, it must be realised that, whatever data are used to measure the prosperity of a region, these will not represent the whole picture. Decaying inner cities are to be found in the South as well as the North, and there are areas within the South in which high unemployment, deprivation and poverty exist. Similarly, in the North there are prosperous areas within otherwise depressed regions. Hence, if evidence is found to support the existence of a North-South divide, this must be seen in terms of measures of 'averages' for particular regions.

This leads to the second problem, which is concerned with the exact demarcation of the North-South boundary. The *South* is generally understood to include the South East and East Anglia. Many studies also classify the South West, the East Midlands and the West Midlands as parts of the 'South'. The *North* on this basis comprises Scotland, Wales, Northern Ireland and the remaining areas of England (North England, Yorkshire and Humberside and the North West) (see Figure 9.1).

When considering the issue of the North-South divide, two questions need to be asked:

(*a*) Does the divide exist?
(*b*) Is the divide widening?

(This chapter studies only the phenomenon of the North-South divide and does not consider its causes. Some of the possible explanations are given in Chapter 10 when regional disparities are studied.)

Figure 9.1: Standard regions

DOES THE NORTH-SOUTH DIVIDE EXIST?

Most economies contain regional disparities – claims about a North-South divide in Britain are contrasted with a South-North divide in Italy, where the South is relatively less prosperous than the North. Whether or not the government could have intervened in the economy by adopting a more active *regional policy*, in order to reduce regional disparities and hence the North-South divide, is considered in Chapter 10. So too is the argument that governments should do the reverse and intervene less in the running of the economy, relying instead on market forces.

There are several ways of considering the relative levels of prosperity in different regions. These are considered below.

In column 2 of Table 9.1, the share of UK GDP accounted for by each region is recorded for 1988. Column 1 in the same table considers the share of UK population accounted for by each region for the same year. If the share of UK GDP accounted for by a particular region is equal to its share of UK population and, if this is true for all regions, then GDP is spread proportional to population throughout the country. However, if the share of UK GDP accounted for by a particular region is higher than its share of UK population, then that region is relatively more prosperous than the average; conversely for a lower figure. Table 9.1 indicates that the South East was the only region that had a higher share of GDP than would be expected from its population size. The economy in the South East (representing 36.3 per cent of UK GDP) dominates the whole economy and its size is more than three times that of any other region (refer also to Figure 9.2).

GDP per head is then compared between regions. A figure of more than 100 indicates that GDP per head in that region is higher than the UK average and, conversely, a figure lower than 100 indicates that the region's GDP per head is lower than the national average. (It should be pointed out that, whereas the figures in columns 1 and 2 are percentages of the whole, so that the sum of the figures in each column is 100, the figures in column 3 are index numbers – comparing GDP per head in a region with UK GDP per head.) A figure of 119.4 indicates that GDP per head in the South East was 19.4 per cent above the average in 1988. Furthermore, the South East can be seen to have been the only region with a figure above the national average – all other regions were below the average (see also Figure 9.3).

Column 4 considers regional unemployment rates as a proportion of the working population. The rate recorded for the South East was under half that recorded for the North of England. Only four regions – the South East, the South West, East Anglia and the East Midlands – produced figures below the national average. Long-term regional unemployment (measured here by those unemployed for more than three years) is often taken as a good indicator of how deep a region's problems may be. When considering the long-term unemployed as a percentage of those unemployed, the same four regions, together with Wales and Scotland, produce figures below the national average. (However, it should be pointed out that the Welsh and Scottish figures are

Table 9.1: A consideration of data for 1988 to investigate whether the North-South divide exists

Region	(1) Share of UK population accounted for by each region (1988) %	(2) Share of UK GDP accounted for by each region (1988) %	(3) GDP per head for each region (UK = 100) (1988)	(4) Regional unemployment as a percentage of the working population (1988 average) %	(5) Long-term unemployment as a percentage of those unemployed (October 1988) %	(6) Average house prices (detached houses) (UK = 100) (April 1988)
UK	100.0	100.0	100.0	8.0	23.9	100
South East	30.4	36.3	119.4	5.2	19.8	119
South West	8.1	7.6	93.8	6.3	17.4	83
East Anglia	3.6	3.5	97.1	4.8	20.7	82
East Midlands	7.0	6.6	94.6	7.2	22.0	58
West Midlands	9.1	8.3	91.1	8.5	29.3	65
North	5.4	4.8	88.3	11.9	26.2	51
Yorkshire & Humberside	8.6	7.8	91.1	9.5	24.1	50
North West	11.2	10.4	93.3	10.7	25.7	59
Scotland	8.9	8.4	93.9	11.2	23.5	54
Wales	5.0	4.2	84.0	10.5	21.0	54
Northern Ireland	2.8	2.2	78.0	16.4	35.8	43

Note: (a) GDP figures exclude the Continental Shelf
(b) 1988 data; provision estimates

Sources: Economic Trends, November 1989, CSO (HMSO); Halifax Building Society; Regional Trends 24, 1989, CSO (HMSO)

Figure 9.2: Share of the UK GDP accounted for by each region in 1988

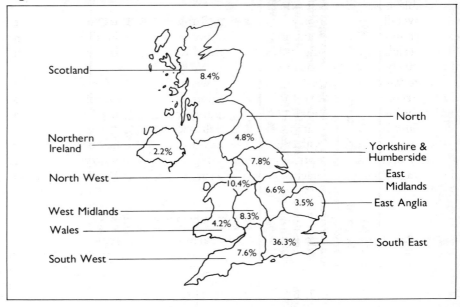

Source: Central Stationery Office; Cambridge Econometrics
From: Sunday Times, 29 October 1989

Figure 9.3: GDP per head by region as % of national average in 1988

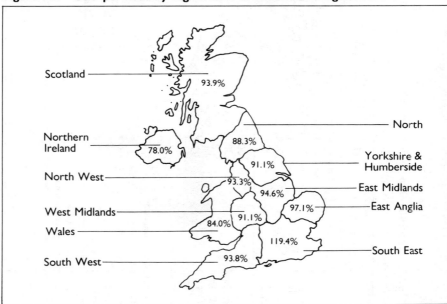

Source: Central Stationery Office

percentages of much higher unemployment rates and are, therefore, not as favourable as might at first seem).

An overall consideration of the data in Table 9.1 appears to indicate the existence in the *South* of an 'inner core' of prosperity (the South East) and an 'outer periphery' (East Anglia, South West and East Midlands), compared with the relatively less prosperous regions of the *North*.

Figure 9.4 considers male average gross weekly earnings. On this map the data is recorded by county and not by region. However, a similar pattern to that described above appears. (The high figure recorded for the Grampian area of Scotland is principally attributed to North Sea oil.)

The most publicised aspect of the North-South divide has been the wide disparity between house prices in different regions of the country. Figures for the average price of a detached house in each region for 1988 are provided in

Figure 9.4: Male average gross weekly earnings, April 1988

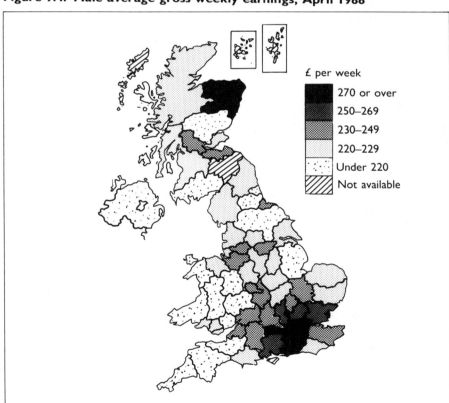

£ per week
- 270 or over
- 250–269
- 230–249
- 220–229
- Under 220
- Not available

Note: a similar pattern is produced for female earnings.

Source: New Earnings Survey (1988), Department of Economic Development, Northern Ireland
From: *Regional Trends 24* (1989), (HMSO)

Table 9.1 (column 6) and indicate that houses in the South East are much more expensive than elsewhere in the country. The difference in regional house prices acts as a major obstacle to mobility of labour. Those wishing to move into the 'South' may be unable to afford to buy a house or may be able to buy only a much smaller house with the money raised from their existing dwelling. There may also be a reluctance to move out of the South, in the fear that if house prices in the 'North' increase at a slower rate, it may be difficult to return to the 'South' at a later date (refer also to Chapter 8, page 107).

HAS THE NORTH-SOUTH DIVIDE WIDENED?

Answering the question: 'Has the North-South divide widened during the 1980s?' is fraught with difficulties and, to some extent, the answer depends on which economic indicators are viewed and the way in which the calculations are interpreted. In particular, conclusions are often drawn with reference to the word 'percentage', but often the question 'percentage of what?' is conveniently ignored. The way in which different conclusions may be drawn from one hypothetical set of data is now shown below.

Hypothetical example showing problems associated with defining North-South divide

Region	Population of working age	Unemployment Year 1	Year 2	Unemployment as % of population of working age Year 1	Year 2
A	200,000	20,000	25,000	10.0	12.5
B	50,000	10,000	12,000	20.0	24.0

In absolute terms, region A suffers more from the rise in unemployment (5,000) than does region B (2,000). However, this does not take into account the different sizes of the populations of working age between the regions. When unemployment as a percentage of the population of working age is taken into account, region A shows an increase from 10 per cent to 12.5 per cent (a rise of 2.5 percentage points) and region B shows an increase from 20 per cent to 24 per cent (a rise of 4 percentage points). On this basis the position of region B has deteriorated with respect to region A. On the other hand one may say that for Region A, between year 1 and year 2, unemployment increased by 25 per cent (expressed as a percentage of unemployment in year 1) and for region B, unemployment increased by 20 per cent (expressed as a percentage of unemployment in year 1). This hypothetical situation illustrates some of the difficulties likely to be experienced when considering the North-South divide and shows why so many conflicting claims have been made about this question.

There are many different measures which could be chosen when trying to assess whether the North-South divide has widened. We shall consider three:

(a) The share of UK GDP accounted for by each region;

(b)   GDP per head in each region;
(c)   Regional unemployment.

The period of time studied is the ten year interval from 1978 until 1988. (1978 was the last full year before the Conservative General Election victory in 1979.)

Table 9.2 (columns 1 and 2) indicates that the share of UK GDP accounted for by the South East, the South West, East Anglia, the East Midlands and Northern Ireland increased between 1978 and 1988. (Again care with the figures is necessary – subtraction of column 1 from column 2 would be meaningless as the figures are percentages of different amounts. Hence column 3 merely registers whether an increase or decrease was observed between 1978 and 1988.)

Columns 4 and 5 show that GDP per head compared with UK GDP per head rose between 1978 and 1988 in all of the five regions listed above except the East Midlands. (It should be pointed out that, if a region's GDP per head declines as a proportion of UK GDP, it does not necessarily imply that the region's GDP per head has declined in absolute terms, but only in comparison with that of the UK.)

Thirdly, changes in unemployment are now considered. The rate of unemployment as a percentage of the working population is recorded for both 1980 and 1988 (columns 1 and 2) for each region (refer also to note section on Table 9.3). The difference between the two figures is calculated for each region. It can be seen that, whilst all regions reflected the higher national unemployment rate, some regions fared better than others. The South East, the South West, East Anglia and the East Midlands were again the regions showing increases less than the national average for unemployment as a percentage of the working population. However, when considering the increase in unemployment in each region as a percentage of the rate of unemployment in that region in 1980, different results are produced. Lower than average increases are recorded in the South West, East Anglia, the West Midlands and the North. (The South East produces an above-average figure because the 1980 unemployment rate was low; even a small increase will therefore appear large proportionately.)

It is clear, therefore, that a conclusion about whether the North-South divide has widened is more difficult to draw from a consideration of unemployment figures than from GDP figures. Any firm conclusions would require much more lengthy analysis than is possible in this book.

The regional differences in house prices have been considered earlier in this chapter (and in Table 9.1, column 6). However, it is clear that the divergence between the North and the South has widened during the period 1981–7 (see Figure 9.5). Nevertheless, it is only fair to say that this marks a period of 'boom' in house prices. Following the end of the boom in 1988, prices fell fastest in regions which had shown the highest increases previously.

One might expect that differences in the level of regional income and employment would be accompanied by a migration of labour into the more prosperous regions. However, the evidence shows that, although there is a drift to the South (see Figure 9.6), there is relatively little migration between regions when compared with movement within the regions themselves. There are many

Table 9.2: A consideration of GDP data to investigate whether the 'North-South divide' has widened between 1978 and 1988

Region	(1) Share of UK GDP accounted for by each region (1978) %	(2) Share of UK GDP accounted for by each region (1988) %	(3) Alteration in share of UK GDP accounted for by each region between 1978 and 1988	(4) GDP per head for each region (UK = 100) (1978)	(5) GDP per head for each region (UK = 100) (1988)	(6) Alteration in GDP per head for each region between 1978 and 1988
UK	100.0	100.0	—	100.0	100.0	—
South East	34.6	36.3	increase	114.8	119.4	increase
South West	7.0	7.6	increase	90.5	93.8	increase
East Anglia	3.1	3.5	increase	95.4	97.1	increase
East Midlands	6.4	6.6	increase	95.1	94.6	decrease
West Midlands	9.8	8.3	decrease	98.1	91.1	decrease
North	5.1	4.8	decrease	91.8	88.3	decrease
Yorkshire and Humberside	8.2	7.8	decrease	94.0	91.1	decrease
North West	11.3	10.4	decrease	97.8	93.3	decrease
Scotland	8.8	8.4	decrease	94.7	93.9	decrease
Wales	4.2	4.2	no change	85.0	84.0	decrease
Northern Ireland	2.1	2.2	increase	77.7	78.0	increase

Note: (a) GDP figures exclude the Continental Shelf
(b) 1978 was chosen as the last full year before the 1979 Conservative election victory

Source: Economic Trends November 1989, CSO (HMSO)

Table 9.3: A consideration of unemployment data to investigate whether the 'North-South divide' has widened between 1980 and 1988

Region	(1) 1980 regional unemployment as a percentage of the working population (1980 average) %	(2) 1988 regional unemployment as a percentage of the working population (1988 average) %	(3) Increase in regional unemployment as a percentage of the working population between 1980 & 1988 [a]	(4) Increase in regional unemployment between 1980 & 1988 as a percentage of unemployed in that region in 1980 [b]
UK	5.1	8.0	2.9	56.9
South East	3.1	5.2	2.1	67.7
South West	4.5	6.3	1.8	40
East Anglia	3.8	4.8	1.0	26.3
East Midlands	4.5	7.2	2.7	57.4
West Midlands	5.5	8.5	3.0	54.5
North	8.0	11.9	3.9	48.8
Yorkshire and Humberside	5.3	9.5	4.2	79.2
North West	6.5	10.7	4.2	64.6
Scotland	7.0	11.2	4.2	60.0
Wales	6.9	10.5	3.6	52.2
Northern Ireland	9.4	16.4	7.0	42.7

Note: Comparison is made between 1980 and 1988 rather than 1978 and 1988 (as for GDP) because changes in method of data compilation invalidate comparisons. It is assumed that the working population remains constant in each region for the purposes of the comparison.

(a) Column 3 = Column 2 − Column 1

(b) Column 4 = $\dfrac{\text{Column 2} - \text{Column 1}}{\text{Column 1}}$

Source: Regional Trends 24, 1989 CSO (HMSO)

Figure 9.5: Change in house prices (1981–87)

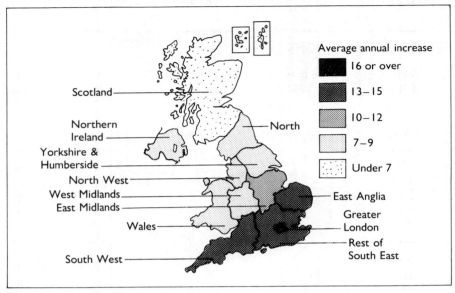

Note: Figures are based on the mix adjusted

Source: Department of the Environment
From: Regional Trends 24 1989, (HMSO)

Figure 9.6: Population changes 1981–8

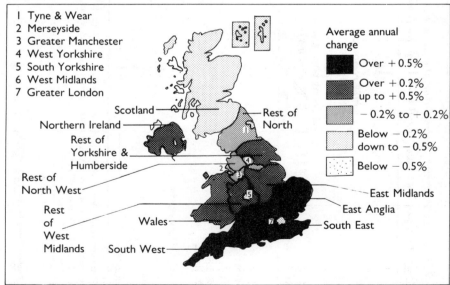

Source: Office of Population Censuses and Surveys; Government Actuary's Department; General Register Office (Scotland); General Register Office (Northern Ireland)
From: Social Trends 20, 1990 (HMSO)

factors which might explain this immobility, of which one certainly is the regional variation of house prices considered above.

POLITICAL IMPLICATIONS

The North-South divide may also be observed when considering the political map of Britain after the 1987 General Election (see Figure 9.7) when previous

Figure 9.7: The General Election (1987) – regional breakdown

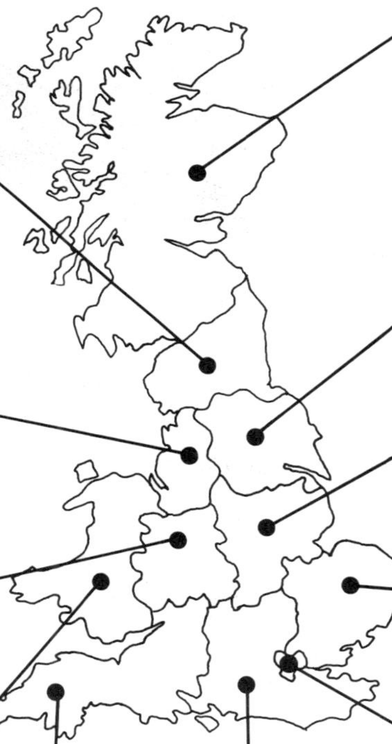

North

	% of vote	Change on 83	Seats
Con	32.3	− 2.3	8
Lab	46.4	+ 6.2	27
All	21.0	− 4.0	1

Scotland

	% of vote	Change on 83	Seats
Con	24.0	− 4.4	10
Lab	42.4	+ 7.3	50
All	19.2	− 5.3	9
SNP	14.0	+ 2.3	3

Northern Ireland

Figures not given because the parties are different

Yorks & Humberside

	% of vote	Change on 83	Seats
Con	37.4	− 1.2	21
Lab	40.6	+ 5.3	33
All	21.7	− 3.9	0

North West

	% of vote	Change on 83	Seats
Con	38.0	− 2.0	34
Lab	41.2	+ 5.2	36
All	20.6	− 3.0	3

East Midlands

	% of vote	Change on 83	Seats
Con	48.6	+ 1.4	31
Lab	30.0	+ 2.1	11
All	21.0	− 2.6	0

West Midlands

	% of vote	Change on 83	Seats
Con	45.5	+ 0.6	36
Lab	33.3	+ 2.1	22
All	20.8	− 2.6	0

East Anglia

	% of vote	Change on 83	Seats
Con	52.1	+ 1.2	19
Lab	21.7	+ 1.2	1
All	25.8	− 2.5	0

Wales

	% of vote	Change on 83	Seats
Con	29.5	− 1.5	8
Lab	45.1	+ 7.5	24
All	17.9	− 5.3	3
Nat	7.3	− 0.5	3

South West

	% of vote	Change on 83	Seats
Con	50.6	− 0.8	44
Lab	15.9	+ 1.2	1
All	33.1	− 0.1	3

South East

	% of vote	Change on 83	Seats
Con	55.6	+ 1.1	107
Lab	16.8	+ 0.9	1
All	27.2	− 1.8	0

Greater London

	% of vote	Change on 83	Seats
Con	46.5	+ 2.6	58
Lab	31.5	+ 1.6	23
All	21.3	− 3.5	3

From: Sunday Times, 14 June 1987

regional electoral trends were reinforced. Even when compared with the 1983 landslide victory, the Conservative share of the vote increased in the South East (including Greater London), East Anglia, West Midlands and East Midlands, and registered only a marginal decline in the South West (albeit with a share of the vote still in excess of 50 per cent). The Conservatives made particularly large losses in Scotland.

The effect of the **first past the post** electoral system exaggerated trends in regional voting patterns, leaving Labour with one seat only in each of the South East (excluding Greater London), South West and East Anglia – out of 108, 45 and 20 respectively. Conversely the Conservatives gained only ten seats in Scotland and eight seats in the North of England out of 72 and 36 respectively. The political fortunes of the Conservative party, based on the evidence of the 1987 General Election, are increasingly regionally-based and reflect to some extent the economic fortunes of the different regions.

COMMENT

This chapter has studied the phenomenon known as the *North-South divide*. For reasons given in the text, all figures should be treated carefully. There are certainly divergences in prosperity apparent between the different regions of the country, with the South East clearly the dominant region, both in terms of its size and economic performance. However, the question: 'Has the North-South divide widened under the Conservative government?' is a difficult one to answer – a limited amount of data has been presented, but the evidence over the ten-year period studied is not conclusive.

The following chapter considers the various policies which have been proposed to deal with regional imbalances and is then followed by a study of inner cities.

10 *The Regions*

BACKGROUND

A *regional problem* is deemed to exist if there are wide disparities between the unemployment rates of different regions. A region with a high rate of unemployment is likely to be characterised by a low level of income, a low growth rate and outward migration. A detailed study of the causes of regional imbalances is complex and lies beyond the scope of this book. However, a dependence on a limited number of industries will cause problems for a region if those industries all decline at the same time. Hence the decline of certain *staple industries* (coal, steel, cotton and shipbuilding) caused problems after the Second World War for several regions (eg South Wales and North-East England) which were heavily dependent on those industries. Similarly, the problems experienced in the 1970s and early 1980s by manufacturing industry (see Chapter 1) caused severe problems in the once-thriving West Midlands, which had been heavily dependent on manufacturing. This is known as the *structural* explanation for regional unemployment.

A second explanation put forward to explain regional disparities is based on *locational factors*. In this situation a region may either have poor **infrastructure** (especially transport) or may be simply located at too great a distance from its main markets, regardless of the quality of transport links. Significant improvements to the prosperity of a region may be noted when transport links are improved. The construction of the M4 motorway to Wales and the 'M4 corridor of prosperity' that followed provides a significant example of this.

However, regional problems in terms of over-concentration and congestion may also exist. Such congestion can cause inefficiencies to develop for firms in that area. In such a situation, it would appear that resources could be used more efficienctly by achieving a more equitable spread throughout the country and governments justify regional policy measures on these grounds. It is claimed that a more even spread of resources will avoid the inflationary problems of excess demand when congested regions encounter capacity constraints and 'overheat'. However, it should also be pointed out that critics of government intervention claim that efficiency is impaired if industry is directed to set up in unsuitable locations.

The existence of regional differences in the UK have already been identified in the study of the North-South divide in terms of GDP unemployment and house prices (refer to Chapter 9). This chapter considers different theoretical approaches to the problem and then considers the changing approach to regional policy under the Conservative government, when compared with the policies adopted by its predecessors.

It can be seen from Figure 10.1 that wide disparities in UK unemployment do exist between the regions. Unemployment in East Anglia at 3.4 per cent is less than half that in the North of England and Scotland (figures for February 1990).

Figure 10.1: Regional unemployment, February 1990 (seasonally adjusted)

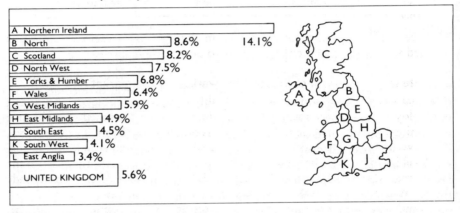

Source: Department of Employment
From: Financial Times, 16 March 1990

THE FREE MARKET OR AN INTERVENTIONIST APPROACH TO REGIONAL PROBLEMS?

The free market approach

In a perfectly operating market economy, the operation of market forces should ensure that disparities in the level of regional unemployment are automatically eliminated without the need for government intervention. This would be brought about firstly by a reduction of wages in the areas of high unemployment relative to those with low unemployment. As a result of wage flexibility it is hoped that firms already in the high unemployment areas would expand and that other firms, attracted by the relatively cheap labour, would be encouraged to set up in those areas, thereby creating employment. Secondly, labour, attracted by the higher wages and better job prospects on offer in the low unemployment areas, migrates thereby reducing the supply of labour and hence unemployment in the high unemployment areas.

Hence, if capital and labour were both mobile and if wages were free to respond to market forces, then the market mechanism would, on its own, correct regional imbalances. Any attempt to interfere with the market process by the government would, in such circumstances, be of no benefit.

It must, however, be pointed out that, for this analysis to be correct, firstly the market mechanism must operate smoothly (ie there must be no *imperfections* in the market) and secondly it must actually *eliminate* disparities between the regions, as is claimed, rather than *reinforce* them. Undoubtedly there are imperfections in the market and, moreover, there are many who believe that market forces, freely operating, will not solve the regional problems. Edward Heath, for example:

> The truth is, as history has so often shown us, that unfettered market forces lead to the rich and the strong growing richer and stronger and the poor and the weak, poorer and weaker until some conflagration in society acted to restore the balance.

The need for government intervention, in the form of a regional policy, is justified with reference to either of the two points listed above.

The case for intervention to improve the working of the market

Regional wage rates may not respond flexibly to the different levels of regional unemployment, as wage rates in many industries are determined by collective bargaining between management and unions on a national basis. The Conservative government's attempts to encourage local wage bargaining in both the coal and steel industries can be seen as an attempt to overcome these rigidities in the labour market, although moves towards such bargaining are often seen by trade unions as attempts to break their collective bargaining power.

Labour and capital are not perfectly **geographically mobile**. In particular, migration of labour between regions is limited by poor information about the jobs available in the low unemployment region, by the expense of moving (especially when the regional difference between house prices is considered – refer to Chapters 8 and 9) and by a reluctance to break family and social ties. In addition, those seeking to move may not possess the required skills. Indeed it appears that migration occurs largely *within* rather than *between* regions. Furthermore, those who migrate tend to be people changing from one job to another rather than the unemployed moving to seek a job – using the language of Norman Tebbit (a former Chairman of the Conservative party) the number of those 'getting on their bikes' is limited. Government regional policy in this context may therefore be seen as an attempt to improve the smooth working of the market. This, broadly speaking, is the Conservative approach to regional problems.

The case for intervention to counter the working of the market

Critics of the *free market* approach claim that market forces may not be able to revive a region with serious economic problems which is in 'cumulative decline'. Such a region is characterised not just by high unemployment, but also by possibly a weakened **industrial base**, poor **infrastructure**, few training facilities, an ageing population and limited ancillary services. There is also likely to be a skills shortage if younger, more mobile, skilled labour has taken the opportunity of employment in more prosperous regions, leaving a residual, less-skilled, ageing labour force. The chance that firms, freely operating in the market, would set up in such an area is small, even when faced with the benefits of cheap labour.

Supporters of this analysis envisage a much more interventionist regional policy stance, in an attempt to control free market forces. Broadly speaking, this may be viewed as the approach of Labour and the Liberal Democrats to regional policy.

REGIONAL POLICY IN THE UK BEFORE 1979

The need for government intervention, in the form of regional policy, to help depressed regions was established in 1934 with the introduction of the Special Areas Act. However, the scale of the intervention during the Great Depression in the 1930s was limited. It was not until the post-war period that regional policy became established as an essential tool in government's drive to achieve 'full employment'. The need for intervention in the running of the economy had been legitimised by Keynes and by the 1944 White Paper on Employment.

A region's need for government assistance was judged principally by the level of regional unemployment, when compared with the remainder of the country. Yet unemployment within a region may not be uniform; there may indeed be some prosperous areas within any particular depressed region. Thus, the necessity may arise to split the region into smaller areas, only some of which will require assistance. In addition, successive governments have recognised the different extent of the problems faced by different areas and, in response, have offered different tiers of help, as part of their regional policy measures. Although it is easy to justify aid to the very depressed areas, it is open to question how far the net should be thrown. If the **assisted areas** are too extensive, then the available resources may be spread too thinly and as a result, be ineffective. Yet, if resources are concentrated too much, the measures will not reach some areas in need of help and anomalies will be created. Resolving this problem has been a recurring theme behind various attempts by governments to redesignate and redraw assisted areas.

UK regional policy has had two components. Firstly, financial incentives have been made available to firms either already based in the assisted areas or intending to establish themselves there – the incentives acting as a 'carrot'. Secondly, the expansion of firms outside the assisted areas has been controlled – acting as a 'stick' – in the hope that investment will be directed into the assisted areas, thereby creating employment.

A large variety of financial incentives have been operated at different times since 1945. These measures have included the establishment of industrial estates with the offer of *subsidised rents*, *tax incentives*, *grants* for capital investment and *labour subsidies*. However, each of these measures has been duly opposed for one reason or another:

(a) Attempts to attract capital into a region, whether in the form of grants or tax incentives, have been criticised for encouraging capital-intensive methods of production, which create relatively few jobs and raise the cost for each job created. However, capital-intensive enterprises may, in fact, have a greater chance of long-term survival and so may be the best way of creating 'real', productive, permanent jobs;

(b) Capital incentives have been criticised because most have been 'automatic' rather than 'discretionary'. This means that incentives were given to all firms, even to those which would have established themselves in the assisted area anyway, without the incentive. Thus complaints have been made that these schemes, by failing to discriminate, are not being cost-effective;

(c) Regional Employment Premium (REP) was used as a labour subsidy from 1967 to 1977. This measure was introduced in response to criticism that capital incentives failed to create many new jobs, and was available to all employers in assisted areas. This meant that REP was spread relatively thinly and it was abolished under pressure from the EC, which viewed it as an unfair subsidy.

To complement the financial incentives ('carrots') discussed above, governments have also operated policies designed to prevent industrial expansion in *non-assisted areas* (ie 'sticks'). Any firm wishing to build a new factory in such an area had first to obtain an Industrial Development Certificate (IDC). Governments hoped that failure to gain an IDC would encourage the firm to move to an assisted area instead. Although many firms did relocate in accordance with the policy of IDCs it was impossible to say how many others invested abroad or cancelled the investment altogether. In addition, questions of national efficiency were raised when companies were prevented from establishing plants in their preferred locations and were instead forced to move to other regions, perhaps at some distance from their main markets or suppliers. Furthermore, whereas the use of IDCs might be accepted by those in the relatively affluent areas in times of rapid growth and full employment, local political pressure is likely if governments attempt to prevent firms expanding in the relatively affluent areas when there is recession and unemployment in the economy as a whole.

The effectiveness of an interventionist regional policy is hard to assess since the extent of assisted areas has frequently been changed by governments. Furthermore, to determine the policy's effectiveness, a comparison must be made between the actual economic position and an estimate of the economic position had the measures not been applied.

Regional policy may be judged principally by the number of jobs created in the assisted areas as a result of the measures adopted. This is usually hard to assess since it will be necessary to exclude jobs which would have been created in the assisted areas anyway without inducements. (From the point of view of the economy as a whole, of course, the *net* creation of jobs is likely to be lower than the number of jobs created in the assisted areas, as a result of the jobs moved from the non-assisted regions.) The cost-effectiveness of the regional policy job creation will depend not just on the cost per job created, but also on the permanence of the jobs and on the possibility of achieving the same result with less expense.

REGIONAL POLICY IN THE UK AFTER 1979

The Conservative government has introduced a series of reforms to regional policy involving the redesignation of **assisted areas**, the introduction of certain specific policy measures and an overall reduction in the scale of the regional policy budget. Advocates of the measures claim that they have been designed to improve the cost-effectiveness of regional policy, although critics claim that they indicate the lack of commitment by a government committed to the working of the market mechanism and reluctant to intervene in the running of the economy.

When the Conservatives were elected in 1979 there were four tiers of assisted areas: *Special Development Areas* (SDA), *Development Areas* (DAs), *Intermediate Areas* (IAs) and *Northern Ireland* (which qualified for special assistance due to the acute nature of the problems in that region). The principal regional policy instruments used were *Regional Development Grants* (RDGs), *Regional Selective Assistance* (RSAs) and *Industrial Development Certificates* (IDCs).

During the first term of the government (1979–83) there was a phased series of changes which involved cuts in the regional policy budget and a gradual reduction in the size of the assisted areas from areas covering 47 per cent of the working population in 1979 to 28 per cent in 1982. The reduction in the areas covered was designed to concentrate aid where it was needed most. RDGs were reduced from 20 per cent to 15 per cent in the DAs, but maintained at 22 per cent in the SDAs. The use of IDCs was suspended in 1981.

The government established twenty-five *Enterprise Zones*, between 1981 and 1984. In these zones, firms were exempted from paying local authority rates and 'red tape' was to be cut to a minimum. It is hard to assess how effective this measure has been, but there is some evidence that many of the jobs created were simply transferred from factories nearby in order to gain the advantages offered by the Enterprise Zones.

During the Conservatives' second term, far more extensive changes were made to regional policy in 1984. In an attempt to simplify the structure of assisted areas, the Special Development Areas status which had been conferred on the most depressed regions was abolished, changing them into Development Areas. The total area to be designated as assisted areas (DAs or IAs) was reduced, as a continuing part of the government's aims to target the aid more effectively, although for the first time the previously prosperous West Midlands was given Intermediate Areas status (see Figures 10.2 and 10.3).

Greater emphasis was placed on discretionary rather than automatic grants in order to increase the cost-effectiveness of regional policy. To this end the government planned to increase expenditure on RSAs relative to expenditure on RDGs (which were limited to a cost per job limit of £10,000). The overall aim of the policy changes was to achieve a near halving by 1987/88 of the

Figure 10.2: British assisted areas at July 1984

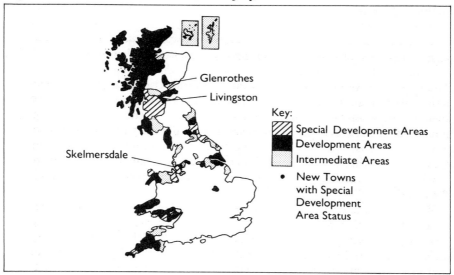

Source: Department of Trade and Industry
From: *Regional Policy: The Way Forward*, H. Armstrong and J. Taylor (1988) Employment Institute

Figure 10.3: British assisted areas at November 1984

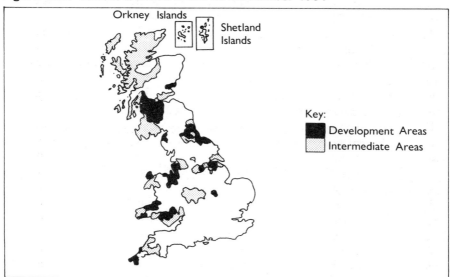

Source: Department of Trade and Industry
From: *Regional Policy and the North-South Divide*, H. Armstrong and J. Taylor (1988) Employment Institute

1983/84 regional aid budget of £700 million (see Figure 10.4).

The trends in regional policy established during the previous eight years were reinforced in 1988 when the automatic Regional Development Grant was scrapped as part of the government's moves towards selective assistance. This change has come about due to the government's belief that much of the RDG was allocated to companies, who would have made their investment in the assisted areas anyway without any government assistance (eg oil-related investment in Aberdeen). Specific grants to small companies employing fewer than twenty-five people were also introduced. Although the White Paper promised to maintain the 'assisted areas map' for the 'lifetime of the present

Figure 10.4: Regional policy expenditure in Great Britain 1972/73–1986/87 at constant (1980) prices

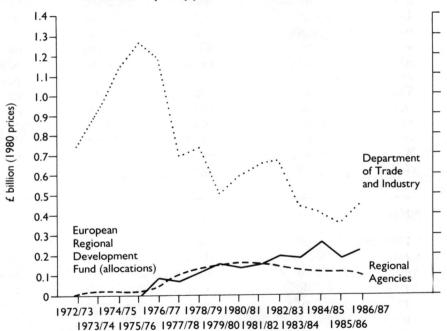

Source: Annual Reports of Industry Act; Economic Trends (HMSO); Annual Reports of Scottish and Welsh Development Agencies; Mid-Wales Development; Highlands and Islands Development Board; Annual Reports of the European Development Fund

From: *Regional Policy and the North South divide, H. Armstrong and J. Taylor (1988) Employment Institute)*

'parliament', the distinction between Development Areas and Intermediate Areas became very small.

A study of traditional regional policy has concentrated on central government measures. Yet especially since the second half of the 1970s, the emphasis has changed, as policy initiatives have come from both the EC, through the European Regional Development Fund, and from the regions themselves, through Enterprise Boards, Development Agencies and local authorities (see Figure 10.4).

In 1988 the EC agreed to a near doubling of its *structural funds* over a four-year period of time. These funds provided resources for regional development, urban renewal and job creation in the EC's poorest regions and had been insisted upon by the less prosperous EC countries as the price for their cooperation during the run up to the completion of the Single European Market in 1992, which was anticipated to favour the more prosperous nations. In addition, in an attempt to avoid distortions of unfair competition, the EC has also become more involved in the monitoring and control of all industrial aid given by member governments – this has included regional aid.

The *Welsh Development Agency* (WDA) is often quoted as the most successful example of a regional development agency. It was heavily involved in encouraging Toyota to establish its engine plant in Shotton (see Chapter 4, page 64). Shotton used to be the home of a British Steel plant, which was closed in 1980 with the loss of 8,000 jobs. The WDA has been instrumental in attracting other high-technology companies into the area, and this resulted in a reduction of local unemployment from 18 per cent to 9 per cent between 1985 and 1989. The WDA is seen as a role model for those who believe in establishing *Regional Development Agencies* (RDAs) in the English regions.

COMMENT

The 1988 measures formed part of a package of moves announced by the Department of Trade and Industry (DTI) to establish itself as a more market-orientated 'Ministry for Enterprise'. Much of the emphasis of recent moves has been placed on job creation in small- and medium-sized firms. Government regional policy may be seen as an attempt to encourage private enterprise to establish itself in assisted areas, in the hope of creating self-generating growth in the long term. It is hoped that the jobs thereby created will be secure and will not become dependent on government assistance for their long term survival.

Set against this are views such as those put forward in the *Guardian* (12 January 1988):

> It is silly to rely too much on market forces to cure regional problems since they were responsible for them in the first place ... The government's main contribution so far has been to cut the regional budget from £1 billion to less than £500 million, to be allocated on a more selective basis. This is barely 10 per cent of the income the government receives each year from selling state owned companies and is not enough.

The free market approach to job creation by encouraging a competitive industrial climate may be seen in the government's attitude to internationally mobile investment projects. A liberal approach to inward investment has been adopted in the UK, in contrast to that adopted in some other EC countries, and the success of this approach is most marked in relation to Japanese investment in car plants in this country (see Chapter 4).

During the high unemployment of the 1980s central government was perceived to be downgrading the importance of regional aid by reducing both its expenditure on regional policy and the extent of the regions covered. The government, of course, would counter these accusations by claiming greater cost-effectiveness and improved targeting for its measures – as has been explained above. However, it would seem true that, during the period of office of the Conservative government, interest has to some extent shifted away from the problems of the regions towards the problems of the inner cities – the topic of the next chapter.

11 *The Inner Cities*

■ What are the problems of the inner cities?
■ The background to Britain's inner city problems
■ Urban policy before 1979
■ Urban policy since 1979
■ Comment

WHAT ARE THE PROBLEMS OF THE INNER CITIES?

There is no simple way of describing what is meant by 'inner city problems', since they cover a wide range of economic, environmental and social issues, the precise mix of which is never the same for any two areas. The problems include many features of economic decline and physical decay often associated with adverse social conditions. Dereliction and decay are prevalent in many inner-city areas and are also associated with a poor quality housing stock, run down factories and warehouses, and inadequate **infrastructure**. Employment opportunities are limited and potential employers find it unattractive to set up in such areas. Inner cities tend to experience *multiple deprivation* – in other words, they are associated with greater than average incidence of poverty, crime, drug abuse, poor health, low educational standards and, in view of high concentrations of ethnic minorities, racial tensions as well. In such areas there is often a feeling of hopelessness and declining community spirit and the areas themselves seem engulfed in a process of 'cumulative decline' – a vicious circle exists, from which it is very hard for the area to emerge (see Chapter 10, page 127).

The problems of the inner cities have been brought to public attention by riots in some cities during the 1980s.

THE BACKGROUND TO BRITAIN'S INNER CITY PROBLEMS

To understand the urban structure of Britain today, one must consider the changes brought about during the Industrial Revolution and further changes thereafter. Towns, especially those close to the ports and the coalfields, attracted the emerging industries of the Industrial Revolution. As the transport facilities available to the workers were limited, so housing for them was built very close to the factories themselves. This period of rapid industrialisation saw the development of large overcrowded cities, which often, as time went on,

FREE TRADE WHARF

Inner city dereliction: around the London docks

merged into urban sprawls or conurbations.

As industrialisation progressed, however, the congestion and overcrowding became increasingly unpleasant features for both employers and workers. In particular, employers found it difficult to expand their businesses, being hindered by both planning restraints and the high price of land, whether for rent or purchase. In addition, within the confines of the inner cities, land for expansion in convenient, and therefore cost-effective, sites near to existing factories was often not available. The movement of factories and workers away from the centre of cities to either the fringe or suburban areas seemed to be increasingly desirable. This process was facilitated by the steadily improving methods of transport available to workers during the Industrial Revolution, which made it unnecessary for them to live in such close proximity to their places of work as had been the case previously. Furthermore the workers were also enjoying rising real incomes, which provided the means to purchase housing in more pleasant areas.

At this stage it should be pointed out that the movement of labour and factories out of a crowded city centre per se is not bound to create problems. To the extent that such a movement reduces overcrowding and congestion, and relieves the strain on the infrastructure of the city, it may well prove beneficial. Unfortunately, however, the migration of both labour and factories has not been even and balanced. Firms which moved tended to be the dynamic, fast-growing enterprises, expanding into new products and using new technology – firms which had both the means and incentive to expand, and for whom the urban environment was no longer attractive. Those which stayed tended to be less dynamic, with weaker long-term prospects, and are said to have experienced *relative decline*.

Similarly the migration of labour out of the inner cities has been selective. Those moving have tended to be professionals and skilled workers, whose higher income and greater **occupational** and **geographical mobility** has enabled them to move to the suburbs, buy their own homes and commute to work if necessary. Thus the population remaining in the inner city areas has had an over-preponderance of unemployed and unskilled workers, many of whom are either young or old. In addition, as young unskilled workers and older workers (who, despite possessing skills in a particular field, may be perceived as being too old to retrain) tend to be relatively immobile, migration of labour out of the inner cities has tended to reduce the size of the working population and, more importantly, the working population as a proportion of the total population. Thus inner city areas are characterised by relatively large numbers of socially and economically disadvantaged people, who may belong to one or more of the following groups: unemployed (in particular long-term unemployed), unskilled or semi-skilled, pensioners, single-parent families and ethnic minorities. The existence of large numbers of people belonging to these disadvantaged socio-economic groups, who may be unable to support themselves fully, increases the numbers dependent on the rest of the community. This inevitably puts a strain on a city's infrastructure and creates a choice between increasing local taxation (thereby making life more unattractive for both residents and businesses) or cutting the level of local services provided (thereby failing to meet social needs and failing to prevent the *cumulative decline* of the area). The extent and diversity of inner city problems has made it inevitable that government responses themselves have been diverse, as governments and the nature of problems have changed.

In the rest of this chapter, a brief comment is made on urban policy before 1979, followed by a more detailed study of the Conservative government's initiatives since that date.

URBAN POLICY BEFORE 1979

During the period since the Second World War, British governments' urban policy may be divided into three stages. From 1945 until the mid 1960s, the main emphasis of government policy was to restrict the growth of urban areas in an attempt to reduce overcrowding and congestion. Measures used included the operation of *green belt* controls to regulate urban expansion into certain areas of the countryside and the construction of *new towns* to act as overspill areas.

During the mid 1960s economists and politicians began to change their analysis of urban problems. Dispersal of people and businesses away from the cities was no longer seen as the best solution. Specific policies to deal with acute social problems were needed and these included improvements to housing and the meeting of specific educational needs of children in inner cities. There was also growing concern about *cycles of deprivation* (a series of social and economic problems from which it was hard for individuals to extricate themselves).

The third stage of urban policy began with the publication by the Labour government of a White Paper entitled *Policy for the Inner Cities* in 1977. This shifted the emphasis of urban policy away from policies aimed specifically at social and environmental problems towards a quest for *economic regeneration*. This was based on a belief that, if the underlying economic conditions could be improved, then the social problems and problems of dereliction would be less.

URBAN POLICY SINCE 1979

The Conservative view contrasted with alternative political approaches

The policies adopted by the Conservative government since 1979 have continued to be based on the belief that the 1977 doctrine of economic regeneration is the pre-condition for eliminating the social and environmental problems of the inner cities. However, the emphasis of the policies has been very different from those adopted by the pre-1979 Labour government and also from the views expressed by both Labour and the centre parties in opposition. In particular, the Conservatives have placed great emphasis on the private sector, in an attempt to develop a partnership between private and public money. However, much of their programme has been directed by central government rather than by the local authorities, many of which are Labour controlled.

Although more recent documents have been produced, a study of comments included by the three main political parties in their 1987 General Election Manifestos is illuminating and illustrates the widely contrasting approaches to explaining inner city problems and the different solutions proposed.

The Conservative Manifesto commented:

> The regeneration of inner cities must be tackled ... the conditions for enterprise and pride of ownership have been systematically extinguished by Socialist councils ... we must remove the barriers against private investment, jobs and prosperity which such councils have erected.

This emphasis on regenerating urban areas by means of the private sector, blaming many of the urban problems on left wing authorities, may be contrasted with the claims made in the Labour Manifesto, which firmly lays the blame at the door of the Conservative government:

> This government has left inner city areas to rot ... Tory cuts in funding and in housing, together with mass unemployment, have turned too many of our urban areas into dingy hopeless places.

The differing emphasis of Labour party thinking, giving a greater role to local authorities, may be seen from their claim that:

Labour's approach will be to develop the partnership between central and local government, with the direct participation of the voluntary and private sectors.

The SDP/Liberal Alliance Manifesto blamed the growth of inner city problems on:

Conservative neglect in central government and Labour control in local government . . . resulting in the development of inner cities . . . as a battleground for the class struggle.

Only hours after gaining a renewed majority in the 1987 General Election, Mrs Thatcher set out the agenda for her third term by claiming:

We've got a big job to do in some of those inner cities, a really big job. Our policies were geared – education and housing – to help the people in the inner cities to get more choice and politically we must get right back in there, because we want them, too, next time.

In this statement, Mrs Thatcher made it plain that, in addition to the higher profile of economic policy to be directed at the inner cities, there were also political overtones involved. This can be seen in part as an attempt to reverse the disastrous performance of the Conservative candidates in many inner city areas in the 1987 General Election. In some major cities the Conservative representation in parliament was wiped out altogether.

As is perhaps inevitable in the superficial comment contained in election manifestos where attaching blame appears to be paramount, the fact that the decline of inner cities has been a long-term phenomenon was neglected. What should perhaps have been considered were the questions: (*a*) has the government been adopting the correct policies to alleviate the problem? and (*b*) have sufficient resources been directed into urban renewal projects?

However, even by *asking* the second question, one is perhaps guilty of prejudging the issue. Conservative thinking is very much based on the notion that 'spending money on a problem' is not necessarily the whole answer (a theme running through this book when commenting on Conservative policy); what is more important is to create the correct environment in which the private sector, comprising businesses and individuals acting in their own interest, will respond. Hence any conclusion which criticised the government for not spending enough on the inner cities presupposes that the more spending there is, the fewer problems there will be. This specific example involving spending on the inner cities may be compared to the government's overall (macroeconomic) view that governments are unable to 'spend their way out of a recession'. (This conclusion was reached by James Callaghan, the Labour Prime Minister, in 1976 and marked the end of the post-war adherence to **demand management** and the rise of monetarism – refer to Chapter 1, pages 13 and 19.)

A leading article in *The Times* (19 June 1987) shortly after the 1987 election clearly summarises the government's position:

The hope is that the inner cities be treated as needing restored self-sufficiency, rather than external propping-up. . . Money is not the problem. Successive governments have poured immense sums into the problem areas with staggeringly little effect. Elected local councils have too often distributed funds and pursued policies in ways that appear calculated to frustrate central government and perpetuate the grievances which keep the council's Labour majorities in power. The government is still feeling its way towards solving these problems. Its battery of different instruments – task forces, development corporations, enterprise zones, regeneration grants and the like – still has an experimental, even improvisational, air. But two principles are consistent: that initiative and private funds should play a full part in the process, and that City Hall (ie local authorities) should have as little as possible to do with control of policy and of the purse-strings.

In addition to facing criticisms of its inner cities policy centred on inadequate funding, the government has also been attacked on a number of other counts. In particular, at one stage there seemed to be a great deal of confusion over which government department was responsible for the overall coordination of policy. In the past the problems of the inner cities had been countered by programmes from many different government departments and so it was unclear who held overall responsibility. The Department of Trade and Industry (DTI) and the Department of the Environment were the main contenders, although the Home Office and Departments of Education and Employment were also involved. The confusion was resolved in favour of the DTI in December 1987, when one of its ministers was given the task of coordinating the government's overall approach. However, following the 1989 cabinet reshuffle, the coordination task reverted to the Department of the Environment in recognition of that department's major spending role in the inner cities.

Criticism has also been expressed that, although the government has attempted to build a partnership between public and private sectors, the local authorities have been largely excluded in favour of central government. Furthermore, the government has been accused of not taking the interests of the existing inner city inhabitants into sufficient account and of not developing an overall integrated approach to regional and urban problems. Instead it has tended to deal with each in isolation.

Specific policies adopted by the Conservative government

The principle of *Enterprise Zones* was established in the 1980 Budget and twenty-five were established between 1981 and 1984. The incentives, which lasted for ten years, included exemption from both local authority rates and development land tax, 100 per cent tax allowance on new investments on buildings, and a relaxation of local authority planning regulations.

However, Enterprise Zones have been judged to be too expensive in terms of 'cost per job created' and the experiment is not to be renewed. In addition, it has been hard to assess how many of the jobs were actually new jobs rather than jobs created by firms moving relatively short distances into Enterprise Zones from existing factories. In that case the *net* creation of jobs would be much less and the cost per job created that much higher.

Urban Development Corporations (UDCs) became the flagship of the Conservative government's attempts to revitalise inner city areas in Britain. The first two were set up during 1981 in the derelict and run-down docklands of London and Liverpool. 'In all practical sense they were to be new town

A housing estate in London's Docklands Development

corporations in old cities', according to Michael Heseltine who, as Environment Secretary, established them. The London Docklands Development Corporation (LDDC) and Merseyside Development Corporation (MDC) were given powers to reclaim land and derelict buildings, with the aim of encouraging the development of new businesses and attracting people back into the area by building suitable houses.

The most striking feature of the UDC programme is that the UDCs are funded by central government, by-passing the (predominantly Labour) inner city local authorities. This gives rise to criticism that the process is undemocratic. On the other hand, it is claimed that there is a reduction in red tape and that central government's private-sector-orientated policies are not interfered with by left-wing local authorities.

The emphasis placed on the role of the private sector in partnership with UDCs can be seen in the attempts of the UDCs to generate private investment as a result of spending public money. Thus public money may be viewed as 'pump priming' the private sector, but the dominant role in redevelopment is to lie with the private sector.

The greatest claims of success for the UDC programme are made on behalf of the LDDC and these claims are now examined. According to a report by the National Audit Office in 1988, the LDDC 'has made good progress towards regeneration of its area and has worked quickly to attract investment ... building up private sector investment in Docklands'. The report also indicated that private sector investment since 1981 was estimated at £2.2 billion. The success of this 'pump-priming' operation can be seen by a 'public-private sector investment ratio since 1981 of 1:9' (ie for every £1 of public money spent, £9 of private sector finances has been forthcoming).

In 1981 only 4 per cent of houses and flats were owner-occupied and, in an attempt to increase this figure, the LDDC intended to build 13,000 new dwellings within 10–15 years, mainly for owner-occupation. However, the housing programme advanced so quickly that the target figure was raised to 25,000 in March 1987. The LDDC has also promoted the Docklands Light Railway and the London City Airport, as means of improving transport and communications, and generally improving the **infrastructure** of the area, which is so important in changing the perception of both potential residents and potential investors.

This appears to represent a major success in 'regenerating' the area and, indeed, any visit to the Docklands will confirm the transformation that has taken place and the general feeling of enterprise and rejuvenation, in what is now a hive of activity. However, the NAO report cautions that:

> The LDDC's success partly reflects its proximity to central London and the deregulation of the City. These special advantages do not detract from the LDDC's performance, but they mean that its achievements will not readily be repeated elsewhere.

It has also been claimed that the LDDC has done little for those already living in the Docklands or working in existing firms in the area. The price of land has escalated as a result of its transformation from derelct docklands into a fast-growing development. This has had a knock-on effect on house prices (most new houses have been built for owner-occupation), putting them beyond the reach of many existing inhabitants. Many of those able to afford to buy such houses are classed as 'yuppies', who may have no roots in the area and do not necessarily work there. The temptation for many existing firms employing local labour to sell up, taking advantage of the high land prices, is therefore great. In addition, the new jobs created in the Docklands may require skills not possessed by the existing workforce. It is therefore important to realise that the figure representing the number of jobs created in the Docklands ignores the fact that some of these jobs might have been created elsewhere, but were attracted into Docklands, and that some existing jobs may have been squeezed out. The potential for tension between East Enders and newcomers is clear and may be seen on the popular BBC television 'soap' of the same name.

Success in the second of the original UDCs in Merseyside has been less apparent. The MDC was located on three separate sites on both sides of the River Mersey and was at a disadvantage because 'the wider Merseyside area suffered from a poor image which deterred prospective developers and investors' (NAO report). The MDC has received acclaim for its refurbishment of the Albert Dock and has also reclaimed land. However, inward investment into the area has tended to concentrate on leisure and tourism, rather than on industry.

The NAO did, however, criticise both UDCs for lapses of management control and criticised the government for not analysing specifically the 'achievement and difficulties' of the first two UDCs before further UDCs were established in 1987 and 1988.

Other government initiatives have included the creation of *City Action Teams* in 1985, designed to coordinate the work of various government departments in specific areas, and *City Task Forces* in 1986, aimed at tackling the problems of acute deprivation in eight small and clearly defined areas.

Conservative plans for regenerating the inner cities during the third term, expected since Mrs Thatcher's statements about the importance of inner cities on election night, materialised in March 1988 as a booklet, *Action for Cities*, rather than in a White Paper as had been expected. Instead of launching any major new initiatives, the government sought to improve the coordination of existing policies. The booklet was aimed specifically at the business community, in an attempt to attract them into inner cities, and was followed by a series of 'working breakfasts' with the business community in several cities. The opposition parties poured scorn on *Action for Cities*, claiming that it did not address the problem of the inner cities and contained no new proposals. There were, however, certain specific initiatives, including the doubling of the size of the Merseyside Development Corporation and the creation of a new UDC in Sheffield (bringing the number established to ten) and the creation of City Action Teams in Leeds and Nottingham.

COMMENT

The treatment of inner cities by the government was attacked in a leading article in the *Financial Times* (8 March 1988), which put the measures outlined in *Action for Cities* into a broader context:

> Other Government policies not counted in the inner city balance sheet are likely to do more damage to the immediate interests of many of the worst-off inhabitants of the inner cities than measures announced (in *Action for Cities*) are to do good. The new Community Charge, or Poll Tax, will be payable by every inhabitant, however poor; the maximum remission will be 80 per cent. The new social security regime will leave some of those at the very bottom of the pile with less income than now. The new housing policies will lead to sharply increased rents, accompanied by a ceiling on rebate expenditure. Some may be 'rescued from dependency' by the combination of such sticks and the *Action for Cities* carrots, but many more will become more dependent than ever.

This view is to be contrasted with a claim by Mrs Thatcher that government policies were 'designed to make inner city dereliction a thing of the past'. This was to be achieved as part of general economic prosperity resulting from Conservative policies, but also by creating the correct business environment in cities, in which enterprise could thrive. A key aspect of these proposals anticipated the reduction in power of inner city Labour-dominated local councils.

It is clearly too early to comment on the overall effectiveness of the Conservative government's policies on inner cities, and firm conclusions will be hard to come by, in view of the different criteria adopted when judging success.

PART 4

OVERVIEW

12 *An Overview of Thatcherism in the 1980s*

The first eleven chapters of the book have focused on specific topics of importance during the period of office of the Conservative government. The final chapter is devoted to an overall study of macroeconomic policy during the 1980s. It is split into four periods of time, each of which contains certain key themes important in the development of Thatcherism. Each subsection is followed by a 'Focus', which concentrates on one particular aspect of policy.

1979–81 STRICT MONETARISM

The election of the Conservative government led by Mrs Thatcher in May 1979 has proved to be a watershed in Britain's economic and political development. The post Second World War period had been dominated by governments (of both major parties) practising Keynesian economics. This involved the use of **demand management** policies and a commitment to maintaining full employment (see Chapter 1, pages 13 and 19). The election of the Conservative government marked a break with Keynesian orthodoxy, which was replaced by an advocacy of *monetarism.*

Monetarists observed a correlation between certain measures of the money supply and inflation and they concluded that there was a *causative* relationship between money supply and inflation. Hence the key to controlling inflation was to control the money supply. Debate about the existence and nature of this causative relationship marked debate between Keynesians and Monetarists during the early years of Thatcherism, although the arguments altered later in the 1980s when the weight given to money supply targets by the Monetarists diminished.

The Conservative government believed in the operation of market forces, and was committed to non-interventionism in the running of the economy. Improving the **supply side** of the economy by liberalisation and deregulation was seen as the key to productivity gains and sustained growth; so too were a reform of trade unions and a reduction of their power. Conservatives were also committed to pushing back the 'frontiers of the state'. This led to a commitment to reduce both government expenditure and taxation. However, the first move on the taxation front in the 'Incentive Budget' of 1979 was intended to shift the burden of taxation rather than reduce it. Income tax (**direct taxation**) was reduced and VAT (**indirect taxation**) was increased from 8 per cent (12.5 per cent on luxury goods) to 15 per cent. This is estimated to have contributed directly to an increase of 4 per cent in the rate of inflation during 1979/80.

The commitment to money supply targets was strengthened in 1980 by the introduction of the *Medium Term Financial Strategy* (MTFS), which produced money supply targets for *Sterling M3* (a 'broad' measure of money) for the next four years.

A combination of high interest rates, resulting from the adoption of monetarist policies, and the existence of North Sea oil resulted in an appreciating currency during the period 1979/81, at a time when inflation in the British economy was higher than the EC average. This made exports less competitive and increased **import penetration** into the British economy. Unemployment soared as the economy sank into recession, rising from 5.1 per cent of the population (excluding school leavers) in 1979 (1.2 million) to 9.9 per cent in 1981 (2.4 million), but the rate of inflation fell from its peak of 22 per cent in 1980.

The government's economic policy and, in particular, its exchange rate policy during this period, has already been considered in greater detail in Chapter 1, where the impact on manufacturing industry has been studied.

FOCUS: THE 1981 BUDGET – the role of fiscal policy?

The 1981 Budget (the third introduced by Sir Geoffrey Howe, Chancellor from 1979–83) proved to be a landmark in the development of economic policy under the Conservative government. The recession, which accompanied the first two years of monetarism, had resulted in a reduction in output, especially in manufacturing industry and a sharp increase in unemployment. Calls, both from within the Conservative party and from outside, were made for a 'U-turn' in the direction of economic policy, at a time when the government was extremely unpopular in the opinion polls. Keynesian orthodoxy advocated a reflationary

Sir Geoffrey Howe, Chancellor of the Exchequer 1979–83

fiscal policy in order to create extra demand and thereby extra production and employment. A U-turn had been taken by the previous Conservative government under Edward Heath. When faced with a 'politically unacceptable' level of unemployment of 1 million in 1971, the economy was reflated and this was accompanied by a relaxation of credit, thereby creating an unsustainable 'dash for growth', often known as the *Barber Boom* (named after the Chancellor at the time, Anthony Barber). This was followed by an inflationary surge.

The Conservative government in 1981 rejected such calls for a U-turn despite a level of unemployment of 2.4 million. (This emphasized the changing emphasis placed on unemployment during the 1980s, when compared with a 'politically unacceptable' level of 1 million in 1971). Not only were calls for a reflation rejected, but the government actually adopted the exact reverse policy, engaging in what Keynesians would term a 'deflationary' budget. However, the government claimed that the effects of this budget were far from deflationary:

> The conditions for sustained growth in output and employment can only be achieved if there is a sustained reduction in inflation. This, in turn, requires a progressive reduction in the rate of increase in the money supply and the *pursuit of fiscal policies consistent with that aim, which avoid excessive reliance on interest rates.*

A downward path had already been set for the public sector borrowing requirement (PSBR), as a proportion of gross domestic product (GDP), in the MTFS in 1980. However, the recession of 1980/81 was deeper than had been anticipated and the rise in unemployment greater. As a consequence the amount of taxation collected was lower than predicted – some had lost their jobs and others experienced a cut in real income – and government expenditure rose to pay 'dole' to the extra unemployed. As a consequence, the 1980/81 PSBR was £5 billion higher than had been anticipated, at £13.5 billion or 6 per cent of GDP.

For the monetarists, a reduction in the PSBR was essential to the success of their counter-inflationary strategy and the Chancellor produced proposals aimed at reducing the PSBR by £3.5 billion. This was achieved principally by increases in taxation. Increases in the rates of income tax were avoided, in order to leave intact the main planks of the 1979 income tax-cutting 'Incentive Budget', but personal tax allowances were not raised in line with inflation, as had hitherto been required of governments (1977 Finance Act). In addition, excise duties on alcohol, tobacco and petrol were increased significantly – by double the amount required to increase them in line with inflation.

The 1981 budget may be seen as an attempt to salvage the MTFS and put economic policy 'back on course'. By rejecting Keynesian demands for a reflationary budget, and indeed by adopting a policy diametrically opposite, the government made it clear that, under monetarism, fiscal policy would be given a limited role, very much subservient to the dominant role given to monetary policy. This was in marked contrast to the priorities seen when Keynesian economics held sway in the era of **demand management**. Shortly after the 1981 budget, interest rates fell by 2 per cent and this was claimed to have vindicated the budget measures.

1981 marked a turning point in the fortunes of the economy. A period of sustained growth began in 1981/82 and lasted throughout the 1980s – the longest sustained recovery seen since 1945. The government claimed that the 1981 budget had helped to create the correct environment in which this might occur, whereas critics complained that the budget was another self-inflicted wound, which depressed the recovery below what it might otherwise have been.

The 1981 budget was also seen as being a further defeat for the Conservative *wets*, who were Conservatives opposed to the more 'extreme' policies of the government and who were principally Keynesians. Many of the wets in the cabinet lost their places in the government in the cabinet reshuffle of 1981. To a great extent Conservative opposition to the content of economic policy (as opposed to the style of the government) diminished from that point onwards.

Nigel Lawson, Chancellor of the Exchequer 1983–89

1982–85 PRAGMATISM AND RECOVERY

The economy began to recover from the depths of the 1980/81 recession during 1981/82. The recovery in production was accompanied by a surge in productivity growth, associated with improved working practices, and also a recovery in the profitability of companies. However, although the renewal of growth increased employment from 1983 onwards, demographic factors meant that unemployment continued to rise until 1986. Inflation fell below 5 per cent in January 1983 and the rate of inflation fluctuated within a narrow margin about this level throughout the period considered (only rising significantly by 1988).

A more 'pragmatic approach' was adopted towards monetary policy. It was announced in the March 1982 budget that two other measures of the money supply would be taken into account as well as Sterling M3 (*M1*, a 'narrow' measure of money, and *PSL2*, another 'broad' measure of money).

FOCUS: THE CHANCELLOR'S 1985 MANSION HOUSE SPEECH
– the end of monetarism?

In October 1985, Nigel Lawson (Chancellor from 1983 until 1989) extended the 'pragmatic approach' towards monetarism and announced

Figure 12.1: Sterling M3 and sucessive targets

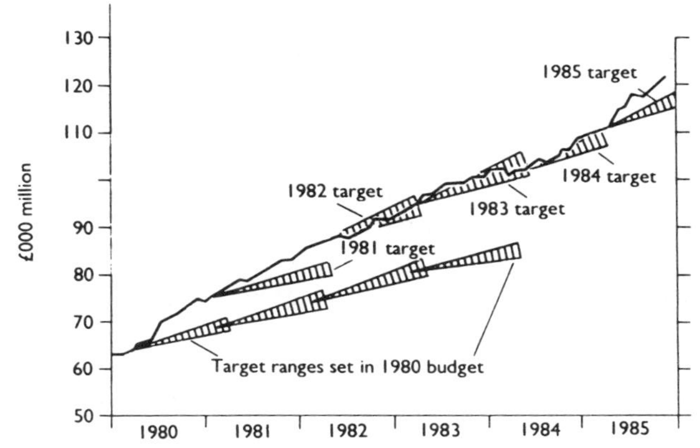

Note: The figures and ranges before November 1981 have
been adjusted to allow for the change in the series.

Source: Royal Bank of Scotland, Economics Office
From: Guadian, 24 October 1985

that the government had suspended its principle measure of the money supply – Sterling M3. The target range for Sterling M3 growth had been 5–9 per cent for the year 1985/86, but its annualised growth over the six months prior to October 1985 was approximately 18 per cent (refer to Figure 12.1). The large rise in interest rates that would have been necessary to achieve the Sterling M3 target was considered neither acceptable nor appropriate, as the Chancellor considered inflation to be 'well under control'.

He indicated that Sterling M3 had grown by 82 per cent during the previous five financial years, but that money GDP had only grown by 54 per cent. This indicated that the velocity of circulation of money – assumed by monetarists to be constant – had decreased. According to Mr Lawson 'We have persistently under-estimated the demand by individuals to hold an increased proportion of savings in liquid form'. Changes in the financial system had affected individual's desire to hold money in various forms and it is clear that the private sector had increased its holdings of *broad money*, not only for spending purposes, but also possibly on a permanent basis, as a means of saving (eg in bank deposits). If this represents a significant trend and, moreover, if the amounts under consideration are liable to fluctuate, then it appears unlikely that Sterling M3 will be linked to future rates of inflation.

Critics of the government saw this as a major defeat for government economic policy, which had had at its core the belief that *broad money* directly affected inflation. In order to try (unsuccessfully as it transpired) to achieve targets for Sterling M3 under the MTFS, interest rates had risen. This created a direct burden on industry and contributed to the rise in the exchange rate during the period 1979/81, which had bankrupted sections of British industry and contributed to the recession. Now this target was being abandoned. The Chancellor announced, however, that changes in *MO* – a measure of *narrow money* – would continue to be monitored (but *not* targeted) and that other measures of money might also be considered, if necessary. However greater emphasis was to be placed on the exchange rate in monetary policy decisions and, in addition, the raising of short-term interest rates would be used to tighten monetary conditions, whenever appropriate.

The abandonment of the Sterling M3 target called into question the government's commitment to fighting inflation, but, according to Mr Lawson, 'The inflation rate is judge and jury'. In other words, if the rate of inflation is low, the government's policy has succeeded, whatever the means used to achieve it and whether or not money supply targets are met.

The decisions to give the exchange rate 'an increased weight in monetary policy decisions' and to 'raise interest rates if appropriate' were not as easy to understand as a single money supply target. The use of various different measures of the money supply was criticised as a means by which the government could select whichever measure happened to suit it in any given year. Furthermore, critics argued that exchange rate policy and interest rate policy were not independent. (This dilemma reappeared during 1988 and 1989 and ultimately led to the resignation of the Chancellor, after conflict with the Prime Minister.)

The Chancellor also abandoned the practice of *overfunding*. In order to achieve money supply targets, the government had sold more gilts than was necessary to finance the PSBR, as a means of contracting the money supply. In future, he indicated, greater emphasis would be placed on short-term interest rates as a means of controlling monetary growth.

1986–88: A GOLDEN AGE?

The rise in retail prices during the twelve months ending in July 1986 was 2.4 per cent. This represented the lowest inflation rate since 1967 and, on the Chancellor's criterion that the inflation rate is the 'judge and jury' of success when assessing counter-inflationary policy, this can be represented as a great achievement.

However, the collapse of the oil price from approximately $30 per barrel in 1985 to under $10 per barrel in 1986, had a dramatic 'dampening down effect' on inflation in the whole of the industrialised world. In the case of Britain, a 'low' inflation rate of 2.4 per cent was regarded as a pleasing figure, even though the average inflation rate for the indutrialised world was also 2.4 per cent – furthermore, inflation was lower in both Japan and West Germany. The decline in the oil price masked an underlying rate of inflation which was less satisfactory.

The rise in average earnings over the twelve months prior to July 1986 was 7.5 per cent. This represented an increase in real earnings of 5.1 per cent at a time when the economy was growing at 3 per cent in real terms. An additional stimulus to consumer demand was provided by rising consumer borrowing and a falling **savings ratio**.

The fall in the price of oil reduced the amount of tax collected from North Sea oil production by approximately £5 billion in 1986/87 compared to 1985/86 but, contrary to expectations, the Chancellor still felt able to reduce the basic rate of income tax by 1p (to 29p), reviving the prospect of the 25p rate promised by the Conservatives in 1979. This provided a further stimulus to demand in the economy.

During 1986, Sterling M3 grew by far more than anticipated. (Its growth during 1986/87 was 20 per cent.) However, relatively little attention was given to this, as Sterling M3 was no longer being targeted. The narrow measure of money, MO, increased within its 4–8 per cent target range during 1986/87. These differing trends of the two measures of money supply can be seen in Figure 12.2.

Figure 12.2: Monetary base (MO) and Sterling M3 (12 month percentage changes)

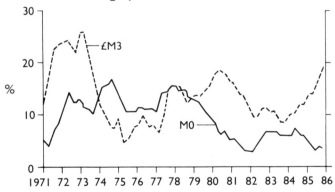

From: Barclays Review, August 1986

The government had re-emphasized in 1985 that the value of sterling was to be given 'greater consideration' when looking at monetary conditions. However, the sterling effective exchange rate index fell from mid 1985 and throughout 1986. Despite this, although sterling depreciated against the Deutsch Mark, the exchange rate against the US dollar increased during this period of time – but this was only because the dollar itself was falling from the unsustainable heights it had reached during the Reagan presidency of 1981–4 (refer to Figure 12.3). A falling exchange rate may be viewed as a reflection of lax monetary conditions in a country. However, it may also be seen to be contributing to inflationary pressures, by means of higher import prices and a removal of the **external discipline** on wage bargainers.

With the benefit of hindsight, it is possible to say that, aided by the oil price

Figure 12.3: Sterling exchange rate for 1984–89

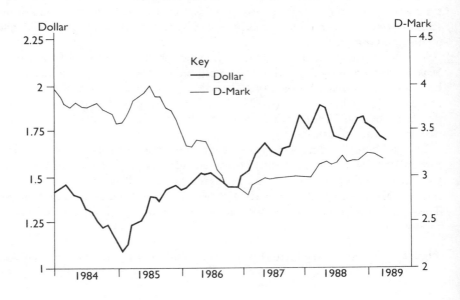

From: *Barclays Review*, May 1989

reduction, the 'judge and jury' measure of counter-inflationary policy (the 2.4 per cent RPI figure) concealed significant underlying inflationary pressures, measured especially in terms of *broad money*, the exchange rate and average earnings.

The **Louvre Accord** in February 1987 attempted to stabilise the major world currencies. This marked a change in the policy established in October 1985, when the **Plaza Agreement** was established in order to bring about a controlled reduction in the value of the US dollar. Although no figures were published, it became clear in the aftermath of the Louvre Accord, that sterling was to 'shadow' the Deutsch Mark within narrow bands and, in particular, sterling should be kept below the 3 Deutsch Mark level. This exchange rate policy was designed to provide stability for exporters and was seen as laying the groundwork for possible entry into the Exchange Rate Mechanism (ERM) of the European Monetary System (EMS).

1987 was an election year and in June 1987 the Conservatives were re-elected for a third term. In the budget which preceded it, the Chancellor was able to reduce the basic rate of income tax from 29 per cent to 27 per cent, but the buoyancy of the economy and the consequent growth of tax receipts enabled him to reduce taxation, while at the same time aiming to maintain his PSBR target at 1 per cent of GDP.

Figure 12.4: Unemployment and prices in the UK

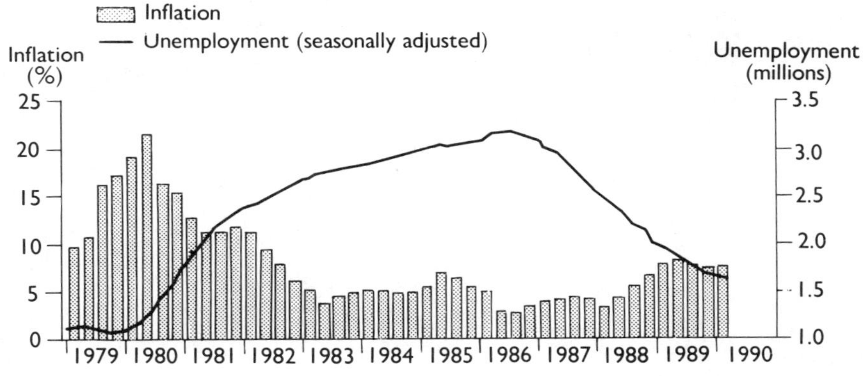

Source: Datastream
From: Sunday Telegraph, 15 April 1990

1987 and 1988 were years of rapid growth, falling unemployment and rising prosperity. GDP grew by 4.8 per cent in 1987 and 4.5 per cent in 1988, compared with an average figure of 2.9 per cent of 1982–6. This led many commentators to claim that the **supply side** revolution was really paying dividends and that the problems of the British economy had been overcome (see Figure 12.4).

There was, however, increasing concern that the economy was *overheating*. 'Overheating' describes a situation in which supply – albeit rapidly increasing supply (as was the case in 1987–8) – is unable to meet the growth in demand. Rising inflation is a symptom of overheating, as is a growing balance of payments deficit on current account. However, certainly in the short term, the emergence of a current account deficit does actually limit the inflationary impact of overheating, as it allows some of the excess demand to be met by imports.

During the summer of 1987, world stock markets appeared to be lacking confidence and there were fears that the **bull market** run of the 1980s had overstretched itself. These fears were confirmed in October 1987 when the world's stock markets, following the lead set by Wall Street, crashed. The *Wall Street Crash* in 1929 – a *financial crash* – was followed by the *Great Depression*, involving slump and mass unemployment across the world in the 1930s – a *real economy crash*. Economists were concerned that the 1987 stock market crash would adversely affect the 'real' economy. As a consequence there was a worldwide reduction of interest rates and liquidity was eased to prevent economic collapse. The confinement of the 'financial crash' to the stock markets of the world without an effect on the 'real' economy was attributed to this policy. However, in the case of the British economy, the easing of monetary conditions further contributed to the existing symptoms of overheat-

Sir Alan Walters, full-time economic adviser to Mrs Thatcher from May to October 1989

ing. Worries of overheating during mid-1987 were abruptly replaced with fears of a depression, but renewed fears of overheating re-emerged during 1988.

However, these fears were not shared by the Chancellor, who substantially reduced taxation in the 1988 budget. The basic rate of income tax was reduced to 25 per cent, thereby achieving the longstanding commitment to this rate, and the top rate of tax was reduced from 60 per cent to 40 per cent. However, using arguments similar to those used the year before, he claimed that the 'strength of the economy has been reflected in rising tax receipts' and that the public sector finances were 'strong'. This enabled him, despite the reduction in taxation, to aim for a budget surplus – a public sector debt repayment (PSDR) of £3 billion, as had actually been achieved in the previous year. This illustrates an interesting aspect about how a government should measure its fiscal stance. The Chancellor based his policies on the size of the PSBR (or PSDR), which allowed him to cut taxation and claim that his fiscal policy remained 'prudent', rather than considering the demand implications of cuts in taxation, which can be seen as contributing to the overheating in the economy and the growing balance of payments and inflation problems.

FOCUS: The decision in March 1988 to 'unpeg' sterling from the Deutsch Mark – conflicting aspects of exchange rate and monetary policies

As mentioned in the previous section, the government attempted to keep sterling linked (within fairly narrow bands) to the EMS currencies and, in particular, to preserve a 3 Deutsch Mark ceiling. This attempt to 'shadow' the Deutsch Mark was successful during 1987 and the early part of 1988. During 1987 the UK foreign exchange reserves rose by $20 billion, as a result of Bank of England intervention in the foreign exchange market, in order to prevent foreign investors from pushing up the value of sterling. As a result of the attempt to maintain a stable exchange rate at a time when there was upward pressure on it, room for manoeuvre in monetary policy was limited. An increase in interest rates, which might have reduced inflationary pressures in the domestic economy, was not possible as it would probably have been sufficient to cause sterling to rise through its 3 Deutsch Mark ceiling. However, by March 1988 the upward pressure on sterling was so great that the government no longer attempted to 'defend' the target and sterling surged upwards. This effectively destroyed the 'shadow EMS band' and delayed plans for entry into the ERM of the EMS. (See Figure 12.5.)

The issue of the 3 Deutsch Mark ceiling had been the cause of differences of opinion between the Prime Minister and Chancellor, both

Figure 12.5: **Uncapping the pound – the performance of sterling against the Deutschmark in 1987 and early 1988**

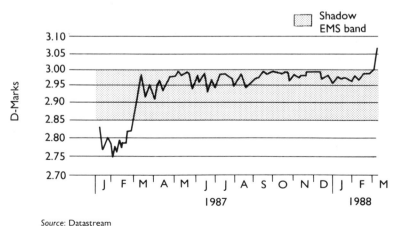

Source: Datastream
From: Guardian, 9 March 1988

before and after the change of policy. Mr Lawson was in favour of stable exchange rates as a prelude both to membership of the ERM and to providing stability for trading. (In addition, a stable exchange rate would provide confidence that high nominal wage increases would not be 'accommodated' by downward movement of the exchange rate at a later date.) Mrs Thatcher viewed the exchange rate differently, arguing for the acceptance of market forces by not trying to 'buck the market'. In the context of March 1988, she welcomed an appreciating currency, which would help to dampen down inflationary pressures. From this it can be seen that both supporters of stable and floating exchange rates claimed that their policies were counter-inflationary.

SINCE 1988: RETRENCHMENT

The continuing strength of the British economy during 1988 witnessed growing inflationary pressures and a sharp deterioration in the current account deficit from £3.7 billion for 1987 to £14.7 billion for 1988. Rejecting alternative economic policies (as discussed in the Focus which follows), the Chancellor, Nigel Lawson, used interest rates as his principal economic weapon to deal with those twin problems.

During the period between March and May 1988 interest rates had been reduced from 9 per cent to $7\frac{1}{2}$ per cent, in order to try to reduce the upward pressure on sterling, but the emphasis of interest rate policy was then altered and the downward trend was reversed. Base rates were raised in steps from $7\frac{1}{2}$ per cent in May 1988, rising in steps over a six-month period to 13 per cent in November 1988 – the last increase in response to a monthly record current account deficit of £2.4 billion reported for October 1988.

It is necessary to explain how the government believed that raising interest rates would help to address the problems of inflation and the current account.

Raising interest rates increases the cost of borrowing. It was hoped that this would reduce expenditure in the economy and hence eliminate overheating. This would reduce inflationary pressures and also reduce the demand for imports, although the demand for domestically-produced goods would, of course, be reduced as well. The government argued that its policies would enable it to achieve a *soft landing*, whereby the problems of overheating would be solved by 'slowing down the economy', without resorting to a full recession, referred to as a *hard landing*. Unfortunately interest rate policy operates as a very blunt weapon and it is impossible to distinguish between different types of borrowing. The end of the house price boom, brought about by rising interest rates, certainly affected borrowing for mortgages, but consumer spending initially proved remarkably resilient to high interest rates. The corporate sector was badly hit, leading to fears that high interest rates would hit investment harder than consumption.

Raising interest rates was not only intended to be effective in reducing inflation and correcting the current account deficit; it was also intended to *finance* the current account deficit, by encouraging short-term capital inflows to Britain, attracted by the interest rate differential when compared with other countries. This point was significant in explaining the further rise in base rates to 15 per cent in October 1989, shortly before Nigel Lawson resigned as Chancellor and was replaced by John Major (see page 158). The change in interest rates occurred in response to a one per cent increase in the West German lending rate. However, a £2 billion current account deficit just published for August 1989 indicated that the increase was needed for other reasons as well – not just to maintain the existing interest rate differential over the West Germans. Financing a current account deficit by short-term capital inflows is inherently unstable, as the capital may be repatriated at short notice. Furthermore, although Britain has huge overseas assets to match the increase in liabilities incurred, financing a large current account deficit by short-term capital inflows cannot continue for ever.

The UK current account deficit for 1989 was £20.3 billion, following the 1988 deficit of £14.7 billion. The rate of inflation at the time of the 1990 budget rose to 7.9 per cent, rising to an eight-year high of 10.9 per cent in September 1990. In the short term, raising the rate of interest in order to reduce inflation, actually *raises* inflation, due to the increased cost of borrowing (particularly for the cost of mortgage borrowing) which is included in the RPI calculations. However, the underlying UK rate of inflation was significantly higher than the average in the rest of the EC.

From this evidence it is clear that a policy of raising interest rates in order to reduce both inflation and the current account deficit does take time to work.

FOCUS: Interest Rate policy – the Chancellor as a 'one-club golfer'?

The reliance of the Chancellor, Nigel Lawson, on high interest rates as the principal weapon to reduce both inflation and the current account deficit was criticized by those who felt that other policy weapons could also be usefully employed, thereby obviating the need for interest rates at levels that were so damaging to the economy.

Traditional Keynesian economics would indicate that fiscal policy should be tightened by either reducing government expenditure or increasing taxation. (This would result in either a reduction in the budget deficit (PSBR) or an increase in the budget surplus (PSDR).) For those who believe that the tax cuts of 1987 and 1988 contributed significantly to the overheating of the economy, a reversal of those cuts would appear to be an appropriate solution. However, for a Conservative Chancellor to resort to such a policy would imply that fiscal policy during 1987 and 1988 had been damaging. It would also call into question the whole Conservative programme of income tax cuts, which began in 1979 as part of the **supply side** policies designed to increase incentives.

Downward movements of the exchange rate have, at various times, been used to reduce current account deficits. However, the success of

John Major, Chancellor of the Exchequer (1989–90). Appointed Prime Minister in November 1990

such policies has been varied and, in any case, a significant depreciation of sterling would increase inflationary pressures, causing further problems. To the extent that the current account deficit reflects structural problems in the British economy (see Sources 1.1 and 1.2, pages 162–7), exchange rate adjustments would be inappropriate anyway.

The Conservative government has relied on interest rates to control the demand for credit. Some critics have advocated the reintroduction of credit controls. *Liberalisation* and *deregulation* of the economy have been principal aims of Thatcherism as part of free market philosophy. One of the first measures adopted by the Conservative government in 1979 was to abolish **exchange controls**, which regulated the flow of money across national borders. Other measures have been introduced by the government subsequently with the same aim of liberalisation. Proposals to return to a system of credit control therefore run counter to Thatcherism. Conservatives argue that, especially in an era of deregulated financial markets, it would be very easy to circumvent controls.

During its time in office the government has abolished hire purchase controls, which affected the demand for credit, and various controls on the supply of credit. Britain is the only EC country, with the exception of Luxembourg, which no longer has 'minimum reserve requirements' as part of its monetary policy armoury. The details of such a scheme lie beyond the scope of this book, but it requires financial institutions to place a designated proportion of deposits with the central bank (Bank of England) so that the central bank can influence monetary policy. Supporters claim that its reintroduction would avoid the need for such large fluctuations in the level of interest rates.

Certainly if moves towards European Monetary Union (EMU) and the creation of a European Central Bank take place, it will be necessary to reconcile the different systems of monetary control in various EC countries.

A EUROPEAN FUTURE?

Debate about Britain's future in Europe came increasingly to the fore during 1989. The Delors' Report on European Economic and Monetary Union, produced in April 1989, envisaged that:

> the creation of a single currency area would add to the potential benefits of an enlarged economic area because it would remove intra-Community exchange rate uncertainties and reduce transaction costs, eliminate exchange rate variability and reduce the susceptibility of the Community to external shocks.

It proposed a three stage transition to economic and monetary union. During the first stage, efforts would be made to achieve greater convergence of economic performance by means of greater co-ordination of economic and monetary policy. It was also envisaged that all EC countries would become members of the Exchange Rate Mechanism (ERM) during this period of time. During the second stage of the Delors' Plan, moves towards a common monetary policy would be accelerated. This would be associated with moves towards a European Central Bank and a narrowing of the margins of fluctuation allowed in the ERM. The final stage would require a commitment to permanently fixed exchange rates. At this point the European Community would be responsible for monetary policy and exchange rate policy (with respect to non-EC countries). Rules governing national budgets would also be formulated.

Such moves were opposed by Mrs Thatcher, although a compromise was reached at the Madrid Summit in June 1989. She agreed to the joint declaration committing the European Community to 'progressively achieve economic and monetary union' and to the implementation of the first stage of the Delors' Plan beginning in July 1990. In addition the conditions for Britain's entry into the ERM – to be known subsequently as the 'Madrid conditions' were laid down, albeit in rather vague terms. A reduction in Britain's rate of inflation was seen as a pre-requisite for entry, but the completion of the single European market and the abolition of exchange controls were also required.

Divisions within the Conservative party, about Europe in general and the ERM in particular, continued to appear. Allied to these were disagreements over exchange rate policy, as described above (see Focus on page 155 and Figure 12.5).

Although Mr Lawson's policy of shadowing the Deutsch Mark was over-ruled by both market forces and Mrs Thatcher in April 1988, the differing emphasis of policy between the Prime Minister and the Chancellor continued and was brought to a head by Mrs Thatcher's appointment of Sir Alan Walters as her full-time economic adviser in May 1989. Sir Alan, who had previously advised Mrs Thatcher between 1981 and 1983, was an ardent opponent of the EMS and of any attempts to shadow the Deutsch Mark.

The Chancellor resigned in October 1989 arguing that 'the successful conduct of economic policy is possible only if there is – and is seen to be – full agreement between the Prime Minister and Chancellor of the Exchequer'. In the sphere of exchange rate policy this was clearly not so. Subsequently in an interview with Mr Brian Walden on LWT (5 November 1989), Mr Lawson argued:

> I believe that the art of a successful economic policy is to have the greatest possible degree of market freedom within an over-arching and overall financial discipline, a framework of financial discipline to bear down on inflation. And the question then is where does the exchange rate fit in, is it part of the market freedom, let it go where it will, wherever the markets are going to push it; or should it be, as I believe and I don't think Alan Walters does, part of the financial discipline to bear down on inflation?

The resignation of Mr Lawson followed shortly after the move of Sir Geoffrey Howe in a cabinet reshuffle in July 1989 from his position as Foreign Secretary to that of Deputy Prime Minister. Thus Mrs Thatcher's two principal ministers involved with European issues – both significantly more pro-European than she – were replaced within a short period.

When Mr Lawson's successor as Chancellor, Mr John Major, announced that Britain was to join the ERM on 8 October 1990, he was accused of taking a 'political decision' since the 'Madrid conditions' had yet to be met – in particular, the UK inflation rate was still greater than the EC average. Critics pointed out that, unless UK inflation fell rapidly, competitiveness of UK firms would deteriorate, which would further contribute to the current account deficit. The value of sterling was fixed at a central rate of DM 2.95, but was allowed a fluctuation band of 6 per cent, compared with the narrower 2.25 per cent band used by most other EC currencies. Entry into the ERM was accompanied by a reduction in interest rates. Bank base rates were cut from 15 per cent – a level maintained for the previous twelve months – to 14 per cent.

Further divisions both between Britain and her European partners and, subsequently, within the Conservative party were witnessed at the European Summit in Rome in October 1990, shortly after Britain had joined the ERM. The EC leaders set January 1994 as the starting date for Stage Two of the Delors' Plan, and envisaged further moves beyond that towards Stage Three and a single currency. Mrs Thatcher attacked such moves with great vehemence claiming that other European leaders were living in 'cloud cuckoo land'.

On 1 November 1990. Sir Geoffrey Howe resigned from the cabinet, blaming both the substance and style of Mrs Thatcher's views on Europe, especially in the aftermath of the Rome Summit. The strong attack by Sir Geoffrey, previously regarded as a loyal supporter of the Prime Minister, despite some differences of view, was a major contributory factor leading to the decision of Mr Michael Heseltine to stand against Mrs Thatcher for the leadership of the Conservative party.

Despite gaining more Conservative MPs' votes than Michael Heseltine in the first round of the election, Margaret Thatcher failed to achieve the margin of victory required in the first ballot (15 per cent more than any other candidate). Faced then with an apparent increase in support for Michael Heseltine and the prospect of defeat in the second ballot, Margaret Thatcher resigned as Prime Minister and Leader of the Conservative party on 22 November. This allowed other cabinet ministers – previously prevented from standing out of loyalty to the Prime Minister – to contest the leadership. The names of Douglas Hurd (Foreign Secretary) and John Major (Chancellor of the Exchequer) were added to that of Michael Heseltine for the second round of the ballot. On 27 November 1990 John Major was elected Leader of the Conservative party and, the following day, became Prime Minister.

COMMENT

During the 1980s, the Conservative government under Margaret Thatcher presided over fundamental changes in the British economy. It sought to raise incentives and to increase competition and consumer choice. At the same time, different attitudes to business and industry have been cultivated by rekindling the profit motive in an attempt to generate an enterprise culture and popular capitalism. The government has stressed the importance of market forces and has adopted a non-interventionist approach to the running of the economy. It has reduced the role of the state and has attempted to introduce a new realism into industrial relations.

Whether the resignation of Margaret Thatcher after $11\frac{1}{2}$ years as Prime Minister marks the end of Thatcherism, or whether its main features will endure, has yet to be assessed.

Essay and source-based questions

I: DE-INDUSTRIALISATION OR INDUSTRIAL REVIVAL?

Essay questions

1 'The production of North Sea oil was bound to cause problems for UK manufacturing industry'. Discuss.

2 Would the adoption of an 'Industrial Strategy' benefit manufacturing industry in the UK?

3 Outline the reasons why parts of manufacturing industry collapsed between 1979 and 1981.

4 'The industrial recovery during the 1980s is a tribute to the Conservative government's supply side policies'. Discuss.

5 'The industrial recovery during the 1980s will not be sustained, and must be seen in the light of the massive loss of capacity during the period 1979–81'. Discuss.

Source 1.1 Producers fail to meet demands of consumers

The deterioration in Britain's trade position with the rest of the world is seen, at one extreme, as a serious structural problem; at the other, as benign and self-correcting. Neither policymakers nor economists can agree on the cause. FT correspondents report on what lies behind the deficit.

1 THERE is no agreement among policymakers and economists about the seriousness of Britain's current account deficit. At one extreme, Professor Wynne Godley and Dr Ken Coutts of Cambridge University regard the deficit as 'a strategic predicament of staggering magnitude.'

5 At the other, Mr Nigel Lawson, the Chancellor, argues that the trade shortfall is not, in itself, a cause for concern. In so far as it reflects imports of capital goods, it is benign and self-correcting; in so far as it reflects excessive growth of domestic demand, it can be curbed by higher interest rates. Inflation remains the real dragon: as and when this is squeezed out of the system, the balance of payments pressures
10 will ease.

Critics note that every significant expansion of domestic demand in the post-war era has led to a balance of payments crisis followed by fiscal and monetary austerity. The fact that an expansion of demand sufficient to get unemployment below 2m has

UK current account as a percentage of GDP

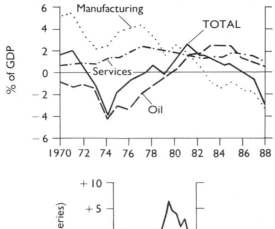

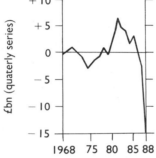

UK current account balance

led to a current account deficit running at an annual rate of £20bn, or 4 per cent of
15   gross domestic product, is regarded as proof that a decade of Thatcher government
has not succeeded in radically improving the supply side of Britain's economy.

Central to the Treasury argument is the claim that this deficit is quite unlike its
predecessors. In the first place, it is not accompanied by a budget deficit; it therefore
reflects the rational decisions of private entrepreneurs and consumers rather than
20   the profligacy of the public sector.

Moreover, the deficit has arisen during an era of capital mobility comparable only
to the pre-1914 Gold Standard years. In such an environment, there is no reason
why countries should not borrow abroad in order to bridge a temporary shortfall of
domestic savings, with the increase in overseas liabilities being more than offset by
25   the foreign assets accumulated during the years of North Sea plenty.

Many economists regard the existence of a budget surplus as of dubious
significance. It has no bearing on Britain's ability to find the resources to service
overseas debts. North Sea assets likewise provide little comfort because they could
not be liquidated quickly in the event of a withdrawal of the short-term 'hot money'
30   flows that are keeping sterling afloat.

In any case, the net foreign asset position will rapidly deteriorate if the current
account deficit is not brought under control.

Capital is certainly far more mobile today than in the 1960s or 1970s. But the
analogy with the Gold Standard years is somewhat forced. Exchange rates are not, as
35   then, irrevocably fixed. And the countries relying on the overseas capital were

typically in an early stage of development. Borrowing made sense for them because they could expect to earn a higher return on capital than more advanced economies and thus repay debts with relative ease.

Britain's present deficit does not appear to fall into this category. First, the
40   shortfall on capital goods is a relatively small portion of the total deficit.

Most of the overseas borrowing has been used to finance consumption. Secondly, the current account deficit is not offset by a healthy long-term capital account – as it would be if the trade shortfall primarily reflected the confidence of overseas investors.

45   Some companies, such as Nissan, have invested heavily in the UK. But Dr Mica Panic, a former chief economist at the National Economic Development Office, points out that the net deficit on long-term foreign investment was equivalent to 2.8 per cent of GDP in 1988.

The balance of payments is thus being propped up by short-term inflows attracted
50   by exceptionally high UK interest rates. That makes Britain vulnerable to sudden changes of sentiment in the financial markets.

But what of Mr Lawson's claim that the deficit is mainly a reflection of a temporary surge in domestic demand? Critics certainly do not accept that if demand is curbed, the UK's problems will be solved. Writing recently in Political Quarterly,
55   Professor Godley and Dr Coutts drew attention to the prolonged deterioration in the trading performance of manufacturing industry. Since 1963, imports of manufactures as a share of gross domestic product have risen at a trend rate of 6 per cent a year. But exports of manufactures as a share of GDP have grown at only 2 per cent.

For many years, the long-term deterioration in manufacturing trade was masked
60   by the buoyancy of other sectors.

Between 1976 and 1985, the oil balance improved by the equivalent of 6½ per cent of GDP.

But in the late 1980s there has been nothing to compensate for industrial weakness: a rising shortfall on manufacturing trade has translated directly into a
65   rising current account deficit.

In terms of production and investment, manufacturing industry has staged a partial recovery since the early 1980s. Profitability is much improved. The problem, argues Dr John Wells, another Cambridge economist, is that manufacturing has not grown significantly faster than the economy as a whole. As a result, the big loss in
70   manufacturing's share of output sustained during the 1979/81 recession has not been made good.

On this view, a significant portion of Britain's trade deficit is deeply structural in character.

It reflects the fact that the composition of output in the economy bears little
75   resemblance to that of demand. In the last decade, production and investment have become heavily skewed towards non-traded goods, yet consumers' appetite for traded goods – especially foreign manufactures – has grown ever more intense.

In the mid-1980s, ministers argued that trade in services would compensate for manufacturing's weakness. But this has not happened.
80   International comparisons appear to support the view that the UK's industrial base is too small for comfort. Manufacturing accounts for under 22 per cent of GDP in Britain compared with 29 per cent and 33 per cent respectively in Japan and West Germany, two countries with very strong current accounts.

In the immediate post-war decades, Britain solved its trade problems partly by

85 growing more slowly than most other advanced economies. This curbed demand for imports.

During the 1980s, the Thatcher Government has striven to reverse the UK's relative decline. But the attempt to keep pace with stronger economies such as West Germany and Japan seems only to have exposed the underlying weakness of
90 the traded goods sector.

Looked at this way, the trade deficit is alarming not because it cannot be reduced (if necessary by a sharp recession) but because it suggests that the rate of growth compatible with balance of payments equilibrium in the longer term is very much slower than that enjoyed in the recent past.

95 Prof Godley and Dr Coutts argued that sustained growth of even 2.5 per cent a year (if permitted by financial markets) would result in a further rapid deterioration in the current account deficit, perhaps to £40bn or £50bn a year. These may look absurd numbers. But in 1986, Prof Godley correctly predicted a £20bn deficit by the end of the 1980s.

100 In the short-term, most economists accept that a period of very subdued growth, if not recession, will be necessary to bring the living standards of the British people into line with their capacity to export goods and services.

But there is much less agreement about the longer term outlook.

To be optimistic you have to believe that deregulation and liberalisation in the
105 1980s have strengthened the UK's supply side even if the benefits are temporarily obscured by macroeconomic mistakes. You have to argue that the trade deficit reflects short rather than long term trends. You have to take the view that the relative size of a country's manufacturing base is not significant.

Pessimists will beg to differ on all three points.

Michael Prowse
Financial Times, *12 October 1989*

1 'In so far as it (ie the current account deficit) reflects imports of capital goods, it is benign and self-correcting; in so far as it represents excessive growth of domestic demand, it can be curbed by higher interest rates' (lines 6–8). Explain.

2 Critics point to the balance of payments position to refute Conservative claims that 'supply side' (lines 11–16) measures have succeeded. Explain.

3 'The current account deficit . . . is not accompanied by a budget deficit; it therefore reflects the rational decisions of private entrepreneurs and consumers rather than the profligacy of the public sector' (lines 18–20). Comment.

4 'There is no reason why countries should not borrow abroad in order to bridge a temporary shortfall of domestic savings' (lines 22–4). Comment.

5 What are the consequences if a current account deficit is financed by short-term capital inflows, attracted by high interest rates, rather than by long-term foreign investment?

6 What is 'the prolonged deterioration in the trading performance of manufacturing industry' referred to by Professor Godley and Dr Coutts (lines 55–6)?

7 Why was this 'long-term deterioration' (line 59) masked for a time?

8 'A significant portion of Britain's trade deficit is deeply structural in character' (lines 72–3). Explain.

9 'Production and investment have become heavily skewed towards non-traded goods, yet consumers' appetite for traded goods – especially foreign manufactures – has grown ever more intense' (lines 75–7). Explain.

10 Services have not managed to 'compensate for manufacturing's weakness' (lines 78–9). Why?

11 'The rate of growth compatible with balance of payments equilibrium in the longer term is very much slower than that enjoyed in the recent past' (lines 92–4). Explain.

12 What assumptions are necessary if one is to be optimistic about the long-term future of the British economy (lines 104–8)?

Source 1.2: Industry still lagging says NEDC chief

1   CONCERN that British industry still suffers from poor quality, worse delivery and burgeoning wage demands – despite more than a decade of a Government bent on fostering the 'enterprise culture' – surfaced at yesterday's meeting of the National Economic Development Council.

5   The round table forum, which brings together government, industry and the trade unions, was discussing a paper, presented by Mr Walter Eltis, NEDC director general, on the deterioration in the country's trade performance.

The Government is hopeful that its counter-inflationary policy will narrow the current account deficit, which measures trade in goods and services, by curbing
10 demand for imports, while British firms look for more business abroad. The deficit was a record £20.8 billion last year.

Mr John Banham, director general of the Confederation of British Industry, told the meeting that the key to improved performance was sustained investment.

The paper acknowledged that exports, excluding oil, had grown by more than 10
15 per cent over the last year – outstripping import growth. But the improvement in exports started from a low base.

The collapse of Britain's traditional surplus on services, such as banking, insurance, shipping and travel, was described as 'extremely worrying', making improved trade in manufactured goods 'crucial.'

20 But Mr Eltis identified unfavourable developments on the wage front which had slowed the gains in productivity in manufacturing and brought unit wage cost growth to an annual rate of more than 6 per cent, compared with less than 3 per cent for leading competitors abroad.

If unit wage costs continue to grow at the current pace in Britain, with an
25 unchanged exchange rate, industry is seen as becoming gradually less competitive, hampering the 'urgently needed' switch from home to export markets.

Mr Nicholas Ridley, the Trade Secretary, chairing the session, observed that all participants agreed it was worrying that unit costs were growing faster than those of the competition.

30 The paper looked at five sectors of industry that accounted for £15 billion of last

year's trade gap – engineering, electronics, construction, clothing and knitting, and tourism and leisure.

While high technology sectors showed the fastest growth and relatively high value-added per worker, other measures revealed the old problem of poor quality.

35 In terms of value-added per tonne, which should indicate the proportion of sophisticated gadgetry in a product, machine tools, pumps and farm machinery scored relatively badly against the leading industrial economies.

The sectoral studies showed up a discrepancy in several industries between the specified quality a product ought to have and the actual quality delivered, recalling

40 the time when British industry became virtually synonymous with bad quality and still worse delivery.

The retail sector, which has done much to raise quality on the home market, was praised in the report for serving consumers well.

But it had left British suppliers more vulnerable in certain industries to

45 international competition than producers in countries which are not 'nations of shopkeepers.'

Mr Robin Leigh-Pemberton, Governor of the Bank of England, shared the concern about the retail sector's effect in sucking in imports. The trade gap, he said, was, however, basically an issue of 'excessive demand.'

50 Drawing attention to the international success of Britain's pharmaceutical, aerospace and chemicals industries, he said that the criterion for manufacturing was achieving 'world class.'

Colin Narbrough
The Times, *5 April 1990*

1 What do you understand by the 'enterprise culture' (line 3)?

2 Explain why 'exports, excluding oil, had grown by more than 10 per cent (in 1989) outstripping import growth' (lines 14–15).

3 What are the implications of the 'collapse of Britain's traditional surplus on services' (lines 17–18).

4 (a) Define 'unit wage costs' (line 24).
   (b) What are the consequences for British industry if 'unit wage costs' rise more quickly than in competitor countries (lines 24–6)?

5 Outline the possible ways in which a 'switch from home to export markets' (line 26) may occur.

6 What non-price factors are identified as contributory to a lack of competitiveness (lines 38–41)?

7 Explain why the retail sector has facilitated the rise of imports in the UK (lines 42–8).

8 The Governor of the Bank of England claimed that that current account deficit was an issue of 'excessive demand' (line 49). Explain this and comment on the view that deeper structural factors account for the deficit.

2: COMPETITION POLICY

Essay questions

1 Should the effect on competition be the only criterion used when deciding whether to allow a takeover to proceed?

2 'The completion of the single market in 1992 makes traditional national takeover regulations irrelevant.' Discuss.

3 Britain's liberal capital laws make it relatively easy for foreign companies to acquire British ones, whereas in some countries the acquisition of foreign companies by British ones is more difficult. Is this lack of 'reciprocity' a cause for concern?

4 'It is hard to see positive benefits from conglomerate mergers, but as they do not adversely affect competition, they should be allowed to proceed.' Discuss.

5 Why has the 'urge to conglomerate' been replaced with moves 'back to the core'?

Source 2.1: Takeovers and 1992

AS BARRIERS to the free movement of goods, capital and labour come tumbling down all over Europe thanks to the 1992 programme, the European market in corporate control has an increasingly anomalous look about it. To date it has been touched only marginally by the tide of liberalisation that is sweeping across the
5 Community. It remains diverse in the extreme. And as a new report by Coopers & Lybrand for Britain's Department of Trade underlines, the obstacles to takeovers in the most member countries of the Community are far greater than in Britain.

That is an understandable worry for directors of quoted British companies who know that Britain accounts for nearly three quarters of all Community takeover
10 activity and remains more open to bids by foreign predators than any other member state. For its part the British Government is anxious to imprint its own enthusiasm for open and efficient markets on the European Commission's programme to remove obstacles to takeovers in Europe. Yet it is questionable whether that constitutes a realistic objective, given fundamental differences of philosophy on the
15 means and ends of corporate activity.

In Britain management is accountable to shareholders; and while directors have been statutorily obliged since the 1970s to take into account employees' interests, their main preoccupation is with increasing earnings and assets per share. In contrast, many continental European countries regard the management's first duty as being to
20 the business, the employees and the company's bankers.

Contested bids

The conflict between the two views is highlighted by opposing standpoints on the value of contested bids. The British regard takeovers as the ultimate discipline over bad management. For the West Germans, whose system of two-tier boards and
25 limited equity voting rights militates against takeovers, predatory bids are inimical to

two key ingredients of their post-war industrial success: management's ability to take the long-term view and harmonious labour relations. And the German banks can provide a more timely discipline than Anglo-Saxon markets – witness the recent departure of the chairman of Daimler Benz at the behest of Deutsche Bank.

30   There is nothing to suggest that the Anglo-Saxon way of holding management to account is inherently superior and plenty of circumstantial evidence that points in the opposite direction. Nor are takeovers likely to play an overwhelmingly important role in West Germany, France and Italy in the foreseeable future given that these countries' equity market capitalisations amount to a relatively small per

35   cent of GDP. In most Community countries family control remains overwhelmingly important and habits of secrecy die hard.

Extreme case

Within Europe, as Coopers & Lybrand point out, Britain is the extreme case. It follows that there are limits to the Government's ability to reshape the European

40   market in corporate control in an Anglo-Saxon mould. There are anyway plenty of worthwhile economic gains to be had from improved information on corporate performance and ownership, which would be of mutual benefit to all member states. These deserve the highest priority. And as much emphasis should be placed on securing the implementation of existing directives on accountancy and disclosure as

45   on measures for the future.

Nor is it clear that Britain's interest lies exclusively in opening up Europe to a British corporate invasion. Against a background of weaker sterling, the London merchant banking fraternity's powerful urge to sell off the British quoted corporate sector to foreigners has some temporary merit. For inward investment provides

50   stable long-term financing for a current account deficit now running at around £20bn a year; encouraging even more outward investment would, in the short term, be singularly inept from a macroeconomic point of view.

At a more fundamental level recent experience in the US suggests that the political consequences of an international market in corporate control are very

55   difficult to manage. In the circumstances it may be no bad thing if Europe's market in corporate control is built brick by brick. Most continental Europeans would not have it any other way.

(Leading article)
Financial Times, *28 November 1989*

I   Explain the meaning of '. . . the tide of liberalisation that is sweeping across the Community' (lines 4–5).

2   Does it matter that Britain is 'more open to bids by foreign predators than any other member state' of the EC (lines 10–11)?

3   Outline the essential differences between the British attitude to 'means and ends of corporate activity' (line 15) and that displayed in many other European countries.

4   Contrast the differing British and West German approaches to dealing with bad management (lines 22–32).

5   Why is it claimed that the German system allows a company to take a 'long-term view', rather than engaging in 'short-termism' (lines 26–9)?.

6 Explain '... these countries' equity market capitalisations amount to a relatively small per cent of GDP' (lines 34–5). How is this likely to affect takeover activity?

7 Why does the 'urge to sell off the British quoted corporate sector to foreigners have some temporary merit' (lines 48–9)? Explain. In particular, comment on why this benefit may be only temporary.

Source 2.2: Brewers may have to sell quarter of Britain's pubs

MORE THAN a quarter of Britain's 80,000 pubs may have to be sold over the next three years under Monopolies and Mergers Commission recommendations yesterday.

In a series of recommendations which would revolutionise the brewing industry,
5 the commission said no brewer should own more than 2,000 pubs and licensed restaurants. Britain's biggest brewer, Bass, owns about 7,300.

The divestment of assets is by far the biggest the commission has recommended in any sector. The report, the result of a 2½-year inquiry, shocked the industry. The Brewers Society called it 'a charter for chaos' which would destroy the traditional
10 British pub.

The commission has decided against urging complete abolition of the tied house system. This means smaller regional brewers, none of which has more than 2,000 pubs, would not be affected.

Lord Young, Trade and Industry Secretary, said he was 'minded' to implement the
15 recommendations, which he said could lead to the sale of 82,000 pubs over three years.

There would have to be talks with the European Commission on other aspects of the report, notably its recommendation for an end to brewers giving free houses loans which depend on the free houses stocking the brewer's products.
20 In 1984, the EC made such loan conditions exempt from a ban on exclusive

Beer sales and market share in 1985

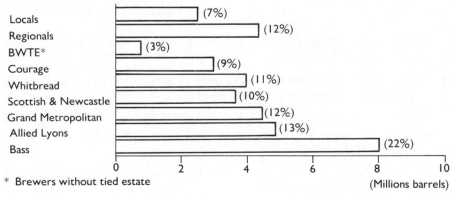

* Brewers without tied estate

(Millions barrels)

Source: MMC

purchasing agreements. The Brewers Society yesterday declined to say whether it would complain to Brussels.

Brewing shares, which fell following the Monopolies Commission decision yesterday not to allow Elders IXL to go ahead with its bid for Scottish and
25 Newcastle, largely recovered after the second report was published.

The City believes the report could lead to some brewers opting to become retailers – notably Allied Lyons, Grand Metroplitan and Whitbread – with others, such as Courage, getting rid of their pubs and concentrating on brewing.

Lord Young said the MMC had found that there was a complex monopoly on the
30 supply of beer. This means a dominant group in the industry has practices which could restrict competition.

He said: 'The MMC conclude that this complex monopoly restricts competition at all levels, against the public interest.'

Main points

35 • No brewer to own more than 2,000 on-licensed premises, including pubs and restaurants.

• Tied tenants to be allowed to sell 'guest' draught beers brewed by companies other than the pub's owners.

• Tied tenants also to be free to buy low alcohol beers, spirits, wines, cider, and
40 soft drinks from the most competitive suppliers.

• No new loan ties, which oblige owners of 'free houses' to sell one brewer's products. It is common for brewers to offer low interest loans provided owners agree to stock their drinks.

• Protection and security of tenure for tied tenants under the Landlord and Tenant
45 Act.

• Brewers to publish and adhere to wholesale price lists.

Findings

• The six leading brewers – Bass, Whitbread, Allied, Scottish & Newcastle, Grand Metropolitan and Courage – produce 75 per cent of the beer sold in Britain, and
50 own 75 per cent of tied houses.

• The relatively high price of lager is not justified by production costs – in some cases lower than those for ale.

Pub and restaurant ownership

	Number of properties	Number to be divested
Allied	6,600	4,600
Bass	7,300	5,300
Courage	5,100	3,100
Grand Metropolitan	6,100	4,100
Scottish & Newcastle	2,300	300
Whitbread	6,500	4,500
Total	33,900	21,900

Source: MMC

- Excessive regional variation in wholesale prices.
- Consumer choice is often restricted, principally because brewers do not allow
55 other manufacturers' beers in their outlets.
- Limited access to pubs and restaurants for independent brewers.
- Beer prices rose 15 per cent in real terms 1979–87, on top of inflation and excluding VAT and duty.

Lisa Wood
Financial Times, *22 March 1989*

1 Explain the following terms:
   (a) 'divestment of assets' (line 7);
   (b) 'the tied house system' (lines 11–12);
   (c) 'free house' (line 18);
   (d) 'loan tie' (line 41);
   (e) 'in real terms' (line 57).

2 Explain the meaning of the phrase: 'a complex monopoly in the supply of beer' (lines 29–30).

3 The brewing industry may be described as a 'vertically integrated industry'.
   (a) Explain this term.
   (b) Describe how the brewers (producers) maintain influence and control over pubs (retailers).
   (c) Give an example of another industry which is characterised by 'vertical integration'.

4 (a) Explain the term 'oligopolistic pricing'.
   (b) Why is lager more expensive than beer?
   (c) What other evidence is there to support the view that 'oligopolistic pricing' exists in brewing.

Postscript
After heavy lobbing by the brewers, the government produced a compromise plan, which did not require enforced divestment or the elimination of 'loan ties'. Critics saw this as a climbdown.

3: PRIVATISATION

Essay questions

1 Why has it proved to be so difficult to assess the performance of nationalised industries?

2 'The Conservative government's privatisation programme has been more concerned with buying votes and raising revenue for the Exchequer than it has been with increasing competition and choice.' Discuss.

3 If the 'market structure' were to be more important than the 'ownership' (ie

public or private) of a company, what would be the implications for privatisation?

4 'The privatisation of "natural monopolies" can never be justified.' Discuss.

5 'The Conservative government's privatisation programme has been a great success.' Discuss.

6 'The Conservative government's privatisation programme has confirmed that industry is always most efficiently and effectively driven by the power of market forces.' Discuss.

Source 3: The Mother of Privatisation

The sell-off of Britain's state industries is becoming a turn-off. Time to return to first principles

IT WAS once the popular mainspring of Thatcherism, but privatisation now threatens to become a political liability. This change has nothing to do with a new blast from the Labour party at the fees paid to the bankers and ad men who have arranged the sale of state industries. Public unease about privatisation has been
5 growing for months, and needs no encouragement from Labour. Few people are persuaded that water and electricity should be sold, and the extravagant efforts of the advertising industry have served only to reinforce their doubts.

This is a pity. Privatisation has been a powerful force for good in Margaret Thatcher's Britain. The sale since 1979 of 54 state-owned companies into the private
10 sector has been a remarkable feat of political will, in the face of hostile vested interests. If you want to find its monument, look at the new dynamism of companies like Rolls-Royce, British Steel and British Airways. Or the increase in the number of share-owners (2m in 1979, 12m now) in Britain. Or the sea-change in public attitudes to a state sector cut by 40% in ten years.
15 The list of credits reflects a range of motives, because the government's reasons for privatising have kept changing. In the beginning ministers stressed efficiency and the tax-cutting merits of a smaller public sector. The sheer scale and success of the British Telecom sale in 1984 then encouraged them to take a shorter-term, more voter-driven view. So while the money the Treasury raises from privatising has
20 remained a constant attraction, Sid has become the star: give the small shareholder preference, guarantee him an immediate capital gain, and you will turn him against any political party that might seek to renationalise 'his' companies.

Over to the regulators
This I-love-Sid approach is at the root of the government's current problems over
25 water and electricity. As the political goals have loomed larger, ministers have come to see privatisation as an end in itself. In fact, it is only one means to a different end: lower prices and better products for the consumer. This confusion hardly mattered so long as the targets of privatisation were operating in competive markets – like British Steel and Jaguar, which should never have been in the public sector in the first
30 place. But as the sale programme has rolled on, it has swept up natural monopolies.
For such companies, it does indeed matter that privatisation should be seen as a method, not a goal. There are often other ways to improve the efficiency of public utilities: better regulation by an independent agency, say, or the franchising of

separable activities to different private managers. The rush to privatise has ruled out
35 such alternatives by default – and has risked the kind of public unease now stirred up
by the water and electricity sales.

Cues for concern have been many and various. The water sale, always pushing
uphill against the public's fond belief that water is as free as rain, raised awkward
questions about past mismanagement by heralding a big jump in the prices charged
40 for water. The electricity sale has more logic, and the merit of boldness. But the
government queered its own pitch by trying to foist nuclear power upon El-Sid.
Worse, it plunged into a complex restructuring with no firm ideas about who should
be the ultimate risk-takers in the business.

Though skilful merchant banking may still steer these two sales through, the
45 damage done to the privatisation idea will remain. To fulfil past promises and leave
the way open for more sell-offs in future, the government must rescue the idea's
credibility by ensuring one thing: the sold-off companies must be regulated in such a
way that they serve their customers better than public ownership did in the past.
State ownership failed mainly for lack of a dependable relationship between
50 government and management, a relationship devised to set the consumers' interest
above all else. Unless that fickleness can be avoided, tomorrow's regulators will be
no less capricious than yesterday's civil servants.

So far, the regulators of the privatised utilities have done a better job than
ministers had any right to expect. But this success owes more to the individuals
55 concerned than to any principles laid down in the deeds of sale. Water and
electricity will be far harder to regulate than telecommunications, where competitive pressures set standards. If the government must stick to its present timetable,
let investors know they are buying a pig in a poke: the regulatory framework that
consumers deserve has yet to be properly devised.

The Economist, *16 September 1989*

1 Why is it claimed that 'Privatisation has been a powerful force for good'
(line 8)?

2 At the start of the privatisation programme, 'ministers stressed efficiency
and the tax cutting merits of a smaller public sector' (lines 16–17). Explain.

3 Why did the government adopt a 'shorter-term, more voter-driven view'
(lines 18–19)? Why might purchases of shares in privatised companies give
the small shareholder a distorted view of the stock market?

4 What are the consequences if the government regards 'privatisation as an
end in itself' (line 26)?

5 What is a 'natural monopoly' (line 30)?

6 'There are often other ways to improve the efficiency of public utilities:
better regulation by an independent agency, say, or the franchising of
separable activities to different private managers' (lines 32–4). Explain.
Would such reforms be likely to succeed if the company remained in the
public sector?

7 'The sold-off companies must be regulated in such a way that they serve the

customers better than public ownership did in the past' (lines 00–00). Explain. How should this be achieved?

8 Why will it be far harder to regulate water and electricity than telecommunications (lines 55–7)?

4: AN INDUSTRIAL CASE STUDY – THE MOTOR INDUSTRY

Essay questions

1 Japanese investment to establish car plants in the UK has been welcomed. Is this an appropriate response?

2 The privatisation of Rover may be viewed as the greatest success of the government's privatisation programme. Discuss.

3 Should the European Community welcome completely free trade in cars?

Source 4.1: Japanese cars in the EC

THE EUROPEAN Community is getting into a deep muddle over how to treat Japanese car sales after 1992. Unless it thinks the issues through much more clearly, it risks taking decisions which will damage Europe's economy and the health of its motor manufacturers, while handing a gift to the Japanese industry.

5   The starting-point of the EC's deliberations is the national limits on Japanese car imports in force in Britain, France, Italy, Portugal and Spain. The European Commission has concluded that these will have to be eliminated by 1992, since they are inconsistent with plans for a single European market. The argument centres on what, if anything, should replace them.

10   The Commission agreed this week on a proposal to negotiate with Japan an EC-wide voluntary restraint arrangement (VRA) as a 'transitional' step on the way to a completely open market. Exactly how such restraints would work, their duration and the level of import ceilings have not been spelled out. Nor has Brussels specified how it proposes to treat cars assembled at Japanese plants in the EC,

15   though it has rejected on legal grounds French and Italian demands that they be counted as European products only if they met a mandatory local content requirement. Apparently unable to resolve these issues, the commission has tossed them into the lap of the Council of Ministers.

Import quotas

20   The Council needs to think hard about its objectives. Quite apart from the widely-observed tendency of temporary VRAs to become permanent import quotas, they would almost certainly benefit Japanese exporters as much as – if not, indeed, more than – European carmakers. In the US, where Japanese car imports have been subject to VRAs since the early 1980s, they have allowed Japanese

25   manufacturers to fatten their margins substantially at the expense of American consumers. VRAs also induce Japanese companies to concentrate on exporting top-of-the range models, on which they make more money than on volume cars. Hence, BMW, Mercedes-Benz and Jaguar would be likely to pay the price for any relief provided to Fiat or Renault.

30   Even that relief would probably be short-lived, since it is hard to see how the EC
could legally prevent Japanese manufacturers from boosting production at European
plants. Nissan is already assembling cars in the UK, and Honda and Toyota also plan
to build plants there. Transitional import restraints would also enable Japanese
companies to establish distribution and service networks in currently protected EC
35   markets in a much more orderly manner than if national restrictions were lifted
immediately.

Increased protection
The biggest mistake the EC could make would be to seek restraints which limited
40   Japanese carmakers rigidly to their current 9.5 per cent share of the Community
market. That would greatly increase protection of EC carmakers. At present, the
anti-competitive effects of import restrictions in countries such as France are offset
by the impact of Japanese exports to open markets such as West Germany. As a
consequence, German manufacturers are obliged to price exports to France at the
45   same level as in their home market, where they face the disciplines of Japanese
competition. For German companies to do otherwise would expose them to
under-cutting by parallel imports.
        A tight Community-wide VRA would remove these disciplines and enable
European carmakers to raise prices with impunity. That would amount to sanction-
50   ing an EC motor industry cartel, whose members would have little incentive to take
the tough actions needed to raise their efficiency and competitiveness to world-class
standards.
        Much the best course for the Community is to take no action on Japanese car
imports and to concentrate on removing all its internal trade barriers by 1992.
55   Purely national restrictions on imports from outside the EC would then become
unenforceable, because they could be evaded by transhipments from elsewhere in
the single market.

(*Leading article*)
Financial Times, *8 December 1989*

I   Why are the Voluntary Restraint Arrangements (VRA)* in force in Britain
and several other EC countries 'inconsistent with plans for a single
European market' (line 11)?

2   Why is there a 'tendency for temporary VRAs to become permanent import
quotas' (lines 21–2)?

3   How do VRAs 'benefit Japanese car exporters' (line 22)?

4   How could Japanese car firms overcome a VRA if a temporary arrangement
became permanent (lines 30–3)?

5   Why would a 'tight Community-wide VRA' amount to 'sanctioning an EC
motor industry cartel' (lines 47–9)?

*   *A Voluntary Restraint Arrangement* (VRA) has been referred to as a
Voluntary Export Restraint (VER) in the text.

5/6: A WELFARE STATE OR DEPENDENCY CULTURE? POVERTY IN THE MIDST OF PLENTY?

Essay questions

1 The Welfare State has resulted in a 'dependency culture'. Discuss.

2 Increased 'targeting' of welfare benefits is essential. Discuss.

3 Poverty in the 'old absolute sense of hunger and want' has been eliminated in the UK. Discuss.

4 If poverty is measured in terms of 'relative deprivation', then poverty will always exist. Discuss.

5 Conservative policies during the 1980s have increased inequality in the UK and, as such, have contributed to an increase in poverty. Discuss.

Source 5/6: Family package for a budget

FIGHTING inflation and demonstrating fiscal virtue are not the only tasks of the British Treasury. The Chancellor and his colleagues might take time off at Chevening this weekend to ponder the fact that the least well off sections of the population have shared very little in the rising prosperity of the last decade and that families
5 with children loom much more important in the poverty picture than before.

Now is the time to start designing a package for 1991–92 onwards, when resumed economic growth will be paying its usual fiscal dividend.

Unfortunately, those who want to face up to this challenge are sharply divided ideologically. The poverty lobby and the mass of *bien pensant* opinion in the centre
10 and left want, among other things, to raise Child Benefit. This is the universal benefit paid across the counter to the 'caring parent' (normally the mother).

The Government pins its hopes on what it calls targeted benefits and its opponents on means tested ones. Chief among them are Income Support and Family Credit. Income Support (which used to be called Supplementary Benefit) is designed
15 to help families without a breadwinner to help families without a breadwinner in full-time employment. Family Credit is designed to top up the incomes of families on low earnings. It is withdrawn at a rate of 70 per cent.

The battle between the two kinds of benefit has implications for the integration of tax and social security in the longer term. For Child Benefit is an embryonic 'basic
20 income' payment, paid out to families with children. Family Credit is an embryonic negative income tax. But, as is made clear in an excellent recent study by the Institute for Fiscal Studies, neither, in its present form, is particularly cost-effective.

The IFS analyses the consequences of alternative measures on the assumption that the Government has an additional £1bn available to help families in poverty. The
25 issue cannot be left to the DSS, if only because the most effective solution involves action on tax as well as benefits.

The case for a straightforward increase in Child Benefit is much weaker than commonly supposed. Because of its universality, it is an expensive benefit, involving an annual cost of £4½bn to provide the modest sum of £7.25 per child, a level at
30 which it has been frozen since 1987. Family Credit, with a budget of around £500m,

provides on the other hand a weekly supplement averaging £25 to 320,000 recipients.

The IFS simulation is at first sight very favourable to the Government's preferred Family Credit. If the whole of the hypothetical £1bn were allocated to Family
35   Credit, it would for instance be possible to double it from £36.35 to nearly £74 per couple. This shows very big redistributive effects, with the largest gain – averaging around £8 per week – for families in the £100 to £160 per week income range.

Unfortunately there are snags. One is the low take-up of selective benefits. One third of the available Family Credit budget is unclaimed and one half of potential
40   recipients do not apply. It takes an average of 23 working days to process a claim. Reassessment takes six months. Thus the benefit is not a secure lifeline for the part-time, casual or seasonal worker. Moreover, the whole process of applying for a selective benefit involves an intense scrutiny of personal means – and the disqualification of people with more than minimal capital sums – all very different
45   from claiming Child Benefit across a Post Office counter.

In view of these problems, the reintroduction of child tax allowances has an appeal to some supposedly non-ideological Tories and is one idea that might actually be mentioned at Chevening. Unfortunately, it would be a step backwards. Child tax allowances were replaced by Child Benefit precisely because they were worth
50   nothing to those who paid no tax and little to those who paid low tax. The IFS simulation of the effects of introducing a £440 per annum child tax allowance shows a roughly uniform gain for families with £200 or more per week, but little or nothing for the least well off. (Moreover the IFS makes the politically unlikely assumption that the child tax allowances will not be available against the higher rates.)
55   The drawbacks of Family Credit and child tax allowances should not however provide an excuse for a crude untargeted increase in Child Benefit. As the IFS points out, Child Benefit would be irrelevant to low-income families if all selective benefits were claimed. The reason for this is that any increase in Child Benefit reduces the child addition both to Family Credit and to Income Support by a corresponding
60   amount.

Even on realistic take-up assumptions the IFS simulations show that overwhelmingly the largest beneficiaries from an increase in Child and One Parent Benefit would be families in the middle and upper ranges. Those with net disposable incomes below £160 per week would gain little.
65   The straightforward taxing of Child Benefit would not help much. Under independent taxation, it would be natural to tax the mother. This would make possible an increase in benefit of £2.80 per week – only another £0.90 more than would be possible without making benefit taxable. The cost would include bringing an extra half a million women into tax and higher marginal rates.
70   Paying Child Benefit to the father and also taxing him would finance a bigger rise in Child Benefit of £4.70 per week. But it would have both the feminist and poverty lobbies up in arms (and reluctantly I might have to join them). Even then much of the gain would spill over into higher income families.

The IFS has, however, produced a scheme which combines the across-the-counter
75   advantages of Child Benefit with the greater selectivity desired by the radical right. This would involve a sensationally large increase in Child Benefit to £34.80 per week, which would continue to be paid to the mother. But it would count as taxable income of the father, if his earnings were adequate. It would, moreover, be withdrawn by applying a specially high marginal tax rate of 65 per cent starting at the

80   bottom of the income tax scale until Child Benefit is exhausted.
     This package has by far the largest redistributive effect. Gains are still limited at
the very bottom because of offsetting reductions in Income Support and Housing
Benefit. But as the chart shows, the greatest gains go to families with relatively low
disposable incomes of £100 to £200 per week. On the other hand, families with
85   disposable incomes appreciably above £300 per week (or above £400 gross) would
lose up to £14 or £15 per week because of the withdrawal of Child Benefit.
     I would not expect the present Government to embrace this particular pattern
and inflict net losses on income groups where many of its already alienated
supporters lie. But on the assumption that there is £1bn to distribute there are
90   numerous ways of eliminating the losses shown on the right hand of the chart. The

Effect of withdrawable increase in child benefit by income range

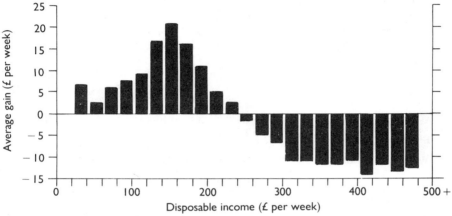

Source: Institute for Fiscal Studies

simplest method would be to tax away not all Child Benefit, but only the increase.
The Government would still be able to have Child Benefit more than doubled to
reach £15 or more.
     A more serious disadvantage is the introduction of high marginal tax rates
95   (amounting to 74 per cent if normal National Insurance contributions are included)
towards the bottom of the income distribution. But this is what is involved in the
selectivity principle, and is already implicit in Family Credit – which would no longer
be needed if the IFS suggestion were followed. The withdrawable Child Benefit has
however the advantage of avoiding the indignity of means-tested applications, and
100 retaining the over-the-counter principle of Child Benefit. The higher marginal rates
could, of course, be reduced to, say, 50 per cent or 60 per cent, but only at the
expense of extending the band across which they would apply.
     The ideal form of cash redistribution would be a Basic Income, related to family
size, for everyone, which would be withdrawn at a uniform rate, corresponding to
105 the ordinary income tax rate as income rises. When that happens, there need be no
quarrel between selectivity and universality; and Basic Incomes and negative income
tax will amount to the same thing. But this ideal would at present involve astronomic
tax rates and it cannot therefore be realised until the utopia (or nightmare) of a
computer and microchip revolution that really does multiply national productivity
110 severalfold has arrived.

Expenditure on families with children 1989–90

	Amount (£bn)	% of toal
Income Support	3.3	40
Family Credit	0.5	6
Child Benefit	4.5	54

Source: Institute for Fiscal Studies

Meanwhile, compromises are necessary. One such compromise, advocated for instance, in the new Social and Liberal Democrat green paper, is the introduction of a small non-taxable basic payment for everyone, which would have to be heavily supplemented by conventional Social Security for the foreseeable future. The other
115 compromise, embraced in this particular IFS proposal, is to have larger basic payments, starting with families with children, but to accept a withdrawal rate higher than the basic rate of tax.

Samuel Brittan
Financial Times, *11 January 1990*

1 What is the meaning of the phrase: 'when resumed economic growth will be paying its usual fiscal dividend' (lines 6–7)?

2 What are 'targeted benefits . . . means tested (benefits)' (lines 12–13)?

3 Why does 'the most effective solution (involve) action on tax as well as benefits' (lines 25–6)?

4 Why is 'the case for a straightforward increase in Child Benefit . . . much weaker than commonly supposed' (lines 27–8)?

5 What are the problems involved in extending the government's Family Credit (lines 38–45)?

6 What was wrong with the former system of 'Child Tax Allowances' (lines 46–50)?

7 What is the IFS scheme which 'combines the across-the-counter advantages of Child Benefit with the greater selectivity desired by the radical right' (lines 74–5)?

8 What is Samuel Brittan's 'ideal form of cash redistribution'. (lines 103–10)?

7: HEALTH

Essay questions

1 'As long as health is provided to the population "free at the point of use", demand for health care will always exceed supply, whatever resources are allocated to it.' Discuss.

2 Analyse the Conservative government's 1989 NHS reforms. What measures would you adopt to improve the health service?

3 Examine the view that, when considering efficiency in the NHS, the Conservative government has been too concerned with cost, rather than with value for money.

Source 7: Medicine and the market

ALL THE main bodies representing the medical profession in the UK have rejected the Government's white paper on health care. The most recent blow for Mr Kenneth Clarke, the Health Secretary, was an overwhelming vote against the proposals by the Royal College of General Practitioners.

5   The Government had hoped the royal college would prove less hostile than the British Medical Association, which is financing an expensive campaign against the reforms. Ministers are likely to receive another battering next week when the BMA hosts a special conference to debate the white paper and the equally controversial new contract for family doctors.

10 Mr Clarke has repeatedly stressed his commitment to the National Health Service and says fears that the next step will be wholesale privatisation are wholly unfounded. So what accounts for the medical profession's hostility? The short answer is that the Government is attempting to bring about a fundamental change in the way the NHS operates – a change which will have profound implications for both

15 doctors and patients. In the past general practitioners and hospital doctors have regarded themselves as part of a nationally planned and co-ordinated health service. No hospital or surgery has seen itself as directly in competition with another – at least not in the sense that Tesco and Sainsbury are in competition. Decisions about resource allocation have been based on professional assessments of need.

20 **Competition**
Mr Clarke wants to change all this. He wants the allocation of resources to be governed by competition, just as it is in much of the rest of the economy. As the white paper puts it: 'The practices and hospitals which attract the most custom will receive the most money. Both GPs and hospitals will have a real incentive to put

25 patients first.' A dose of competition, in other words, will do this fusty institution a power of good. The doctors, like the lawyers, are bound to resist the sweeping away of restrictive practices, but no reforming government can afford to take such self-serving objections too seriously.
The competition argument is extremely appealing, especially for those who have

30 strongly supported the revival of the market in the 1980s. But while the NHS can certainly be modernised, the case for putting doctors and hospitals explicitly in competition with each other needs to be examined with great care. Both economic theory and empirical studies suggest that it will often not be the best way to improve the quality of medical care. Nor is it likely to reduce costs.

35 **Innovation**
Those who find it hard to accept that health care really is 'different' should ponder a few numbers. The principal argument for competition is that it reduces costs while encouraging innovation. Yet consider the international record. The US, the country with the most competitive system, has by far the highest costs: it spends around 12

40 per cent of GDP on health care compared with 8 to 9 per cent in Europe. Britain, the country with the least competitive system, has the lowest costs, spending less than 6 per cent of GDP. Yet there is no evidence that the average Briton is less healthy than the average West German or American. Nor is the UK record on innovation poor: in many fields the treatment available in the UK is among the best
45 in the world.

The moral is not that the NHS should be preserved unchanged like a stately home. There is always room for improvement. Many of the white paper proposals – such as the need for more sophisticated information and management systems – are sensible and uncontroversial. The crucial issue, however, is whether fragmentation of the
50 health service and direct competition between hospitals and doctors will raise quality and reduce costs. So far Mr Clarke's case has been based on rhetoric rather than solid argument or research. He did not consult before he published the white paper and he rejects pilot studies and trials. His untested plans are 'non-negotiable'. In the circumstances, the doctors are right to kick up a fuss.

(*Leading article*)
Financial Times, *Friday April 21 1989*

1 What are the implications of a shift in decisions about resource allocation in the NHS from 'professional assessment of need' to 'competition'? (lines 18–22)?

2 'The principal argument for competition is that it reduces costs while encouraging innovation' (lines 37–8). Explain.

3 Why might competition in the health service not reduce costs (lines 30–45)?

4 What criteria would you use to analyse the success of the government's health service reforms?

8: HOUSING

Essay questions

1 'The Conservative government has no effective policy to deal with homelessness in the UK.' Discuss.

2 'Mortgage interest tax relief should be abolished.' Discuss.

3 'The extension of owner-occupation during the 1980s has not been wholly beneficial.' Discuss.

Source 8: The surge in house prices

THE RATIO of house prices to incomes in the south east of England has risen steadily since 1982 and now stands only a fraction below the spike reached in the inflationary boom of 1973. Jeremiahs, their appetites whetted by last year's stockmarket crash, are hinting that the bubble must burst soon. Borrowers, they
5 say, are over-extending themselves in the misguided hope that capital appreciation will continue to dwarf debt-servicing costs. A disastrous crunch can be averted only

if steps are taken to limit the generous flow of cheap credit to the market.

The concern is understandable, but possibly a trifle exaggerated. The stock of houses is not easily altered in the short run. Quite modest changes in demand can 10 therefore cause extremely rapid price movements. Bursts of house price inflation – or disinflation – are not necessarily signs of impending doom. They do not necessarily imply correspondingly violent gyrations of broader measures of inflation, such as the retail price index. The factors, such as rising incomes and falling interest rates, which push up house prices also inflate demand for other goods. The 15 difference is that in other markets supply can adjust more readily to the increased demand.

Much of the present excess demand for housing reflects innocuous and predictable trends. When the baby-boom generation of the 1950s and 1960s reached maturity, the scramble for desirable houses in prosperous parts of the country was 20 bound to intensify. The pressure has been exacerbated by the well-established trend towards smaller families. People are marrying later, divorcing earlier and living longer. As real disposable incomes rise, families are also understandably demanding a better standard of housing; many are able to afford two homes.

The demographic pressures, of course, have been aided and abetted by financial 25 deregulation. When building societies had a virtual monopoly of the mortgage market, they were able to ration finance. Once monthly lending limits were reached, intending purchases were simply forced to wait. The onset of vigorous competition has eliminated the queues and transferred power to the home buyers.

Demographic changes were unavoidable. Deregulation was desirable even if it was 30 likely to cause transitional difficulties. But could the Government have countered these changes in demand with supply-side reforms? The short answer is probably not. Even if the present plans for accelerated house construction in the south east had been implemented at the turn of the decade, the resulting incremental increase in the housing stock would probably have done little to dampen the price explosion. 35 A more ambitious building programme than is now contemplated might have had greater impact, but arguably it would have been undesirable on environmental grounds.

The Government could certainly have used fiscal levers to influence the supply/demand imbalance. Mortgage interest relief could have been phased out 40 entirely in the past nine years. Alternatively, the old schedule A tax on the imputed income from home ownership could have been reintroduced. More controversially, capital gains tax could have been extended to principal residences. Various taxes on the value of land have also been advocated and could have been introduced. It is regrettable that the Government has instead resolved to abolish local property 45 taxes, a move that can only increase the relative desirability of housing as an investment.

But it would be foolish to pretend that fiscal changes – either now or in the past – would have had an enormous impact. Direct credit controls are the most powerful weapon at the disposal of the authorities. Their use to break a dangerous speculative 50 bubble would not be a betrayal of market principles. The difficulty is in deciding if or when to act. The authorities must hope that the present inflationary boom will ease of its own accord. This is possible: lenders are becoming more aware of the prudential risks and borrowers may decline yet heavier servicing burdens. But there is certainly no room for complacency.

(Leading article)
Financial Times, *31 May 1988*

1 What does the 'ratio of house prices to incomes' show (line 1)? What would you expect to happen to this ratio during a house price boom?

2 Explain the phrase: 'over-extending themselves in the misguided hope that capital appreciation will continue to dwarf debt-servicing costs' (lines 5–6).

3 'Quite modest changes in demand can therefore cause extremely rapid (house) price movements' (lines 9–10). Explain.

4 The growing demand for housing is explained by 'demographic pressures' (line 24) and 'financial deregulation' (lines 24–5). Explain.

5 How would an increase in the supply of the housing stock have affected the house price explosion (lines 32–4)?

6 How could the government have used 'fiscal levers to influence the supply/demand imbalance' (lines 38–9)?

7 'Direct credit controls are the most powerful weapon at the disposal of the authorities' (lines 48–9). What does this mean? Do you envisage any problems with the operation of such a policy?

8 Why might an inflationary house price boom be expected to 'ease of its own accord' (lines 51–2)?

9/10 THE NORTH-SOUTH DIVIDE
THE REGIONS

Essay questions

1 What evidence would you use to support the claim that the 'North-South divide' has widened during the 1980s?

2 Have Conservative policies contributed to a widening of the 'North-South divide'?

3 'The best policy to help depressed regions is to encourage the free operation of market forces, in the hope that investment – both domestic and foreign – will be attracted to those regions.' Discuss.

4 'The Conservative government claims that the reduction of resources allocated to regional development does not reflect a downgrading of the importance of regional policy, but rather a more effective use of the funds available.' Discuss.

5 'Present regional policy is inadequate and there should be a substantial injection of funds into the regional programme, if the problems of the regions are to be addressed seriously.' Discuss.

Source 9/10: North and South

RELEASE of the 1986 employment estimates on Thursday (see figures below) suggests that regions outside the South East, East Anglia and the South West have borne the brunt of a net decline of 1.6 million jobs since 1979; the southern regions which contain nearly half the population account for only 6 per cent of the employment decline.

5 While there may be considerable arguments about the precise figures, the numbers have already been used by the Labour Party's regional affairs spokesman and will no doubt also strengthen the arm of Conservatives like Michael Heseltine, Peter Walker and Edward Heath who have been pressing for more attention to be 10 paid to the North-South divide. But the reality is well known: some of it is inevitable – though it is also capable of being improved by assistance it is not now getting.

Regional breakdown of the 1.6m employee jobs lost and gained between June 1979 and 1986

East Anglia	+23,000
South East	−73,000
South West	−39,000
West Midlands	−301,000
North West	−278,000
Yorkshire/Humberside	−266,000
The North	−215,000
East Midlands	−118,000
Scotland	−149,000
Wales	−130,000
Northern Ireland	−64,000

There are many facets to the changing distribution of jobs in Britain that underlie these figures. Perhaps the most obvious is the shift out of manufacturing into services. But it is important to remember that manufacturing employment started to 15 fall absolutely from the mid-1960s, with the pace of decline accelerating after 1973 and really plummeting after 1979. The North has borne the brunt of this decline not only in traditional issues like steel, shipbuilding and heavy engineering but also in some of the new industries attracted to those areas with government assistance during the 1960s. The West Midlands with its heavy dependence on the car industry 20 has also been affected by the general decline of manufacturing.

Services, in particular public services, partially compensated for the decline of manufacturing jobs in the regions up until the mid-1970s. But since then the public sector has ceased to fulfil this role. At the same time, the cumulative effects of high levels of unemployment have inevitably fed through into a declining demand for 25 consumer services in the North. Moreover, the North has not benefitted signifi cantly from the growth of services to business where demand is generated from company headquarters in London.

Perhaps more significant than the shift from manufacturing to services has been the changing occupational structure of employment. Take examples: Tyne & Wear 30 and Berkshire. The table opposite shows that the former area has a heavy emphasis on low level industrial occupations, 'craftsmen' and low level services and it is these types of employment which have been most affected by technological change. By contrast Berkshire, which does contain a significant amount of manufacturing activity, has a stronger representation of higher level industrial occupations.

Skills quotient 1981

Grade	Berkshire	Tyne & Wear
Managerial	1.07	0.79
Higher service	1.19	0.85
Higher industrial	1.62	0.89
Lower services	1.02	1.09
Craft/Foremen	0.89	1.22
Lower industrial	0.80	1.01

(The quotient is the proportion of the local employed workforce with the specified skills divided by the national proportion with that skill: a quotient of 1.00 defines the national average.)

35   THESE CONTRASTS represent deep-seated structural differences between a blue collar North and a white collar South that have been building up over many decades. The differences feed through into the ability of areas to generate new economic activity through industrial innovation in existing businesses and in new business foundations – because it is groups like R & D workers and financial managers who
40   play a key role in product innovation and new business formation. And each new merger wave seems to result in a further reduction in the number of headquarters in provincial cities as duplicate research and administrative departments are combined in London and the South East.

The distance-shrinking ability of telecommunications seem at the same time to
45   make it easier for companies to control production in the North from London, while continuing to enjoy the rich network of personal contacts between the financial institutions, government and the media that the capital offers. These same technologies also make it easier for financial institutions to tap regional savings for the benefits of the international financial system.

50   How inevitable are these tendencies and can government do anything to counteract them? Regional disparities are a feature of most market economies and past attempts at intervention have not proved very successful, partly because they have treated symptoms rather than deep underlying causes and have sought immediate effects. The free marketeers in the government look to a downward
55   pressure on wages in the North, and shortages of skills and land in the South, to encourage the diversion of some industry. But there are few signs of this happening and every indication that, as in the past geographically specific skill shortages will hold back economic growth and contribute to inflationary pressures in the economy at large.

60   THERE are also doubts as to whether a policy of diverting growth to the North is sufficient on its own to re-build local economies capable of self-sustained economic development. Hence the demand for development agencies modelled along the lines of the Scottish Development Agency which lead in the attraction of new industries and link them with measures designed to build on existing strengths and stimulate
65   new enterprise formation.

Those arguing for regional development agencies do so on economic as well as social grounds. It is increasingly recognised that many of the obstacles to successful

economic adjustment in the UK are local as well as national in character. For example, new technology is installed in particular offices and factories and the
70 relevant skills and know-how are still transmitted through personal relations between customers, suppliers and training agencies. The decline of the North therefore represents a major constraint on the economy at large, not just because of transfer payments associated with unemployment and social security benefits.

Prior to an election, the political will to do something about the regional problem
75 is most likely to arise in the South. Here there are increasing pressures for some re-introduction of regional planning as the demand for land development threatens many of the attractive residential environments which the nation's managerial elites hold dear.

But even if the political will exists, any attempt to introduce effective regional
80 planning in the UK is beset with difficulties. One major obstacle is in the departmental organisation of central government. Careful examination of the prosperity of the South reveals that it is not entirely dependent on private enterprise: the high technology end of defence expenditure, government research laboratories, mortgage tax relief, commuter subsidies to British Rail, and the
85 expansions of London's Airports are all major elements of public expenditure which *incidentally* have strengthened the economy of the South East.

The regional problems strike right at the heart of the way in which Britain is governed: and it is one of those issues which politicians and administrators prefer not to deal with in any fundamental way.

John Goddard

1 'The regional problem is really a manufacturing problem, which is located in certain regions.' Comment on this statement in the light of the figures produced (see lines 12–34 and Table E5).

2 Why are the 'deep-seated structural differences between a blue collar North and a white collar South' (lines 35–6) so important?

3 What are the consequences for the regions if fewer firms locate their headquarters outside the South East (lines 42–4, but refer also to Chapter 2).

4 What policies are adopted by free marketeers in order to alleviate regional disparities? Why have these policies not been effective in the view of the author (lines 54–9)?

5 What are the arguments for establishing Regional Development Agencies (lines 66–73)?

6 Explain the statement: 'Careful examination of the prosperity of the South reveals that it is not entirely dependent on private enterprise (lines 81–3). What are the implications of this statement for regional policy?

II: THE INNER CITIES

Essay questions

1 The Conservative programme to overcome inner city problems will only succeed if local authorities and local people are more closely involved. Discuss.

2 'Many inner city areas are in such a state of decay that they will never recover unless there is a large injection of public resources.' Discuss.

3 Examine the view that the Conservative policy on inner cities has addressed the wrong issues and has caused more problems than it has solved.

4 The Conservative government's programme for the inner cities has placed great emphasis on private initiative and enterprise and has turned away from years of 'throwing money at problems' and 'misguided interference by local authorities'. Discuss.

Source II: URBAN REGENERATION AND ECONOMIC DEVELOPMENT: THE LOCAL GOVERNMENT DIMENSION

Report Summary

Although the UK economy continues to grow rapidly, urban problems remain. They differ from place to place in character and intensity. Sometimes whole inner cities are affected, in other places there are deep pockets of deprivation alongside
5 prospering communities, elsewhere the problem is located in urban fringe estates. Some of the most intractable problems are as much social as economic.

There is now little argument about the position that private-sector-led growth is the main long-term answer to urban deprivation. Those local authorities which attempted to operate their own 'planned economy' strategies now recognise the
10 need to support rather than resist local business initiatives and acknowledge the primacy of economic development as the long-term answer to deprivation.

But there remains a case for intervention by government. Central government accepts this case, though it emphasises the importance of a careful definition of the circumstances in which intervention is justified. This is where environmental
15 problems, public good issues or externalities inhibit the natural operation of the market.

Local government has an important role to play in this intervention. In part that is so because of its responsibility for the main local services, such as education, planning, roads, and housing, but also because it has specific powers to support economic
20 development. Just as importantly, local authorities identify closely with the interests of their local area and can generate leadership and inspire confidence over a sustained period.

The most critical need is for the three major actors in urban regeneration – central

government, local government and the private sector – to pull together. This does
25 not always happen now.

Audit Commission
(HMSO), 24 January 1990

1   'There is now little argument about the proposition that private-sector-led
    growth is the main long-term answer to urban deprivation' (lines 7–8).
    Discuss.

2   What is the meaning of the 'primacy of economic development' (line 10)?

3   Examine the case for intervention by government in urban initiatives.

4   How has the Conservative government's programme for the inner cities
    involved local government? What changes are proposed in the Audit
    Commission report (lines 23–5)?

12: AN OVERVIEW OF THATCHERISM IN THE 1980s

Essay questions

1   What were the government's counter-inflation policies in the early 1980s?
    What were the consequences of those policies?

2   How may cutting government spending, whilst the economy is in a
    recession, ever be justified?

3   Outline the conflicting views which led to the resignation of the Chancellor
    in October 1989.

4   Why did the high growth of the mid 1980s prove to be unsustainable?

5   Did a realistic alternative exist to the government's high interest rate policy
    in the late 1980s?

Source 12.1: A monetary muddle

THE WEEK that saw the Government's tenth anniversary in power has been
extraordinarily quiet on the main battle front: the economy. Apart from warning
shots from transport union artillery, the Government has found itself in an economic
lull. Mrs Thatcher could enjoy the celebrations and treat the Vale of Glamorgan
5   by-election result as a typical mid-term difficulty.
        The calm is illusory. The battle to control inflation that was fought between 1979
and 1982 is being fought once more. The circumstances may be easier and the
enemy less ferocious, but the fact of a return engagement is ominous. The
Government's natural supporters are likely to be the least forgiving. They will judge
10   the Government not only by its ability to defeat inflation, but also by the casualties
incurred in the battle. For after 10 years in power those casualties will rightly be
judged unnecessary.
        Nor can the Government's dwindling popularity be easily dismissed. It has lost its
lead over the Labour Party after a long period of economic expansion that

189

15 culminated in two years of economic growth at over 4 per cent. It should be basking in the admiration of the electorate. Instead, support is weakening before the extent of the likely economic deterioration has hit the voters. Moreover, the current account deficit may still be too large and the rate of inflation too high to allow use of the fiscal surplus in the time-honoured fashion when the next election approaches.

20 **Lessons for future**
How did the Government get itself into this fix and what lessons should be drawn for subsequent policy? Particularly important must be a reconsideration of the goals and instruments of monetary policy, the heart of macroeconomic policy throughout the Thatcher era.

25 Ten years ago the Government believed that the strategic objective of curbing inflation would best be achieved by monetary control. These tactics were successful, but only after a bloody war of attrition. Just as the British generals of the Second World War determined to eschew the tactics of the First, so Mr Lawson abandoned the rigorous monetarism that had led his predecessor to costly victory.

30 During Mr Lawson's long period of generalship both objective and tactics have changed out of recognition. The often repeated goal of eliminating inflation is no longer credible. Nobody knows what the Chancellor means when he says that 'interest rates will stay as high as is needed for as long as is needed. For there will be no letting up in our determination to get on top of inflation.' Does this mean
35 inflation at 4 per cent to 5 per cent a year (a rate at which the value of money halves every 15 years)?

Equally important, and closely related, have been changes in monetary tactics. The exchange rate was brought into ever greater prominence. But domestic monetary targets were not eliminated altogether and no firm public commitment was made to
40 a particular target for the exchange rate (for example, by participation in the exchange rate mechanism of the European Monetary System). The policy culminated in the attempt to keep sterling below DM 3, which was introduced in secret and led to open conflict with the Prime Minister in March 1988. At that time – and, indeed, for months thereafter – British monetary policy was in total disarray.

45 **Clear objective**
What are the lessons of this experience? The first and most obvious lesson is that, if more than one indicator is used, then it is still more important than otherwise to be clear about the strategic objective. Domestic monetary indicators and the exchange rate can give contradictory signals. One can only anticipate what the Government
50 will do when the indicators conflict, if one knows what its overriding aim actually is.

The second lesson is that an effective policy is one to which the Government as a whole is committed. The final lesson is that a strategic objective that is disregarded when policy is formed will in time be completely discredited.

After 10 years in power the Government faces far more than a little local
55 economic difficulty. One of its main achievements is threatened by its own past mistakes.

The Government should at last make a serious effort to make the time ripe for full participation in the EMS. The goal must be a rate of inflation consistent with the maintenance of competitiveness against major competitors over the long term, at a
60 stable exchange rate. The implied target is zero inflation in unit costs in the production of tradable goods. Given long term productivity trends this, in turn,

means earnings rising at no more than 5 per cent to 6 per cent a year. That the
economy is now so far from this position and moving further away by the month,
shows how far from victory is the Government in what it has itself claimed as its
65   major battle.

(*Leading article*)
Financial Times, *6 May 1989*

1   'The current account deficit may still be too large and the rate of inflation
    too high to allow use of the fiscal surplus in the time-honoured fashion
    when the next election approaches' (lines 17–19). Explain.

2   'Ten years ago the government believed that the strategic objective of
    curbing inflation would be best achieved by monetary control' (lines 25–6).
    (a)   Explain the meaning of this statement.
    (b)   Why did the Chancellor subsequently feel obliged to abandon 'rigor-
          ous monetarism' (line 29)?

3   Why is the 'often repeated goal of eliminating inflation no longer credible'
    (lines 31–2)?

4   How does a high interest rate policy affect inflation, both in the short run
    and in the long run?

5   Why did the attempt to keep sterling below DM3 cause monetary policy to
    be in 'total disarray' (line 44)?

6   'Domestic monetary indicators and the exchange rate can give contradictory
    signals' (lines 48–9). Explain.

Source 12.2: Supply-side reforms leave 'important weaknesses'

BRITAIN has pursued supply-side policies with greater rigour and determination
than most other major industrial countries but important weaknesses still remain,
according to the OECD.

   In its annual report on the British economy the agency says the momentum of
5   structural reform needs to be maintained at the same time as bringing inflation on to
a downward course.

   The OECD says that relating many benefits to income continues to mean high
marginal tax and benefit withdrawal rates for the small number of people caught in
the poverty trap.

10   Other benefits such as company cars continue to be relatively lightly taxed. It also
believes that the mortgage interest relief represents 'a significant tax distortion.'

   Although significant progress has been made in dismantling quantitative import
restraints in recent years, various import impediments remain.

   Britain has, for example, about 600 bilateral arrangements under the Multi-Fibre
15   (Arrangement) and industry-to-industry agreements to limit imports of cars and
commercial vehicles from Japan.

   The OECD says implementation of recent education reforms will remove
deficiencies in work-related education of schoolchildren. It makes clear that more
must be done, however.

20   'As long as only a small proportion of people receive formal education beyond

191

school leaving age, the basis for the workforce to take full advantage of modern work organisation and production techniques will remain inadequate,' says the OECD.

25 The same sense of a job only half done pervades the OECD's analysis of the Government's privatisation programme. 'The full range of benefits which could potentially be drawn from privatisation does not seem to have been realised yet.'

In particular, the organisation criticises the way corporations such as British Telecom and British Gas have been sold intact. 'A shake-up of the structure of privatised industries would have strengthened forces of competition and facilitated 30 regulation.'

According to the OECD, the government should have separated the natural monopoly part of the companies to be privatised from those parts where competition is possible. It also should have separated natural regional monopolies from each other.

35 The creation of independent production units would have limited the extent to which cross-subsidisation and vertical integration could be used for anti-competitive purposes.

The splitting of the corporations into regional units would have given regulators a better idea of the price that the industries could command for their products or 40 services.

The OECD notes that in future privatisations the electricity industry will be restructured and the water authorities sold as separate companies.

In the case of electricity, however, an element of integration between competitive and non-competitive activities will remain in most of the corporations.

45 The group applauds the Government's efforts to make the public sector more efficient. 'The United Kingdom has taken a leading role in this area' with the introduction of modern management and efficiency monitoring techniques and increased competitive and financial pressure on public sector management.

It recognises that greater attention to output and performance has replaced 50 preoccupation with inputs and cost control. Large-scale devolution in operational matters is also envisaged in the near future.

However, the OECD says further work needs to be done on improving management information systems as a base for assessing how resources are allocated.

55 The group says substantial savings have been achieved where private sector companies have been able to compete with the state in the provision of services.

The planned introduction of competition in the delivery of health care and education represents 'a novel approach to the use of market incentives within the public sector,' the OECD says. 'Provided that public-sector production units are 60 prevented from engaging in monopolistic practices and that consumers take advantage of the internal market, the new approach is likely to stimulate efficiency.'

Economics correspondent
Financial Times, *11 August 1989*

I Which 'supply side' measures have been adopted by the British government (line 2)?

2 What is the 'poverty trap' (line 9)?

3 Why does mortgage interest relief represent 'a significant tax distortion' (line 11)? What are the consequences of this for the British economy?

4 What are the consequences for the British economy of 'industry-to-industry agreements to limit imports of cars' (line 15)? What would be the outcome if such agreements were scrapped?

5 Which single improvement to education is highlighted by the OECD (lines 17–18)?

6 Why have 'the full range of benefits which could potentially be drawn from privatisation ' (lines 25–6) not been realised?

7 Explain: 'The creation of independent production units would have limited the extent to which cross-subsidisation and vertical integration could be used for anti-competitive purposes' (lines 35–7).

8 How has the government attempted to 'make the public sector more efficient' (lines 45–6)?

Note Material in this article refers to various chapters in the book and not just to Chapter 12.

Glossary

Absolute deprivation
A measure of poverty made with respect to some degree of physical need (eg what is required to keep an individual above the subsistence level). (Refer also to *relative deprivation*.)

Asset stripping
A charge levied against a firm that takes over another and then sells off some of the constituent parts. It is likely to be most pronounced if there are job losses and in situations where businesses are sold off and closed down, in order to facilitate, for example, property development on the site.

Assisted areas
Areas in Britain which are provided with government aid/assistance, in view of the severity of their economic problems – measured in terms of persistently high levels of unemployment or low levels of income.

Benefit culture
See *dependency culture.*

Sir William Beveridge
Wrote what became known as the 'Beveridge Report' in 1942. This led to the development of welfare services in the post-war period as part of the Welfare State.

Big Bang
The name given to describe the changes in the City of London prior to October 1986. These changes involved extensive deregulation of City institutions and practices, and liberalised many existing restrictive practices. The Big Bang was intended to keep London as one of the foremost world financial centres.

Bull market
A term used to describe a situation in which there is a persistent upward trend in average share prices. The bull market of the 1980s came to an abrupt halt with the Crash of October 1987.

Competitive tendering
Occurs when firms are obliged to bid for (ie 'tender' for) a contract. The contract will be awarded to the lowest tender offer.

Concentration
The degree to which a small number of firms dominate a particular industry (measured normally in terms of market share).

Cross-subsidisation
Occurs when a firm directs profits from a profitable operation to support or subsidise an unprofitable one.

Crowding out
Occurs when the public sector grows at the expense of the private sector. This occurs either through the capital market (the higher interest rates needed to finance the public sector reduce private sector investment) or through the labour market (attraction of labour from the private sector to the public sector). If this is so, then it questions Keynesian demand management policies.

Dawn raid
Occurs when a predator company makes a concerted move to acquire a stake in another company, before the financial markets have properly opened for business.

Demand management
As used in the 1960s and 1970s, involved adjustments to the government's budgetary stance, in order to increase or decrease aggregate demand, in an attempt to achieve 'full employment'. Changes to taxation and public expenditure were known as 'fiscal policy'.

Demarcation dispute
A dispute between groups of workers over which group does which job. Such disputes tend to occur in industries in which there has been technological change. As a result of this, workers who have traditionally been involved in a particular production process, may now find themselves superceded by another group with different skills. Demarcation disputes have often resulted in disputes between unions.

Dependency culture
Associated with right-wing economists, mainly from the US, during the 1980s. It describes a situation in which recipients of welfare benefits become less reliant on self-help and more dependent on the state, thereby hindering their ability to break loose from reliance on the benefits. Also called *benefit culture*.

Direct tax
A tax on the income of individuals or companies. The main forms of direct tax are income tax (on individuals) and corporation tax (on companies). (Refer also to *indirect tax*.)

Economies of scale
Occur when the average cost of producing a product falls, as output of the product increases.

Enterprise culture
Fostered if the merits of popular capitalism are accepted. (Refer to *popular capitalism*).

Exchange controls
An attempt by a government to influence the value of its currency. The government attempts to control the purchase and sale of foreign currencies by residents of its country. Exchange controls were abolished in Britain in 1979, as a result of the Conservative government's free market thinking, and also in an attempt to reduce the value of sterling, which was appreciating at the time.

Abolition of exchange controls in all other EC countries was one of the conditions imposed by Mrs Thatcher before Britain would enter the ERM.

External discipline
(on wage bargainers) Occurs when a rising exchange rate forces management to make cost savings in order to remain competitive. These cost savings may involve productivity improvements or a reduction in a firm's willingness to grant wage increases, both of which would reduce inflation. This contrasts with a situation in which wage bargainers feel able to claim high wage increases, in the expectation that a declining exchange rate will regain lost competitiveness. A similar effect may occur if there is confidence that the level of an exchange rate will remain stable. UK entry into the ERM in October 1990 may be seen as an attempt to impose an external discipline on the economy in order to reduce inflation.

External growth
(of a company) Occurs when a firm merges with another. Growth targets are likely to be achieved more quickly than through *internal* or *organic growth*.

'First past the post' electoral system
A system in which Members of Parliament are elected by choosing the candidate who gains most votes in a particular constituency. This works against the interests of smaller parties, who may gain a reasonable share of the total vote, but very few seats. Compare with *proportional representation*.

Fixed costs
Costs which do not depend on the level of output (eg the rent of a factory or the heating costs of an office). Also known as *overheads*.

Free at the point of use
Implies that there is no direct cost to the recipient of the service (eg a visit to a GP or hospital). The term often appears somewhat misleading, as it may imply that the service is really free – it must, of course, be financed from government revenue.

Geographical mobility of labour
Represents the willingness and ability of workers to move from job to job in different areas. Compare with *occupational mobility of labour*.

Golden share
A mechanism whereby the government provides protection from takeover to recently privatised companies, usually for a finite period of time. The government commitment to the whole concept of golden shares was questioned when Ford was allowed to takeover Jaguar and when BP was allowed to takeover Britoil.

Headquarters effect
High technology and highly-skilled jobs are likely to be associated with the headquarters of a company. Firms often keep key production processes and decision-making in their headquarters.

Import penetration
Represents the importance of imports in a particular sector. As trade barriers are reduced, one would expect countries to increase their trade with one another and, therefore, import penetration would be expected to rise. Problems may be caused when import penetration rises particularly quickly in certain sectors.

Imputed income
(on a house) Represents the notional benefit gained by living in one's own house. It may be assessed by measuring the amount of rent one would consider paying for the use of the house. In some European countries, this notional amount of income is taxed, but this is not so in the UK.

Incomes policy
Represents an attempt by a government to control the rate of increase of money wages, by setting a maximum figure. Some incomes policies have been voluntary (ie by agreement with unions and employers); others have been statutory (ie imposed). The Conservative government under Edward Heath operated a statutory policy between 1972 and 1974. The Labour government under Wilson/Callaghan operated a voluntary policy (the Social Contract) between 1975 and 1979. Incomes policies were anathema to free market thinking and formed no part of Conservative economic policy during the 1980s.

Indirect tax
A tax on expenditure. The main forms of indirect tax are VAT and excise duties (ie taxes on alcohol, petrol, tobacco). (Refer also to *direct tax*.)

Industrial base
The underlying strength of the industrial sector of a country. This will affect the sector's ability to compete and to prosper in the long-run and will also affect its ability to withstand short-run reductions in demand. The industrial base will be strengthened by raising investment (especially that devoted to research and development in areas of high technology) and by improving industrial training.

Industrial strategy
The term has various meanings, but generally involves an interventionist government industrial policy with support for certain industries. This support is likely to focus on certain key sectors in an attempt to spot winners. It formed an important part of government economic policy during the 1960s and, to a lesser extent, during the 1970s. It is principally, but not exclusively, associated with Labour governments.

Inflationary expectations
Represent people's beliefs about the likely rate of inflation. As the inflationary wage-price spiral is largely self-perpetuating, expectations about higher prices encourage higher wage demands by pushing up firms' costs and resulting in price increases, thereby producing a self-fulfilling prophecy for the initial

expectation. This emphasises the importance of reducing inflationary expectations.

Infrastructure
The infrastructure of a region includes provision of transport (roads, railways, airports) energy supplies (electricity, gas), communications (telephone services) and water. Improvements in infrastructure are often a pre-requisite for economic growth in a region.

Internal growth
See *organic growth*.

Internal market
(in the health service) Occurs when health authorities are able to buy and sell services from and to one another. This allows the benefits of specialisation and *economies of scale* to accrue and avoids expensive duplication. The objective is to improve the service provided to the patient and to reduce the costs of providing it. In order for the internal market to operate, it is essential that health authorities price their services on a commercial basis. In the past, local authorities have not been used to pricing their services, but an efficient allocation of resources requires costs to be calculated as a pre-condition.

Louvre Accord
An agreement signed in February 1987 between the G7 countries (G5, Italy and Canada) to stabilize the value of the US dollar and other major world currencies. This marked a change in policy from that made in the *Plaza Agreement*.

Management buyout
Occurs when all or some of a company's management team organises the purchase of the company from its existing owners. (This might be the government or it could be a company which is selling off a subsidiary).

Means tested benefits
Benefits which are given to an individual dependent on his 'means', which may be based on income or wealth. This contrasts with universal benefits, which are given irrespective of income or wealth.

Mixed economy
An economy in which there exists both a private and a public sector. The mixed economy was accepted by all major political parties in the UK in the post-war period. This consensus has only been broken during the 1980s, as the Conservative government rolled back the frontiers of the state.

Natural monopoly
An industrial structure in which technical factors suggest that it would be very inefficient to tolerate the existence of more than one firm in the industry. (Eg if competition in sewage disposal were to exist, it would require different networks of pipes).

No-strike deal
In exchange for signing a 'no-strike deal', a union is likely to be granted various

concessions by the management such as sole negotiating rights (a *single-union agreement*).

Occupational mobility of labour
Represents the willingness and ability of workers to change occupations. Compare with *geographical mobility of labour*.

Oligopoly
A market dominated by a small number of large firms (eg sales of petrol).

Oligopolistic pricing
It is impossible to predict the outcome of pricing decisions in an oligopolistic market. This is because the behaviour of a firm in such a market depends on the behaviour of other firms in the market. The fear is that firms in an oligopoly situation will collude and raise their prices. (Refer also to *oligopoly*.)

Organic growth
Often termed *internal growth*. The term describes a situation in which a firm retains its existing structure and increases its production. This may be achieved either by concentrating on products already in production or by diversifying into other areas. Organic growth is contrasted with *external growth*, which occurs when a firm merges with another firm. With organic growth a firm is likely to achieve its growth targets less quickly than when external growth is experienced.

Overheads
See *fixed costs*.

Pendulum arbitration
A form of arbitration used when negotiation between management and unions fails to provide an agreement acceptable to both sides. The arbitrator has to accept either the position of the management or that of the unions. The purpose of such arbitration is to encourage moderation, by discouraging unrealistically high pay claims from the workforce and unrealistically low offers from the management, in the expectation that a traditional arbitrator would eventually 'split the difference' between the two positions.

Petrocurrency
A currency whose value is significantly affected by the fortunes of the oil industry in that country. Hence if the price of oil rises, the value of the currency rises and vice versa. North Sea oil conferred petrocurrency status on sterling in the early 1980s during the build up of oil production. Sterling lost this status during the mid-1980s, as other factors became more important in determining the exchange rate.

Plaza Agreement
An agreement signed in September 1985 between the G5 industrialised countries (USA, Japan, West Germany, France and UK) to reduce the value of the US dollar. (Refer also to *Louvre Accord*.)

Popular capitalism
A Thatcherite term describing the way the Conservatives have tried to identify

the 'average person' with the benefits of capitalism. To this end the Conservative government has tried to increase ownership of shares and property. In addition, it has sought to stress the importance of profit and capital to the smooth running of the economy. (See also *enterprise culture.*)

Poverty trap
Exists when a low-paid worker receives a pay increase, but then, as a result of paying tax and losing his entitlement to various means-tested state benefits, he finishes up worse off, or only marginally better off. This acts as a disincentive to removing oneself from poverty.

Predatory pricing
A situation in which a firm lowers its prices to eliminate its competitors and then raises them once the competition has been eliminated. In such a situation the consumer is not likely to benefit in the long run.

Proportional representation
A system of electing members of parliament whereby seats in parliament are allocated according to the number of votes received. Compare with *First past the post electoral system.*

Rationalisation
Occurs when a firm eliminates inefficiencies, such as duplication of resources or underused plant. This may involve plant closures and redundancies, and is often to be seen in the aftermath of a takeover.

Reciprocity
Occurs when British companies are able to bid for foreign companies with as much ease as foreign companies are able to bid for British ones. Britain's capital laws are more liberal than those in many other European countries. This gives rise to the claim that there is a 'lack of reciprocity'.

Relative deprivation
A measure of poverty which views it not in terms of absolute need, but rather in terms of needs relative to others in the community. (Compare with *absolute deprivation.*)

Restructuring
The amalgamation of various firms within an industry, in order to be able to face a different market environment. (Eg the need to face foreign competition may provoke mergers, in the hope of gaining economies of scale.)

'Right to manage'
A slogan of the 1980s associated with the attempt to reduce the power of the trade unions, which had been built up during the 1960s and 1970s. Management strove to impose its will on the wage bargaining process, working practices and the introduction of new technology, without as much reference to trade unions as previously.

Satellite plant
A low-technology operation that merely assembles the finished product from

components brought in, often from abroad. Such plants perform low value-added operations, involving relatively unskilled workers. Also called a *screwdriver plant*.

Savings ratio
The proportion of income which is saved. When considering personal savings, this is generally represented as a proportion of personal disposable income.

Screwdriver plant
See *satellite plant*.

Security of tenure
Protects a tenant from eviction from a rented property. Security of tenure provisions have been introduced to protect the tenant against the landlord. However, in the long term, it has often worked against the tenant, as landlords have been reluctant to continue letting a property when it has become vacant.

Short termism
Occurs when management fails to give sufficient weight to long-term factors in its decision making. This might involve a failure to invest or to commit money to research and development projects, because the pay-back time is too long. Short termism may occur because of myopic management or because banks are unwilling to lend for anything more than a short period. It can also occur if management fears that a takeover might be pending and, as a result, is reluctant to commit itself to long-term expenditure, preferring instead to use its resources to achieve a boost in the short-term share price.

Single-union agreement
An agreement between the management and one union, whereby that union is granted sole negotiating rights for the factory. In exchange for this, the union often has to agree to various points as specified by the management, eg a *no-strike deal*.

Stop-go cycle
A term which was used a great deal during the 1960s. Whenever a government reflated the economy too quickly, inflation rose and the current account of the balance of payments deteriorated. This was followed by deflation of the economy in order to reduce demand. The resulting cycle of economic activity was known as the 'stop-go cycle' and was often associated with attempts by governments to reflate before an election, only to deflate afterwards.

Supply side
Supply side policies have made up a major part of the thinking of free market economists during the 1980s and are to be contrasted with *demand management* measures. These policies include measures to improve the working of the labour market by the reduction of the power of trade unions, reductions in taxation and the reform of the benefit system in order to increase the incentive to work.

Synergy
A word used to describe the favourable effects which may occur if two merged

companies 'gell' together. This may arise from shared management philosophy or a common process used.

Targeting
Welfare benefits have been increasingly targeted during the 1980s. By doing so, it is hoped that real need may be readily identified and dealt with. The danger is that increased targeting will avoid meeting the needs of certain groups.

Transmission mechanism
Describes the process whereby changes in the supply of money affect the rate of inflation. This may operate in various ways, but in the context of this book, it describes a process whereby control of the money supply affects *inflationary expectations* and thereby wage bargaining and prices.

Unemployment trap
Exists when an unemployed worker is better off as a recipient of social security, than taking a low-paid job. It acts as a disincentive to seek employment.

White knight
A company which is approached by another which is under threat of a takeover from a third party. The company is invited to propose a friendly merger in order to thwart the third party.

INDEX